Representing Talent

Representing Talent

Hollywood Agents and the
Making of Movies

VIOLAINE ROUSSEL

The University of Chicago Press   Chicago and London

The University of Chicago Press, Chicago 60637
The University of Chicago Press, Ltd., London
© 2017 by The University of Chicago
Published 2017
Printed in the United States of America

26 25 24 23 22 21 20 19 18 17   1 2 3 4 5

ISBN-13: 978-0-226-48680-2 (cloth)
ISBN-13: 978-0-226-48694-9 (paper)
ISBN-13: 978-0-226-48713-7 (e-book)
DOI: 10.7208/chicago/9780226487137.001.0001

Library of Congress Cataloging-in-Publication Data
Names: Roussel, Violaine, author.
Title: Representing talent : Hollywood agents and the making of movies /
    Violaine Roussel.
Description: Chicago : The University of Chicago Press, 2017. | Includes
    bibliographical references and index.
Identifiers: LCCN 2016057354 | ISBN 9780226486802 (cloth : alk. paper) |
    ISBN 9780226486949 (pbk. : alk. paper) | ISBN 9780226487137 (e-book)
Subjects: LCSH: Theatrical agents—California—History. | Theatrical
    agencies—California—History. | Motion picture industry—United
    States—History—20th century. | Hollywood (Los Angeles, Calif.)—History.
Classification: LCC PN1993.5.U65 R75 2017 | DDC 384/.80979494—
    dc23 LC record available at https://lccn.loc.gov/2016057354

♾ This paper meets the requirements of ANSI/NISO Z39.48–1992
(Permanence of Paper).

For Nick

Contents

An Agent at Work

How do agents contribute to the making of movies and other entertainment products? To be introduced to the unknown world of Hollywood agents, what better way than letting one of them tell us the story of a movie with which he got intimately involved? One of the few movies that made recent film history, *The Silence of the Lambs* remains to this day "one of only three films that won the Oscar for the five main categories, and the only thriller that ever won a best picture" (see table 1).[1] However, like many other big hits, this movie almost didn't get made.

In 2014, I met with Robert (Bob) Bookman—the motion picture literary agent who sold the rights to the book from which the film is adapted—in one of the popular restaurants of Beverly Hills where Hollywood professionals are used to discussing projects and negotiating deals around lunch or drinks. There, the veteran agent, expert of the Hollywood machinery, shared the details of the epic story that led to the production of this film, the obstacles that had to be overcome, and the long and chaotic process of assembling the various pieces that made up such an unprecedented success. He immediately highlighted the paradoxical fact that "it was so difficult to get to sell the rights [. . .] given its later success." Yet it's not a unique example. The notion that "all hits are flukes" is familiar to the entertainment industry (W. Bielby and D. Bielby 1994). As Bookman put it, "It's just amazing that, kind of like grass growing through concrete sidewalks, there are these miraculous things that happen." This story sheds light on the erratic creation of a

Table 1 *The Silence of the Lambs* (1991) in Sum

Directed by	Jonathan Demme
Produced by	Kenneth Utt, Edward Saxon, Ron Bozman
Screenplay by	Ted Tally
Starring	Jodie Foster, Anthony Hopkins, Scott Glenn, Ted Levine
Distributed by	Orion Pictures
Country	USA
Budget (source: Box Office Mojo)	$19 million
Box office, domestic + foreign (source: Box Office Mojo)	$272.7 million
Awards	*Academy Awards, won:* Best Picture, Edward Saxon, Kenneth Utt, Ron Bozman; Directing, Jonathan Demme; Actor in a Leading Role, Anthony Hopkins; Actress in a Leading Role, Jodie Foster; Writing (adapted screenplay), Ted Tally *Academy Awards, nominated:* Film Editing, Craig McKay; Sound, Tom Fleischman and Christopher Newman *Golden Globes, won:* Best Performance by an Actress in a Motion Picture–Drama, Jodie Foster

hit, making visible in a paradigmatic way some of the elements that allow for the improbable to become real.

This story is told from the point of view of a motion picture literary agent; that is, an agent who represents writers and directors and sells "material"—the rights to a book, a screenplay, a spec script (speculative screenplay, or a noncommissioned, unsolicited screenplay)—to production professionals. When our story begins, Bob Bookman is already a well-respected and influential "player" in the industry working at Creative Artists Agency (CAA), then indisputably the top talent agency, run by Michael Ovitz at the time. He is armed with experience both as a former literary agent at International Creative Management (ICM, now ICM Partners), a powerful company especially in the field of literary agenting, and as a former studio executive: although he left the production side after six years to go back to agenting and join CAA, this experience afforded him valuable connections and an intimate understanding of studio dynamics.

In the late 1980s, Thomas Harris, the author of the famous Hannibal Lecter book series, is represented by a powerful New York literary agent, Morton Janklow, who is known for his client list of best-selling authors. *The Silence of the Lambs* is the second novel of this series. Thanks to his preexisting connection with Janklow, Bob Bookman receives the mandate to sell the rights to the book to a studio and becomes one of Harris's representatives. The first novel of the book series, *Red Dragon*, was turned into the 1986 film *Manhunter* (directed by Michael Mann and starring Brian Cox as Hannibal Lecter). The rights to the book *Red Dragon* were initially bought by Warner Bros., but, as it often happens, the studio eventually decided not to make the movie and to put it in "turnaround," an arrangement by which a project can be moved from the studio that initially owned/developed it to another studio that decides to produce the movie. This time, Dino De Laurentiis picked it up and inherited the conditions of the Warner Bros. initial deal. *Manhunter*, distributed by the De Laurentiis Entertainment Group and produced by Richard Roth, didn't meet with box-office success. This initial failure became an impediment to later attempts to adapt Harris's novels. Another obstacle was the lack of popularity of the genre—a thriller and horror/crime film—in the eyes of studios at that time. This reveals some of the important elements that one needs to bear in mind to understand "what it takes to get a movie made."[2] This case study introduces us to the complex process by which a piece of written material becomes a movie.

This is when the marathon of the motion picture literary agent to sell the rights to *The Silence of the Lambs* starts. This marathon involves multiple layers of players caught up in an intricate game. Bob Bookman first needs to go to De Laurentiis, whose contract with Warner Brothers stipulates a "first negotiation/last refusal" right. Such a right reserves for the producer who optioned a novel in a book series the first opportunity to purchase the movie rights to the sequel.[3] De Laurentiis passes on the sequel. The agent then has to "deal with the marketplace." This means circulating the book and examining offers from potential buyers on the production side; trying arousing interest on the part of others; and assessing the value and "right price" of the material, taking into account a combination of contradictory elements: the unappealing genre of the book, the failure of *Manhunter*, and—on the opposite end—the fact that *The Silence of the Lambs* has now become a *New York Times* best seller. This evaluation process is a collaborative one: Bookman, Harris, and Harris's New York book agent, Janklow, agree not to accept a few offers that they receive from independent producers, judged to be "too low" financially.

The effort to shop a film project around to potentially interested "buyers" can be coordinated by a literary agent when the writer/director is the key piece of a package, like in the present case, but also by a talent agent who represents a star, by a star's manager, or by a team made up of several of these participants, depending on each particular situation. As our case study illustrates, this process sometimes proves to be a long and difficult marathon, when a project struggles to find a producing home, is put on hold for years, and might have to change form to finally meet the interest of a studio or a financier. The buyers to which the project gets offered are not randomly selected; it's not about chasing all studios and producers in town either. Part of the agent's role is therefore to evaluate the *type* of movie that the project is meant to be, and to match its genre, budget range, and intended type of audience with the areas of specialty and preferences of the studios at the moment. It is part of an agent's early work to imagine, categorize, and price artworks, as we will explore in details in later chapters.

Back to *The Silence of the Lambs*. Despite the efforts of the agents, the town remains silent; no studio steps up to buy the rights to the book. The following developments show how important the ties the agent cultivates with his counterparts can be. Bookman's connections at the studios allow him to get some precious information and to use his relationships with a studio head—in this case, at Paramount—to try inflecting the studio's negative perception of the book. When a piece of material is submitted to a studio, it is given to a reader, who usually doesn't have decision-making power, for evaluation; this evaluation is called "coverage":

I had heard that Paramount had very negative coverage. [. . .] So I called Ned Tanen, who at the time was the head of Paramount, and I said, "I've never asked you to do this before, but I understand that you got very negative coverage of *Silence of the Lambs*. I'm not going to ask *you* to read it, but I'm going to ask you to give it to a reader who has different sensibilities who you really trust. Just see if there's a difference, okay?" He calls me three days later: "You'll never guess what happened! The second reader loved it, gave [it] 'highly recommended'—we're still not buying it." That was how difficult it was.

The next development rises from the interrelations linking agents together, especially within the same agency and at CAA—known to be organized under Ovitz's influence in ways favorable to "team agenting." Team agenting now exists in all large talent companies: forming teams around the stars so as to multiply the connections the stars can have with agents internally is a strategy to win the artists' loyalty and to retain them even if their "point agent" leaves the agency; it is also meant to provide better and more extensive service. In addition, team agenting facilitates the task of "packaging" several agency clients in the same movie. In our case study, Bookman's colleague, longtime CAA agent Fred Specktor, contacts him with an offer from one of his star clients, Gene Hackman:

Fred Specktor called me and said, "Are the rights to *Silence of the Lambs* still available?" And I said yes, and he said, "Gene Hackman wants to buy them. He wants to produce it, he wants to direct it"—he'd never directed a film—"and he wants to play Hannibal Lecter. [. . .] And he's gone to Orion"—which was then sort of at its peak as a production company—"and Arthur Krim"—who was a beloved, extraordinary man, chairman of Orion—"has agreed to be his partner." So we negotiated a *very*, very big deal.

The cohering effect of having a star like Hackman committed to the project soon produces additional aggregation mechanisms: producer Robert Sherman, a former agent to Hackman turned studio executive and then producer, who has also been a professional counterpart to Bookman for a long time, agrees to join the project. The chain reaction continues with the addition of Ted Tally as a scriptwriter—here again, the agent playing the role of oiling the machinery by connecting key participants:

I got a call from Arlene Donavan, whom I worked with at ICM in the '70s—again, a great person—and she said, "I represent Ted Tally"—who was a very successful playwright at the time, just starting to write screenplays—and she said, "Ted Tally is obsessed with *Silence of the Lambs*, how do I get him the job?" I said, "Call Bob Sherman." She called Bob Sherman, he hires Ted Tally. So, now, I get a call from Fred Specktor. He says, "You won't believe what happened!" I said, "What?" He goes, "Gene's pulling out of *Silence of the Lambs*." I said, "Why?!" He said, "His daughter read the book and called him and said: 'Daddy, you're not making this movie.'"

We see here the making and possible collapsing of the "gravitational field" that forms around a star for a given project. This is also often how "film packaging" happens. Far from deriving solely from "star power" or "star charisma," this aggregation dynamics implies the activation of preexisting ties, which sometimes combines with the effects of trajectories of professional mobility between the representation and the production sides (agents turned studio executives or producers, especially). Such long-lasting relationships between professionals who circulate between various organizations, positions, and sectors of the industry create tightly woven webs of intertwined ties. The agent's activity, which starts very early on in the filmmaking process, both relies on his inclusion in such webs, and contributes to further weaving the thread: some of the collaborations reactivated or initiated here will repeat and strengthen on later occasions. As solid as the aggregate formed around a project may look, it always remains vulnerable: any of the key pieces can pull out at any time, and the entire project may or may not survive it. Hackman's defection is a hard blow. Sustaining enough "attraction force" to keep the remaining players involved and the "gravitational field" in place is not an easy task. Participants' perceptions are challenged: "Is the movie real?," "Is it really happening?" become nagging questions. In this context, the agent works at consolidating participants' optimistic anticipations, in line with his client's and his agency's best interest.[4]

In our case study, the project survives the withdrawal of the initial star, as Arthur Krim at Orion Pictures agrees to take on the entire project. Bookman and Krim then convince another of the agent's clients, director Jonathan Demme, to join the team. The fragile imagined endeavor has regained some strength, and casting can start. Demme and Krim argue about the best actors to hire for the main parts, in transactions that the agents describe as typical of the casting process, and they compromise on Jodie Foster (Orion's choice) and Anthony Hopkins (Demme's).[5] Most pieces are now in place. The movie has become probable; it looks "real."

One tricky question, inherited from the history of the film series, remains: the "first negotiation/last refusal" right included in the initial *Manhunter* production deal meant that, if the producer, Dino De Laurentiis, refused to acquire the movie rights to *The Silence of the Lambs*, the sequel could only be made under the condition of changing all the characters and placements that appeared in the first movie; the name Hannibal Lecter and all others, in particular, would have to be modified. For this reason, at this stage of the process, De Laurentiis has kept a decisive say as far as the making of the sequel is concerned. The director, Jonathan Demme, mandates his agent to get De Laurentiis's permission to use the original character names in his movie. Bookman engages again in negotiations with De Laurentiis to convince him to go against the restrictive policy set up by Warner Brothers,[6] successfully so. This arrangement would later allow De Laurentiis to produce two sequels to *The Silence of the Lambs*: *Hannibal* in 2001 and *Red Dragon* in 2002.[7] As Bookman reports, "back-to-back, all the subsequent Hannibal Lecter film and television [projects] have all been controlled by Dino and then by his estate. He would never have made them if *Lambs* had different names."

Orchestrating preproduction, from a central position in a highly collective game, is the domain of the motion picture literary agent. When production starts, his role comes to an end. The rights are sold; the key elements are in place for the next phase to start. The director and the production team complete the cast and the technical team, a stage at which agents from "boutique" companies who represent actors and actresses hired for smaller parts and below-the-line personnel get into the game with a more limited participation in terms of both time and scope. Literary agents like Bob Bookman rarely visit movie sets, and they are "not really involved during production, not at all. From an agent's point of view, it's over." Production (the shooting of the film itself) and postproduction (editing; addition of music, sound, and visual effects; and all other stages that occur after the last day of shooting) run their course, marketing and publicity strategies surround the release of the movie, critics and box office speak, award season arrives. The consecration of *The Silence of the Lambs* is unprecedented, shifting the trajectories of a number of the participants. But the effect on the agent's resources, path, and credibility is more elusive in the eyes of Bookman:

It had a big effect on Thomas Harris in terms of the value of his material; it had a big effect on Jonathan Demme—his next movie was *Philadelphia*, which otherwise wouldn't have been an easy movie to make; it had a big effect on Ted Tally, who became a very in-demand screenwriter. It certainly had a big impact on the actors in it, right? The only effect on me, I guess, was . . . it's kind of an intangible. I mean, obviously positive, but I don't think you can *measure* it in a way you would measure those other things. Who knows what client came to me because of that, or what client didn't leave me because of that, you know? Or how much of a factor it was in other things, as opposed to a hundred percent of something. It's just part of the ebb and flow of business from the agent's point of view. [. . .] Within the agency, everybody always knows who did what. But you can't put your finger on something [happening], say, because we also represented Anthony Hopkins. There were a lot of factors, so, I don't know.

What participants know has happened becomes an element of their evaluation of the individuals involved, of their trustworthiness and their "taste," confirmed by the success and the consecration of the movie; it contributes to making up and strengthening participants' reputation as well as their power to act and provoke action in others, analyzed in the following chapters. These shared experiences manifest preexisting interconnections; they *make* ties and networks as well. Only part of these interconnections materializes in the legal form of a contract or in any official way. Informal relationships matter just as much as the size and influence of the agency one belongs to (here, the top one, CAA) or the position held in this organization. In fact, informal relationships and their history dictate, to an extent, the effective meaning and impact of the formal titles attached to organizational positions—as I will explain. The "episode" of the making of *The Silence of the Lambs* gets integrated into the succession of small events that make up the collective history of Hollywood. This film story puts a particular system of players and organizations under a magnifying glass, revealing the central role that literary agents can play as early "coordinators" in the process.

Other categories of agent are in a position to act as project orchestrators in this way. It is typically the case of talent agents whose clients are big Hollywood names, but also of "independent film agents" hired by the major agencies to package, find financing, and represent film projects that are too small for the studios, especially international coproductions. Talent agents are the ones we usually have in mind when we think about this profession: they represent actors and actresses at all levels, from big movie stars who can get a film made on sole name power to unknown performers who struggle to secure an acting job. The top talent agents of the biggest companies who handle "bankable" stars, such as Ben Stiller at William Morris Endeavor (WME), Will Smith at CAA, or Gwyneth Paltrow at United Talent Agency (UTA), play this key role of coordinating the initial steps of the making of certain films on behalf and in collaboration with the star. In addition, unlike literary agents, whose job is over when production starts, these top talent agents often stay alongside their client throughout the entire process, beyond postproduction, up to the release of the film and the associated promotion effort. Talent agenting as they experience it contrasts with the mere activity of pitching lesser-known actors for jobs once the casting process has started, which talent agents at smaller companies perform. Later chapters will address the diversity of specialized agenting roles that lead these professionals to come into the mix at different stages of the filmmaking process.

More generally speaking, the case of *The Silence of the Lambs* illustrates the dense structure of interrelations implied in the making of a film. Financial, legal, and creative dimensions get intertwined. The vertical division of labor between talent representatives, artists, and production professionals combines with horizontal ties linking individuals and organizations located in these different functional domains of the film industry. Such ties can be official or informal; they can include information exchange, other forms of active cooperation, give-and-take strategies in which returning the favor can be put off for a long time, and even looser forms of (symbolic) association or nonaggression pacts. Only part of these interconnections responds to a project-based logic, gathering various participants in the making of a movie for a limited period of time, with no guarantee that any of these ties will be recurrent. By contrast, while *The Silence of the Lambs* was being orchestrated, Bob Bookman and the other agents were also juggling several other projects and clients, and managing lasting relationships with counterparts, forming more stable professional configurations with them.

In addition, the successive stages that lead to the existence of the movie are not always well described by the traditional division between preproduction, production, and postproduction phases. Agents are for the most part present during what is usually identified as preproduction. At the same time, our case study shows that the timeline is in fact often more complex (see figure 1). Bookman's job didn't end when he closed the production deal for Harris's book; we know that the transaction process still had a few more episodes to go. Because it significantly increased the likelihood that the movie would become real in the eyes of the participants, it was a turning point and a transition to another stage of the process. As we know, however, it was only later on—after Gene Hackman pulled out, and the agent and the producers managed to "repair" the cohesion of the network around the project[8] with the addition of the director and the lead actors—that the elements were in place for the film to go into production. Only then had it become "real."

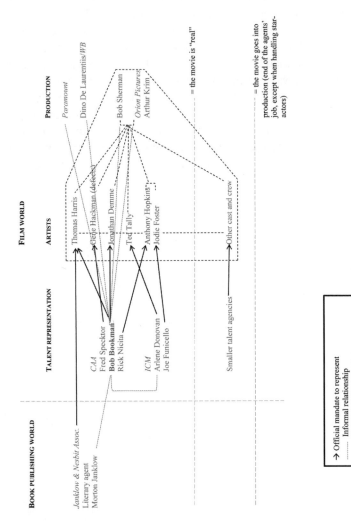

1   Interrelation system for *The Silence of the Lambs*

ONE

Introduction

Thousands of agents work in Los Angeles, either in one of the few major companies—large organizations, such as the famous WME or CAA, whose acronyms are part of the Hollywood dream, as they are known to represent the biggest movie stars in the world—or in one of the hundreds of boutiques that employ only a handful of agents.[1] Being an agent in these different contexts corresponds to huge variations in terms of work experience, level of salary/bonus and compensation structure, and type and status of clients and of their potential employers. Small agencies can specialize by segment and niche (for instance, representing actors of a certain age group or ethnicity, or film/TV technicians) whereas big ones are internally compartmentalized entities that are simultaneously active in most domains of agenting. This range of possibilities translates into contrasting experiences of agenting.

At the same time, several mechanisms unify the agenting profession. There are common conventions to the practice of agenting, as well as shared professional images. The profession activity is relatively strictly regulated, unlike the much more informally organized role of personal manager. Agencies are licensed by the state in which they are located; Los Angeles–based agencies have to receive the approval of the California State Labor Commissioner. A second level of regulation takes place with the Association of Talent Agents (ATA), which organizes many of the agencies in LA and New York and claims to speak on behalf of the profession, to the industry unions and guilds—such as the powerful Screen Actors Guild and American Federation of Television and Radio Artists (SAG-AFTRA),[2] the Directors Guild of America (DGA), and the Writers Guild of America (WGA). The agencies typically receive as a commission 10 percent of the amount that they negotiate for each of their clients' contract. Nowadays, agents are not allowed to produce— although, as we will see, they are increasingly involved in production-like activities—but they officially have the monopolistic right of seeking work and negotiating deals on behalf of their clients, and to cash the remuneration attached to this activity.

The Invention of Agenting

The professional definition of agents and agencies is the result of a historical process. Kemper's work on the emergence of talent agencies in the 1920s and 1930s (Kemper 2010, 2015) provides us with elements for understanding the birth of "agenting"—as agents themselves call their activity. His work shows that agents sprouted up in the 1920s from the studio system, and as a subsystem to it, in two combined ways: the first generation of agents sprang for the most part from within the film business itself (many were former producers or studio employees); and the conditions for agenting to form as a specialized activity, autonomized from studio tutelage, were created by the stabilization of studio infrastructure and operations themselves. Studios were growing entities that already had to organize the rapid increase in the flow of their production and distribution activities. Delegating talent representation to "independent agents," who remained closely tied to studios since their business depended on such relationships, was not without benefits for the studios. It also protected them against the suspicion—made explicit and debated in the trade papers—that the internalization of talent scouting and management would lead the studios to serve their own interest over that of the artists.

However, the idea that the development of independent agencies would simply respond to a utility function dictated by market laws would be misleading. This process was really anything but obvious or natural at the time. Agents were not immediately or easily accepted as legitimate intermediaries in the film business. This is apparent, for instance, in their conflicts with studios and in the attacks on agents' undue power/profits regularly published in the press throughout the 1930s. Agents had to struggle to establish the validity and merits of their intervention. At the same time as they were developing their ties with studio executives and asserting their systematic presence behind the scenes, they were publicizing their strategic role by placing ads in trade journals or releasing agency pamphlets highlighting their connections to stars and other key talent. By doing so, they were selling the *perception* of their relationships with artists, production professionals, and studios as organizations, as much as they were making use of these connections themselves. They were gradually constructing their position as "sellers"—that is, unavoidable counterparts to "buyers" on a free market. Their successful negotiations with talent unions (especially the Screen Actors Guild), leading to the signature of franchise agreements between the guilds and the agencies in the late 1930s, were also decisive in signifying their accreditation as professional players, individually and collectively, in Hollywood. Meanwhile, during the same decade, the transactions bringing together agents and studio executives had become increasingly routinized, to the point of defining a norm; studio executives were referring unrepresented talent to the agents they were used to working with, strengthening the new vision that a "fair negotiation" implies the representation of the talent by an independent agent.

By the end of the 1930s, collective perceptions had shifted. Agents were now commonly seen as legitimate intermediaries performing a "valid economic service" and fulfilling a necessary function in the industry.[3] This perception is in line with the definition of Hollywood as a disjointed and opaque market in which supply and demand of talent require intermediation. This mental framework of the "Hollywood market" was gradually defined in the same process by which professional groups formed and fought for their recognition: the professional constitution of the main industry forces in play (the major studios and their smaller competitors, the agencies, the talent unions, etc.) is inseparable from the formation of the mental repertoire with which they name and construe what they are doing. The definition of agents as market intermediaries is thus the outcome of a historical process, and not the necessary effect of immanent market laws: it is the result of interdependences, alliances, and competition between groups that progressively clustered, during the 1920s through the 1940s, into a specific professional system. Today's Hollywood still rests on the interdependence structure that formed in this period, in spite of the changes that have occurred within it.

Changes that have occurred since then—the growth of agencies as organizations and the strengthening of the agents' role in Hollywood that this book elaborates on—make the study of contemporary agenting all the more necessary. Agents are central participants in what happens and what gets manufactured in Hollywood. They are said to "sign, sell, and service" talent. However, beyond just placing clients into jobs and negotiating associated deals, they shape artists' careers and profiles in a very profound way and participate in the early orchestration of projects—all the more when they work at the biggest companies and are able to assemble the various elements of a project in a film, television, or digital "package." "Packaging" is the key activity of putting together the critical elements of a project then sold altogether to a studio or a network.[4] What agents do therefore goes way beyond fulfilling a gatekeeping function and filtering the massive amount of aspiring artists who converge on Los Angeles. In fact, for most of the agents who operate in the major agencies, agenting is not about gatekeeping at all. It's a much more complex and decisive role that the following pages unveil.

Filling a Lacuna in the Sociology of Hollywood

Despite what I just said, the creation of a movie is usually attributed to a small number of visible participants: a star actor, a director, or sometimes a big producer is supposed to be the driving force of the process, coming up with an idea that is soon turned into a cinematic product. In such a simple story, agents are either purely and simply forgotten, or they are treated as minor players, strictly standing on the commercial side, brokering the deals. Sociological studies of Hollywood reflect for the most part this perception.

Besides the question of celebrity and stardom,[5] artists' careers have captured most of the scholarly attention, with a perspective that approaches Hollywood in terms of project-based organization (Faulkner and Anderson 1987; Jones 1996; Rossman, Esparza, and Bonacich 2010). Cultural products that are manufactured in Hollywood—films and television shows especially—have also attracted sociological interest, be it from the angle of their recognition as legitimate "high art" (Baumann 2007) or their transformation and shaping by globalization dynamics (D. Bielby and Harrington 2008). By contrast, studies looking at what happens "behind the scenes" remain rare, and when they exist, they primarily focus on the production side, be it by shedding light on the history of the studio system (Schatz 2010) or the independent film world (Mann 2008; Ortner 2013; De Verdalle and Rot 2013). Recent works have started to explore less legitimate areas of entertainment production, such as reality programming in television (Grindstaff 2002) and "below-the-line" workers in film and television (Caldwell 2008; Mayer 2011). Talent representatives and agents, however, have consistently been missing from attempts to decipher the dynamics of the film/television world and to identify its participants. The profession has largely been ignored by art historians and scholars, more inclined to analyze the content of films than the professional configurations leading to their fabrication. In spite of a few pioneer incursions into the agency world in the form of specifically focused articles (W. Bielby and D. Bielby 1999; Zafirau 2008),[6] the social sciences have not yet offered a systematic analysis of the activity of contemporary Hollywood agents.[7] This book has this ambition.

Understanding agents' contribution to the making of artists and artworks implies considering their relationships with other professional groups that populate "Hollywood." This book approaches Hollywood as an occupational space holding together various types of participants whose activities collectively make entertainment products. Its epicenter is located in Los Angeles, and even in specific areas: all the most powerful agencies have their headquarters in Beverly Hills, or nearby, in Century City. Agents and production professionals who work in New York often mention the necessity to live "around Los Angeles time" (in the words of an interviewed agent) and to adjust to what happens there. So do other "media capitals" (Curtin 2010) such as London, Paris, Dubai, Beijing, or Vancouver in which participants adapt and respond to what they perceive as Hollywood, while Hollywood professionals may also work at conquering foreign territories and audiences. Hollywood is thus the dominant pole of the interdependence system that these diverse media centers form, even though local cultural production has more autonomy than the model of cultural hegemony suggests.[8]

"Hollywood" is also the name of a unique configuration: nowhere else in the world are the activities of film- and entertainment-making institutionalized and professionalized to the same extent. Hollywood is indeed an "industry" in which agencies that employ several thousands of people and are active in many different sectors of entertainment (including motion picture, television, theater, music, book publishing, digital media), as far as the biggest companies are concerned, face a few large studios able to produce and distribute worldwide, and which are part of powerful media conglomerates. In addition to such giants, midsize and "boutique" agencies, management companies, law and publicity firms, smaller mini-major studios, and independent production and distribution companies populate this occupational space. They compete and cooperate for the transaction of projects and artists who number in the hundreds of thousands, aspiring to professionalization in Hollywood. This second group of smaller players forms what the second chapter of this book analyzes to be "Little Hollywood," in contrast to "Big Hollywood."

I will expose later in more detail the composition and structure of this Hollywood game. What matters here is to consider that it forms *a differentiated sphere of activity*. In other words, it is one of the specialized spheres of action, characterized by the relative autonomy of their specific dynamics and "rules of the game," that together compose contemporary societies like ours (Bourdieu 1976; Luhmann 1982; Alexander and Colomy 1990). "Hollywood" is, as a professionalized world, characterized by a set of common norms and institutions, specific vocabularies, and shared experiences and references known by the players. At the same time, this world appears as internally segmented and hierarchized, and so is the agency system within it. Firstly, activities are partly organized around specific types of media (motion picture, television, digital, etc.) even though the boundaries between them are regularly—and increasingly often—crossed by some of the participants. Secondly, functional division of labor delineates different occupational groups that form Hollywood's professional system: artists, talent representatives, casters, producers, distributors, and financiers (or studios that concentrate the last three types of activity). These groups cooperate and compete, defining the frontiers of their activity and sometimes engaging in jurisdictional contests (Abbott 1988). Thirdly, within the group of talent representatives, agents, managers, and lawyers deal with one another in cooperative or competitive ways, or are just held together by interdependence mechanisms.[9] Fourthly, the agency world has its own internal structure and divisions: small agencies contrast with large corporate entities, while, in the latter, the formal hierarchy of positions combines with a high level of compartmentalization of activities. The departmental structure of the large agencies separates motion picture (talent or literary) from television (scripted versus reality programming), as well as from digital, music, theater, branding, gaming, sport, independent film financing/packaging, books, commercials, and so on. Careers tend to confine "expert agents" into specialized domains of operation, whereas their artist clients often need to cross over various media and creative genres. The question of the place of agents and agenting work in professional configurations will therefore be omnipresent.

I consider art to be collective work and occupational dynamics to be what directly frames the contribution of various categories of participants making cultural products. Approaching Hollywood as a professional sphere has often led to separating creative from noncreative personnel within it. Becker's famous approach to the art worlds (1982) includes this partition of "creative" versus "support personnel," the agents being a priori assigned to the second category. Similarly, the few existing studies of middlemen and brokers in culture industries often analytically separate creative from economic power and spheres of activity, even when they strive to explore their intertwining. The perspective of the production of culture also relies on such a division by approaching cultural forms as determined by modes of production and infused with the ideologies they convey (Crane 1992; Ohmann 1996; Du Gay 1997; Peterson 2004): the focus is placed on the hold that economic mechanisms have on cultural production, which ultimately defines cultural production as an economic process.

The approach in terms of cultural intermediaries that has recently developed in Europe and the United States also comes with an implicit model of the market in which brokers and middlemen—including production, distribution, and representation professionals—operate. But these studies insist on the social and cultural processes that shape economic practices in cultural industries (Faulkner 1983; Nixon and Du Gay 2002; Negus 2002). However, agents are not their focus,[10] and when agents are incidentally mentioned, it is still mostly as incarnations of economic constraints and of the power of entertainment corporations over creative activities.[11] The idea of tension between a "commercial pole" and an "artistic pole" structuring the fields of cultural production is also central to Bourdieusian approaches (Bourdieu 1996). In this perspective, the cultural intermediaries that agents are—especially when they operate in the most lucrative segments of Hollywood—is readily associated with the commercial pole. Even though my approach to Hollywood as a structured and specialized sphere of activity is coherent with Bourdieu's theory of fields, I diverge from his conclusions as regards such a dual structure of this field, organized around the tension between "mass production" and "art for art's sake" and between the possession of economic capital and that of symbolic capital.

The following chapters show not only that commercial and creative dimensions are closely intertwined in agenting activities—which wouldn't be particularly groundbreaking—but more important, that conceptualizing the structure of cultural industries with this opposition is in fact deceptive. I will explain, on the contrary, *how* both artistic quality and economic value inseparably emerge from the activity of interdependent Hollywood professionals. I thus pursue and adapt to the specifics of this book, the agenda that Viviana Zelizer (2005) outlined for a sociology of social relationships and practices that, at the same time, make markets and make art. Consequently, studying agents in "show business" won't mean thinking "business" against "show." It implies understanding how the creative process operates while forming economic relations. Relationships that agents build and engage in are commercial ones from end to end, at the same time as they are creative ones from all quarters. This book takes seriously the inseparable nature of show and business in "show business," and explores the key role of agents at the intersection of economic and symbolic power in Hollywood.

Facing Stereotypes

Art, including movies and television shows, contributes to our perception of what an agent is.[12] Agents themselves also face such stereotyping. In film and television especially, "the agent" oscillates between two typical characters standing at the opposite ends of the Hollywood power scale. It is, on one hand, the somewhat shabby and risible character incarnated by Woody Allen in *Broadway Danny Rose* (1984)—Rose, whose one-man agency represents countless unpromising clients, gets caught in a love triangle involving the mob; or, with a different but still comedic tone, the character of the down-on-his-luck agent for child actors, Howard Holloway (Clark Gregg) of *Trust Me* (2014), who discovers a young acting prodigy and ends up being the victim of his unwillingness to transgress his ethics and use the same low blows as his competitors so as to "swim with the sharks."[13] Such characters evoke, by contrast, the merciless and (symbolically and economically, if not physically) violent nature of relationships in Hollywood, translated via the practice of talent representation. They also embody the dominated end of the Hollywood spectrum and the desperate quest for salable talent.

At the other end of the spectrum, images of success in agenting are built around the stories of a few industry moguls and of star handlers who created their own "empire,"[14] an extension of the historical figure of the powerful impresario which was not always clearly distinct from that of the producer in the past. The character of Ari Gold (Jeremy Piven), the frenetic "super-agent" of the HBO television series *Entourage* (2004–11), partly modeled on the real-life CEO of WME, Ari Emanuel, embodies the elite agent, a top executive in the age of large corporate agencies. A number of the stereotypical traits ascribed to agents are aggregated here: Gold's hyperactive and exuberant personality, the ruthless pursuit of his own professional interest (under his warm and caring exterior toward clients), his brutal behavior with agency employees—all of this reveals and fosters the social imagery of the agent. Like its fictional representations, the social figure of the agent is a questionable one, suspected to be at once superficial and insincere, ruthless and impervious to empathy, indifferent to art and economically self-interested (and manipulative for that purpose).[15] References to the agent as a "shark" who "can't feel other people's pain" and as a "parasite" who "doesn't make anything" and yet benefits from the substantial profits sometimes made in cinematic production were indeed made by some of the producers interviewed for this book.

These are elements of a stereotype. Stereotypes are neither entirely true nor false; as in the Thomas theorem, they are "real in their consequences." Confronted with the social reality of the stereotype, agents have no other choice than reacting to it and working (with) it. They know that they face discrediting images that attach them exclusively to the commercial side of Hollywood.[16] These representations are the facets of a "spoiled identity," a "stigma" (Goffman 1963) that agents can never completely avoid and that they respond to, including by spontaneously distinguishing themselves from it in the context of our discussions:

As I was growing up, [I heard] the portrayal of an agent like a lawyer, that they're these horrible people that are just flashy and arrogant, and just about wanting to get rich and things like that. I'm sure there are agents like that, but at the end of the day, it's really a tough job, and it requires these certain skills, which are: you have to be a people person, you have to have compassion for other people, and understand other people—not just your clients, but everybody else in the industry that you work with—and you have to be able to work with a lot of different types of people. (Freelance agent, below the line, October 2010)

In the context of interaction, agents work at renegotiating their professional identity by reversing the stigma threatening them. For instance, a former lawyer turned owner of a below-the-line agency mentioned having left his initial job precisely to avoid being "paid to be a jerk for the rest of [his] life."[17] Another agent, who works at one of the largest agencies, insisted that the notion that agents "don't have very good integrity" is "the biggest misnomer about agents," concluding: "So, if I could have great integrity, that's more important than any dinner I can go to." (October 2010)

The underlying opposition between art and commerce, agents being placed *exclusively* on the business side of "show business," is a key element here. Besides the moral suspicion associated with their activity, this is what they reject the most vigorously. The association with commerce is of course not a discrediting attribute per se. That it takes a discrediting connotation in this professional context is in fact revealing of the symbolic hierarchy that makes up "worth" in Hollywood. The equalization of agenting with the commercial pole of cultural production *opposes it* to the aesthetic and artistic logic supposedly driving other participants, especially the artists that the agents represent. Such a symbolic division of labor assigns commercial practices to agents and places them not only at a distance from creative dimensions, but *in a conflicting position* in that regard. They are thus suspected to think as "vulgar salesmen," taking away from the "purity" of the cinematic or aesthetic endeavor. Adapting the remark that Bourdieu and Nice (1980, 262) made regarding "the art dealer or publisher, 'cultural bankers' in whom art and business meet in practice," I could say that agents' position in Hollywood similarly "predisposes them for the role of scapegoat."

Although such a symbolic boundary separating creative from noncreative personnel, art from commerce, is internalized by the agents—who are willing to embrace the identification with commerce to a certain extent—they show a more complex positioning. The literary agent below highlights the difficult balancing act that he has to perpetually accomplish, using the metaphor of the "bridge" he has to cross repeatedly, expressing at the same time the strength of the social definition of art and commerce as intrinsically distant and opposite elements: "The best description I've ever been able to come up for what I do, is: there's a creative reality over here, there's a business reality over here. I live my life on the bridge, and I spend all day and night long scuttling back and forth [on] the bridge, trying to get the creative reality and the business reality out to shake hands, which is a deal that might lead to a movie" (midsize agency, March 2013). If mastering both "sides" is sometimes described by the agents as a feat that makes them valuable and even indispensable to the functioning of the industry, agents usually establish a clear hierarchy between the business and the art of agenting, putting their creative contribution at the forefront. This can be done by insisting on their belief in talent and their interest in art, which distinguishes them from simple dealmakers and ordinary salesmen: since talent is not an ordinary product, the person who sells talent cannot be a salesman like any other. Many interviewees profess their lack of personal interest for the deal-making process per se, in contrast with their passion for what relates directly to art-making. The latter is what led them to work in entertainment, whereas they learned only later the commercial and legal "tricks of the trade" making up secondary skills, with the implication of being less important. However, in practice, the "creative element" can never be fully disconnected from the business of agenting—what this senior agent calls "the transactions"—and agenting has to be performed on the edge of this tension: "The transactions are the simplest part of what we do, especially with all the support that we have with seniority, experienced agents and lawyers everywhere, it's just easy. What's hard and what's interesting is the creative collaborations and the storytelling to create the transactions" (big agency, December 2013).

This book thus investigates the two-faced activity of Hollywood agents.

In the Field with Hollywood Agents

When I started doing spadework for this study, the lack of preexisting scholarly accounts of agents' activity confronted me immediately—how little information and data were already available. Beyond dissecting journalistic sources (especially the industry trade press) and secondary sources such as books or articles published by and about Hollywood professionals, I needed more direct, firsthand access to the reality of agenting. Because I approach agenting from the analytical standpoint that practices are determined by perceptions (which themselves are constantly reshaped through experience), it was crucial for me to understand the frames of meaning and conventions that Hollywood professionals share, and to grasp what being an agent means for the concerned. This dictated my choice of qualitative methods: interviews and in situ observations. My intention to investigate the agency world was initially received with skepticism. Talent agenting was deemed to be impenetrable, known for its culture of secrecy, mixing reference to confidentiality (of financial, professional, and personal information that agents indeed keep) and a "mystique" of hidden power. However, I was eventually able to penetrate it.

I conducted 122 open-focused interviews with agents in various areas of specialty and types of agencies; former agents and trainees; plus a few of their work counterparts so as to get their perspective on agenting (including studio executives, independent producers, managers, lawyers, publicists, actors, directors, and writers). The interviews were complemented with five in situ observations at agencies and alongside agents. Three observations took place in the organizational setting of different types of companies with their owner's approval: over a three-week period in a management company in Beverly Hills, led by a former agent of one of the very large agencies (May 2012); several days in a boutique agency established on the border of Beverly Hills, by the side of a female agent representing actors and actresses (April 2013); and a few days as well in a three-agent below-the-line agency whose clients were film and television crew members, located in downtown Los Angeles (March 2013 and February 2014). In addition, two agents let me shadow them repeatedly while they were performing their daily agenting activities: one was a senior agent from one of the major agencies who allowed me to witness a number of interactions with his clients, his agent colleagues, and his counterparts at studios (2012–3); in the other case, in the spring of 2012, I observed a talent agent in a small company (five agents) in his search for potentially new clients via showcases or "workshops for actors" aimed at casting directors and talent representatives. These experiences were irreplaceable opportunities to grasp the daily reality of agenting at the most granular level, giving me access to dimensions that interviews cannot well describe. This fieldwork all took place in Los Angeles between 2010 and 2015.

In this context, on repeated occasions, I was faced with the stereotype of the insincere agent, mentioned above, in the form of doubts (from outside the agency world, of course) regarding the reliability of what agents told me during interviews and, more general speaking, the question of how much they can be believed. Doubtless, they are professionals of speech who are skilled in the use of language and storytelling—a characteristic that they share with political representatives and journalists, as well as various types of intellectuals and artists. However, this does not mean that what they say is not revealing, or that it is insincere in their own eyes. In a perspective in which understanding people's perceptions and representations is key to analyzing their action, being attentive to what agents say (about what they themselves are and what they do) is, on the contrary, absolutely necessary. In addition, the number and diversity of the interviews I conducted allowed me to compare them with one another (and to place them in the light of interviews with artists and production professionals who are not necessarily inclined to paint an idyllic image of agents and agencies), as well as to compare the interviews with what I directly observed when I shadowed several agents, ensuring that the analysis does not remain prisoner to an idealized vision of agents' activity.

Being immersed in agents' everyday life through fieldwork led me to see beyond the legal definition of the activity and the official divisions supposedly drawing clear-cut lines in the industry, such as those separating representation from production and "commercial" from "creative" activities, distinguishing managers from agents, or dividing the making of a movie into the successive phases of preproduction, production, and postproduction. These lines are more blurry in practice: they are moved and crossed, and overall collectively drawn by the participants. This book reveals how. In addition, there is much more to agenting than the stereotypical images: we usually think of the agent as the aggressive white male who represents actors and actresses and works either as an independent who handles just a few clients or as a top corporate executive in a suit, tinted with the glamourous and frantic attitude attributed to Hollywood. The reality of agenting is more diverse. Agents represent many of the Hollywood professions, from actors, directors, and writers ("above-the-line" creators) to professionals of film and television crews ("below-the-line" personnel, from cinematographers to makeup artists), producers, or "reality world" personalities (in TV and digital media). Beyond individual talent, they may also represent projects and companies, as well as manage "talent" in areas other than the ones usually associated with Hollywood, which are not the focus of this book: athletes, models, video game creators, and so on. They therefore form a segmented and specialized profession. Specialization mechanisms mean that small companies tend to focus of one specific dimension of agenting, or a "fringe business"; or these mechanisms manifest themselves in the advanced division of labor and compartmentation characterizing large "full-service" agencies, which are present in the core areas of representing the most visible talent, all the while developing "ancillary businesses." Regardless, each agent typically handles a long list of clients, from several dozens to more than 100 or 150. And they do a lot more in practical terms than just negotiating deals. Ethnographic work precisely revealed agents' daily experience and their dependence on both the organizational settings within which they operate—the agencies—and the personal ties that they must constantly create with other categories of Hollywood professionals. From the perspective of the agents and through their eyes, the invisible structure of relationships organizing action in Hollywood comes to light.

How an outsider can get access and penetrate the agency world is telling. I started as such: an outsider at several combined levels by virtue of being a French scholar without any prior connections in Hollywood. Several elements helped me open doors for fieldwork: speaking with the authority of science and taking seriously an activity that had not attracted scientific attention before was valued by the agents because it meant shining light on them in a way that was not putting them at risk of being exposed for disclosing confidential information, especially since participants were protected by anonymity. Coming from Paris was an additional element making the interview request both exotic-chic and distant enough from Hollywood gossip and routines to feel even safer. The notion of venturing into unexplored territory with this book was also an efficient selling point to capture the agents' interest, as it is a selling point that Hollywood professionals themselves commonly use. Getting recommendations from initial interviewees quickly proved to be decisive to enter deeper into Hollywood circles and to figure them out. The help of a few established agents was also instrumental for opening more doors, either directly through recommendations or indirectly because mentioning their name was often a door opener in itself. It revealed how strategic is, in this world, the ability not only to know people and show that they know you, but to understand who can really reach whom and what the informal hierarchies that these associations delineate are. This fieldwork experience allowed me to delimit the subgroups and games making up Hollywood described in this book. It made the division between the world of small agencies and that of major ones all the more obvious, giving flesh to the structure organizing the agency world, assigning specific counterparts to agents at each level. It also shed light on the ways in which agents at all levels define hierarchies among their clients in a business in which, as the saying goes, "20 percent of the clients pay 80 percent of the bills"—granted that, in fact, an even smaller percentage probably really does.

The path I followed to get access to agents—from those working at small boutiques who do not deal with stars or negotiate extremely lucrative contracts to some of the "super-agents" and owners of the giant agencies—was somewhat comparable to an accelerated version of the trajectory of agency assistants: they have to start at the bottom of an agency, learn to map Hollywood and recognize its divisions (by function, organization, prestige, and career), speak the language and the subvocabularies characterizing different areas of practice, accumulate relevant connections and use them judiciously and in a timely manner, behave as expected in specific context of interactions, understand the importance of building stable ties over time versus pursuing only immediate profitability—all of which concur to being identified as a credible counterpart. This is also how in situ observations resulted, from winning the trust of some interviewees. It involved, to a certain extent, feeling my way in like beginner agents do, connecting and communicating like they do, walking in their steps and using the informal norms and patterns that reveal themselves to anyone who has to learn agenting on the job in Hollywood. Only from there is it possible to understand what "having a relationship" means *in this particular sphere of action*, and what the current transformations of this world really imply.

What This Book Unveils: Agents and
(E)valuation Communities

This study turns new light on a relatively unknown profession that contributes in a decisive way to what gets made in Hollywood. While being
specific to the occupational system in which contemporary talent agents
operate, the findings presented in this book have a more general analytic
impact. They fall within the scope of an *occupational sociology of worth*
that approaches Hollywood in terms of the professional configuration
within which the "quality" of people and projects is evaluated at the
same time as their "value" is defined. Agents are among the participants
in this collective evaluation process.

Such configurations form at the confluence of relational mechanisms
and institutional dynamics. On one hand, the logics of agenting depend
on participants' placement within the organizational system of the agencies. Agents are situated in organizations—from which they draw unequal resources and hierarchized identities—and agencies themselves are
located within two distinct systems of cultural production; the world of
small agencies (in particular vis-à-vis the production side) is very different from the sphere of the major players to which the few big agencies
belong. On the other hand, agenting is performed in transorganizational
circles: beyond the boundaries of the agency, what matters for the agent
is to create and maintain strong ties with relevant counterparts who are
potential "buyers of talent" (studio or network executives, producers,
casting professionals, distributors—depending on the level on which an
agent operates), allies in the transaction of talent and projects (managers,
lawyers, financiers, and so on), and of course actual and potential clients.
These different categories of Hollywood professionals compose specific
(e)valuation communities that determine, through their activity, which
artistic projects and careers get shaped. Participants in such communities are engaged in both the evaluation of the aesthetic worth of projects
and the definition of prices for artistic labor and material. This concept
of "(e)valuation communities" is here at the heart of the approach. However, it is the interconnection with understanding relationships in Hollywood—what they mean and imply for the participants themselves—that
makes up the analytical apparatus that the book proposes.

This approach is what ties together in the following pages the analysis of the "culture of work" proper to Hollywood—what "trust" is in this
context, how reputation and professional legitimacy are created, how

professional powers operate and work together—and that of the "work of culture" here in play; that is, the decisive effects that the studied activities have on the making of art and of creators. What is at stake is to grasp what makes the agents' power to affect which artists we get to know and admire, and which entertainment products get offered to audiences or never see the light of day. Investigating what agents do therefore confronts us with questions that resonate with more than just agenting or Hollywood: how "charisma," "taste," and even "talent" are collectively defined, made, and assigned to participants—artists as well as those, such as agents, who we are used to thinking of as "non-creative"; and what the "influence" of Hollywood's top players exactly means and does. These questions go beyond the specialized world that I explore in empirical detail here. This is also what makes the analytical tools forged in this context relevant, in my opinion, to further work in other social worlds, beyond just entertainment industries.[18]

This book unfolds in the following way. The second chapter sets the scene and clarifies what "Hollywood" refers to in terms of organizational system, and where agents and agencies fit within it. I elaborate on the idea that Hollywood consists of two interdependent but different occupational spheres, to which the distinction between "Little Hollywood" and "Big Hollywood"[19] refers: the many boutique agencies and their specific counterparts on one hand, and the major agencies, the big studios, and the other dominant Hollywood players on the other. This chapter looks at the recent transformations of Big Hollywood; it assesses what the parallel processes of corporatization, concentration, and diversification of agencies and studios implies for the practice of talent representation. Together with this introduction, this chapter provides the foundation for understanding what comes next.

Chapters 3 through 6 form the real core of this book. Chapter 3 shows how agents are trained and "made professional" in talent agencies. Beyond the relevant socialization mechanisms for understanding how agents do their job and come to shape artistic careers and projects, this close look at professionalization processes also reveals the relational dynamics that tie together talent representatives and production professionals from the start of their careers, forming "generations" in Hollywood. This chapter introduces the dual logic that structures action in this professional sphere: each agent is positioned in the organizational system of the agencies, and belongs to transorganizational circles that bring together, on a long-term basis, talent representatives, artists, and production professionals. Learning to build and maintain strong ties with clients and production counterparts is decisive for an agent's existence and success.

Chapters 4 and 5 precisely explore the meaning of "relationships" in Hollywood and approach agenting as relationship work. Both sincere and strategic, relationship work is at the heart of agenting activities. Chapter 4 focuses on the types of ties that agents construct with producers, casters, and studio executives, who are the primary "buyers of talent" with whom they transact. Winning the trust of production professionals conditions the agents' existence and success in their own eyes and is therefore crucial. Chapter 5 explores the way in which agents create intimate bonds with artists, performing emotion work with them and constantly working at drawing the boundary between "being friendly" and "being friends" with their clients. This chapter sheds light both on the agents' dependence on the artists that they represent and draw their professional legitimacy from, and on the forms of power that they hold over their clients, even when they handle the most successful stars. These two chapters show that even if relationship work takes very personalized forms, it goes beyond building one-on-one ties; it involves larger mechanisms of mutual reliance that form the groups agents belong to in Hollywood.

Chapter 6 focuses on what gets made through the activity of the transorganizational circles uniting talent representatives, artists, and production professionals: these Hollywood (e)valuation communities are collectively engaged in the evaluation of quality and the definition of value of people and projects. I show *how* this happens: first, how agents participate in the collective recognition and shaping of "promising " or "good" creative content leading to the production of a movie; and second, how agents price talent (in spite of referring to it as incommensurable) according to shared conventions, and how they contribute to setting economic standards. This chapter demonstrates that economic and symbolic dimensions of value creation in Hollywood are co-constitutive, in contrast with approaches that put the opposition between a commercial pole and an artistic pole at the center of the analysis of fields of cultural production.

Chapter 7 draws from the case study of independent film agents to shed light on the process by which (e)valuation communities form and transform at the same time as new agenting roles are created, and to show how such changes relate to the emergence of new artistic genres and profiles, as well as to the construction of associated markets. Understanding how these agenting changes take place as a whole helps us grasp the ongoing transformation of show business that all Hollywood players experience and contribute to bringing to reality.

TWO

Mapping Hollywood

The differential impact that agents can have, both creatively and economically, depends on their position and placement in the agency system and in the structure of Hollywood at large. Hollywood is not one but two, not entirely disconnected but clearly distinct, systems of cultural production. This chapter describes them and identifies the place and role of agents within them. It elaborates on the relationship tying agencies and studios, their recent interdependent transformations leading to the new power configuration that participants currently experience. This is the context in which agenting takes form and meaning today.

Agenting in Big versus Little Hollywood

Just as Hollywood is not a single profession but a professional sphere tying together talent representatives, production/distribution professionals, and different types of "talent,"[1] it doesn't indicate a particular media, even though cinema and movie stars attract a large part of the attention. Trying to understand the activity of talent agents (that is, actors' agents, whose name is used as a synecdoche for the entire profession) separately from that of literary agents (representing writers and directors), or what motion picture agents do independently from what television agents do, for instance, would be extremely artificial. If such fields of specialty exist and structure the activities of agents and their counterparts, it is in their relationships that careers and projects get made.

The agency world is therefore a complex space, organized following several intertwined lines of division: individual agents, organizations (agencies), and informal circles linking agents to other categories of professionals making up Hollywood (for instance, managers, lawyers, producers, casting directors, talent). What we call *talent agencies* refers in fact to contrasted types of organizations in a field nowadays characterized by a high level of division of labor and specialization. Empirical observation allows us to quickly recognize—just as the protagonists themselves do—that agencies belong to one of two distinct systems of cultural production. I name them after the categories defined by Faulkner (1983) of Little Hollywood and Big Hollywood, without following strictly the approach that this author developed to characterize them.

In this book, Big Hollywood refers to the individual and collective entities that dominate this game. On the agency side, this includes the major agencies that alone gather thousands of employees—that is, the giant agencies WME and CAA, followed by competitors UTA and ICM—and a few midsize agencies such as Gersh or Paradigm. Such sizable agencies represent "star clients" of various statures and enter into business (alongside the main law firms and the most reputable managers) with the executives and heads of the studios and as well as with major players in the independent world. Their transactions concern the most lucrative projects, as well as those that have the greatest chance to earn professional recognition from artistic authorities. In contrast, Little Hollywood forms a galaxy of smaller players: in Los Angeles, hundreds of agencies with only a few employees coexist with one-(wo)man (or two-agent) shops, which regularly come to existence but can also quickly close doors, depending on the ebb and flow of the business—and sometimes on the misfortune of a single project or client. These agents represent developmental talent and artists who have fallen out of favor, as well as specific categories of talent (children, seniors, below-the-line personnel, etc.). They interact mostly with casting professionals—television casters or casting directors in charge of modest film projects or hiring for smaller jobs in bigger productions—and sometimes with independent producers.

Big and Little Hollywood are thus two different relational systems, although connected ones, of course, in terms of their complementary participation to the making of cultural products: most of the time, a television show or a movie requires the intervention of both Big and Little Hollywood professionals, in different ways and at different moments. They gather separate categories of players, as far as the triangle between artists, agents, and producers is concerned. They therefore form parallel hierarchies of talent, representation professionals, and production professionals. Both Little and Big Hollywood are professionalized realms. However, they don't cover the integrality of creative activities that can lead to the making of a video, a show, or a film; new technologies and digital platforms have allowed for the expansion of a (semi-)amateur world at the margins of Little Hollywood. Because, in this "Very Little Hollywood," those who make art do not usually make a living out of it, agents do not operate in this sphere of activity. This "Very Little Hollywood" thus remains outside of our present field of study.

This also implies that agents are not involved with the making of a certain type of "indie movies." However, the distinction between "studio movies" and "indie films" is not an obvious boundary allowing us to delineate the perimeter of agents' activity, as far as the film world is concerned. Agenting spans both the domain of big studio movies and that of independent films, to an extent. Indeed, *independent film* refers to anything that isn't entirely taken on by a studio from production to retail. It thus excludes only the big tentpoles, often franchises or sequels, that are nowadays the major source of profits for the studios. It includes different categories of movies, from films made within the studio system, even if it is by the specialty film division of a studio (for instance, Fox Searchlight's *12 Years a Slave*, which won an Academy Award for best picture in 2014) to international coproductions involving the complex coordination of private and public film financiers, domestic and foreign distributors, and international creative personnel. Such " midlevel" budget movies (ranging from $15–40 million) have a lot to do with central industry players based in Los Angeles, including agents and agencies. By contrast, a third category of "indies" is formed by much smaller films with an extremely limited budget (just a few millions, and sometimes less than a million), which are always at risk of being restricted to the limits of amateur production. It is these very small productions that remain outside the frame of this study; as Sherry Ortner (2013) phrased it, they are "not Hollywood"—or, I'd rather say, they are not made within the *professional* system that we explore here, and agents are rarely, if ever, involved with such projects.

More generally speaking, the boundaries of Little Hollywood define the limit of professionality. Very Little Hollywood's amateurs, for the most part, aspire to entering the professionalized entertainment industry and joining its more mainstream avenues (for instance, making television shows rather than videos they post on the Internet or web series). "Signing" with an agency is one of the signs and mechanisms of such a professionalization. Part of Little Hollywood agents' know-how has to do with spotting those who have gained enough credit and stature with previous achievements in the amateur space, and to bet on their ability to make them into salable talent. This construction of professionality is not an obvious or an easy thing. On a purely statistical basis, the odds of succeeding in this attempt to becoming professional (that is, in Weber's [1958] terms, to make a career and a living out one's activity) are not in one's favor. As an illustration, we can roughly estimate that about six thousand films are made yearly and domestically, out of which only 10 percent get released (659 movies in 2013[2]) and 1 percent becomes profitable.[3]

If, in terms of pure statistical probability, an actor or actress's average chances to book a job are very slim,[4] they are indeed quasi-inexistent without being represented by an agent (or possibly, at the start of a career, by a manager), given the fact that talent representatives monopolize the access to casting and production professionals, and can practically submit actors for open parts through the online interface of Breakdown Services.[5] Little Hollywood agents are consequently in a position to pick and choose among a large crowd of wannabe professional talent, and they are then the ones in charge of mobilizing their counterparts on the production side to try getting their clients "in the room" with a casting director, or someone able to hire them. In folk categories, small agencies are known to be an "outgoing-call business," because their employees are constantly on the phone "selling" their clients—that is, working to convince casters to have a better look at a résumé or video, and to meet with a client—by contrast with the "incoming-call business" of larger agencies that receive phone solicitations from buyers interested in their already known and successful clients. Of course, agents at the biggest companies also have to be proactive and reach out to their professional counterparts. However, in the typical division of an agent's activity between "signing, selling, and servicing," the latter is mostly a concern for Big Hollywood agents, because it is preconditioned by the selling of talent. Getting clients a job comes first, before servicing them can even become an issue.

Because agents in Big and Little Hollywood operate in contrasted organizational contexts, in relationship with distinct categories of professional counterparts, we could go as far as to say that they *practice different professions*. The existence of such large and powerful companies as CAA or WME, each of them employing several thousands of people, representing high-end international talent, and making transactions with major studios is unique to Hollywood. More generally speaking, the agents who work at one of the major agencies—among hundreds of employees, in a compartmentalized and bureaucratized environment, servicing a group of already established clients usually shared with colleagues of the same specialized department—have a very different daily experience of what "being an agent" means, in comparison with that of the agents managing on their own all the activities of developmental clients at a small boutique. Different types of professional self-concept thus coexist and differentiate Little from Big Hollywood agents.

These contrasted professional definitions correspond to a diversity of roles that agents play in the making of artistic careers and in the creative process. Let's illustrate this with the case of talent agents. They populate the entire scope of the agency business, from tiny boutique agencies to the largest companies, such as WME and CAA. However, their daily activities and their contribution to the creation of a movie are radically different, depending on their placement in the agency system and, correlatively, on their clients' level of professional and commercial success. Motion picture talent agents who represent "A-list artists" play a more extensive and influential role than their counterparts who don't. Agents who belong to the biggest companies are in a position to package a star in a project and can therefore be in charge of "pitching a project," as opposed to "pitching a client" for a given role when a movie is being cast. Their involvement spans the entire time frame of a project. In many ways, they stand at the top of the professional hierarchy in the agency business: they can practice agenting "on a higher level," as one interviewee put it.[6] Building and maintaining close ties primarily with casting directors, as well as with directors, is at the heart of the talent agent's job when his or her clients are likely to be cast in supporting roles, at the casting stage and not earlier in the process. For the agents who handle stars, on the contrary, the relationships that matter the most link them to the studio heads and top executives who make earlier decisions.

The big agencies, which total hundreds of employees if not more, are characterized by a high level of specialization and compartmentalization. This division of labor makes "team agenting" all the more necessary. Cooperation follows organizational formats: daily meetings punctuate the life of an agency. Some meetings include motion picture talent agents; others, all motion picture specialists (for instance, literary, talent, sometimes together with independent film financing specialists). Teams can also be formed around a genre (comedy, etc.), and so on. During such meetings, "covering agents" play a key role. Indeed, in large agencies, recently promoted agents do studio "coverage," which means that they maintain relationships with executives at a few designated companies and collect information on the projects that they develop. This precious information is then shared with other agents during departmental or interdepartmental agency meetings: what studios are thinking of making, and which agency clients could be "packaged" and sold to them, or attached to an existing "package" if the project has already reached the casting stage of development—these are the questions discussed "in the room," to use the vocabulary of the agents.

Smaller agencies don't have the same contact with the studios to find out about projects. They have to rely on the acting job offers publicized by casting directors through the electronic system of Breakdown Services and submit their clients' résumé and material through the same channel. This same information reaches the whole agency system at once; so at this level, which concerns smaller roles, agents don't make a difference by getting the information first, but by activating their preexisting relationships with some of the casting professionals—that is, following up by phone and other means. Specialized agents (who represent film technicians, visual effects specialists, etc.) and talent agents in small agencies are included here for a short while in the brick-building game of making up the cast and crew of a movie, and, if successful, they negotiate the corresponding deal for their client. When these deals are closed, the job of talent agents who do not service a star is for the most part done.

In sum, unlike Big Hollywood agents—who can act as project architects through packaging and handling star talent—smaller agencies enter the fray only later on, when a film has been green-lighted and the casting phase begins, struggling then to get a job for the (lesser known or unknown) clients that they have sometimes personally "discovered" and brought into professionality. Consequently, these two classes of agents symbolically construct the relevance and importance of agenting in different ways. The generic figure of the agent is *imagined into existence* at the intersection between the two typical representations of the Little Hollywood talent scout on one hand, and the Big Hollywood super-agent on the other hand.

As far as the agents' practices and perceptions are concerned, the professional spheres of Little and Big Hollywood are characterized by their relative autonomy toward one another. Between the protagonists of these two worlds, there is more mutual ignorance and, to a certain extent, mutual indifference than competition or relational self-definition. Because the names of the top Big Hollywood players are well known—especially those who personify organizations, such as Ari Emanuel, Bryan Lourd, Jeremy Zimmer, Jeff Berg, or Chris Silbermann[7]—and because their coverage by the press creates public narratives about their paths and initiatives that contribute to the master narrative regarding the industry as a whole, Little Hollywood agents know about them in the same distant way as they know about their star clients. This distant familiarity is not comparable to the insider's intimacy with the game he or she is a part of. Shadowing and interviewing Little Hollywood agents allowed me to observe their fascination for the unknown that the activity of Big Hollywood players represents. Several times, participants in the study asked me to tell them about the life of the major agencies since my investigation was giving me an access to this world that Little Hollywood professionals didn't themselves have. However, this didn't mean that what was happening in Big Hollywood was directly relevant to their activity.

For Big Hollywood participants, on the other hand, Little Hollywood was for the most part practically invisible. This invisibility must be understood in the most literal sense, as a result of the irrelevance of Little Hollywood's existence to their own activity and its insignificance with regard to their own space of reference; that is, the specific interdependence system within which their perceptions form, their strategies take on meaning, and their activities have consequence. The agents of the largest companies in turn referred to midsize agencies (such as Paradigm or Gersh, and their 50 to 150 agents[8]) as the small players in the field, disregarding the existence of most or all of Little Hollywood, and drawing the symbolic boundary of their world in relation with the ability to package projects and represent "name talent."

The "Big" and the "Little" are therefore relationally defined, and the limit separating the two can be strategically moved by participants in context. Although Hollywood professionals share common perceptions of the power structure they belong to (that is, either Little or Big Hollywood) and know their place within it, they also engage in classification struggles and work at promoting partly different orders of worth, in line with their own position and interest. Agents working at midsize agencies such as Paradigm or Gersh are, for instance, often inclined to rearrange symbolic hierarchies by including their company into a larger pool of "big agencies": they refer to the "Big Six" or "Big Five" to define more inclusively the contours of the organizations that matter in Hollywood. By contrast, WME or CAA agents commonly point to a dual leadership in agenting, while UTA employees name three major agencies, including their own company, in this top game. The insiders' perception of the weight and worth of organizations has also varied recently, over a short period of time: all players agree that the top of the game, which used to gather several agencies of relatively comparable power until the late 2000s, now consists of fewer entities, growing in size and becoming more corporate.

My approach to Big and Little Hollywood and the relational structure they jointly form is distant from the representation of Hollywood as made of concentric circles of which Big Hollywood constitutes the "core." Such a representation can be found in network studies of the entertainment industry, which have been discussed elsewhere in more detail (Roussel 2015a). One of the prevalent characteristics of network analyses of Hollywood is indeed to bring up the question of what stands at the center of this space: networks tend to produce center-focused models. More generally, even though equating centrality and importance is not intrinsic to network theories, it is widely assumed that highly central actors are more powerful, especially in information networks (the highest degree of correspondence making up this centrality). Consequently, who or what occupies a central position becomes a key preoccupation affecting how one interprets the relational structure that networks form. The core seems to represent the most consequential ties and the most dominant entities. It is in that sense that Big Hollywood and, within it, the core largest talent agencies stand at the center of concentric circles of which Little Hollywood and its countless boutiques constitute the periphery (to borrow the notions of Faulkner [1983] and W. Bielby and D. Bielby [1999]). Indeed, for Faulkner, Big Hollywood is the center of an echelon-like organization of activity, forming a recurrent set of interlocks among specialists, whereas Little Hollywood is typically made of an isolated series of nonrecurrent ties among one-shot participants in film creation. Both spheres pile up in a concentric structure in which Big Hollywood fulfills the general function of stabilizing the game and reducing uncertainty within it.

Even though this interpretation might speak to the imagination, picturing Big Hollywood as the core of a unified system is in fact a deceptive metaphor. What such a representation suggests is not confirmed by ethnographic observation. As far as agents are concerned, even though the composition of professional clusters differs in Big and in Little Hollywood, the activity in the later space does not show less cohesion, or looser, more erratic, and isolated ties. Rather, what is striking is the relative autonomy of each of these spheres toward the other regarding the organization of key recurrent interactions. Circulations and career mobility between Little and Big Hollywood, as far as middlemen and brokers are concerned, are also extremely limited.

In addition, the question of what stands at the center of the Hollywood system and governs it has a lot of affinity with the historical narrative that we are familiar with regarding the central place that the studios once occupied in the film industry and then progressively lost (Schatz 2010). It is a common perception in the film and television industries themselves that the dissolution of the studio monopoly and the fragmentation of the activities that they initially concentrated led to the rise of the agency's centrality and power, at least until the glorious time of the 1980s and 1990s. However, today's reality proves to be more complex. Only recently has the American agency business come to be led by such giant corporate entities that are simultaneously active in many sectors of the entertainment industry as well as beyond the domestic market. Parallel to this, production professionals have also witnessed decisive transformations. I will now outline the main aspects of the structural changes that have reorganized the agency and the studio businesses and redefined talent representation itself.

"The Other Side": Interdependent Transformations of Studios and Agencies

To the players and the observer alike, the making of film and television projects appears as a two-sided game; that is, a structurally adversarial system in which talent representatives and production professionals are tied together in antagonistic positions. Agents perceive, and describe during the interviews, being on the opposite "side" from the producers, studio executives, and casting professionals who are their permanent counterparts (counterparts, but "not partners," as a top talent agent of one of the largest agencies pointed out during our interview). The structural tension between agents and production professionals derives from their competition for the control of talent, on both economic and creative levels. This studio head explained why developing direct relationships with artists is "extremely important":

It's one of the most important things for someone in my position. Otherwise, the agent will always control your *access*. That's their job, to control your access, and my job is politely to not let them control my access. So that *I* can talk to [big director's name] directly without having to talk to his agent. It's probably why someone like me, after all these years, is valuable. That's my value, that's one of my values—that I have relationships with the talent directly. And I can call them up and I can get to them and so yes, that is extremely important. It's one of the most important things to develop on the production side. For *exactly* that reason, so that you can get *around* the agents who are going to have their own agendas. (February 2014, his emphasis)

In the battle over talent, the stakes have first to do with creative control; that is, from the producer's perspective, with the control over what makes the value of a *project*. As an agent put it during an interview, studios "traffic in content," whereas agencies "traffic in artists." The value of an artist makes that of his or her agent. An agent's agenda when transacting with the production side is thus not focused on a single project and its expected (box-office/critical) success. For production professionals, on the other hand, having and keeping a hold on a film project is crucial and takes the form of either owning the material from the beginning of a project, or gaining the cooperation of a star whose name is the basis of the projected value of a movie (and who might bring in material too). The chairman of a studio expressed this dual strategy as follows:

The leverage battle is over who has control of the talent that makes a project that somebody wants to make. The agencies get that control because they represent [the talent]. Outside financers get that control because they have money and they give it to them without any restrictions. Studios get that back in two ways. One: they invest in properties, so they [own] the material to a much greater degree than anybody else. Hundreds of projects at every studio, that's their investment—number one. And number two, they battle the agencies for those relationships, so that both agencies and studios have relationships with the talent. (March 2014)

The antagonistic positions of the production and the agency sides also respond to the strictly economic dynamics of the transaction of talent: one interviewed talent agent pointed out that production professionals "are not [our] partners, [because] it's a marketplace" in which the agent-seller and the producer-buyer structurally stand on opposite ends. Agents are the guardians of the "business side of the artists" and make "the bad side of artists worse,"[9] in the eyes of the studios—that is, those who negotiate the most favorable deals for the artists against what production teams see as their best commercial interest. According to their technical and legal professional definition, agents sell talent on the basis of an economic interest they share with the artists, since the agency receives 10 percent of its clients' contract earnings. The structural economic tension between artists and production professionals is thus incarnated by the agents in that sense, as a mechanical result of their mission of talent representation.

The tension between agents and producers is also more direct and stems from the ways in which these professionals evaluate their own worth in comparison with their counterparts of "the other side." Agents sometimes think of production professionals as their more creative equivalent, playing a role that they initially imagined would be their own career path. Producers and studio employees can envy the more stable and lucrative position that some successful agents occupy. This structural opposition manifests itself in diverse ways and impacts the making of artistic careers and products differently depending on the balance of power between the two "sides" at a given moment in time. Since the late 2000s, as many agents explained, lucrative deals and offers from the production side have rarefied so that "buyers are above sellers" and "sellers are in need." In this context, agents no longer think of themselves as being in the dominant position that they sometimes experienced in the previous decades, when a $20 million deal for a top star was not uncommon. By contrast, the suspicion and scorn that some production professionals openly expressed toward agents during our interviews probably reveal their perception of holding a dominant position.

This new order of things derives from changes in studio policy during the 2000s that production professionals have noted. For instance, successful producer Lynda Obst describes in her book *Sleepless in Hollywood* (2013) the emergence of what she calls "the new abnormal," referring to her initial feeling, at the start of her career, that Hollywood was a strange world that she had gradually gotten used to, and to the rapid transformation of this "old abnormal" into something radically new in the first decade of the new millennium. The "old abnormal" captures the idea that the functioning of production companies and studios was anything but truly economically rational. The standard practice for studios was to buy material extensively, including without any specific project to develop it in the near future, merely to prevent the risk of it being owned by a competitor in the event it would become of interest at some later point. The economic vitality of the industry made it possible for production entities to opt for such a stock policy: accumulating material that for a large part wouldn't end up in development; developing projects which wouldn't necessarily ever be green-lighted, to just see how they turn out and what "sticks"; taking risks every year with a few "quality movies," knowing that box-office success was highly uncertain.

Not only was this surplus policy made possible by a favorable economic context prior to the financial crisis of 2007/08, it was strongly rooted in the routines and pragmatic norms of the industry. In a world in which visible failure must first and foremost be avoided,[10] preventing public embarrassment and "saving face" (Goffman 1955) are a priority. In the case study of *The Silence of the Lambs* developed in the prologue, the provision in Warner Bros.'s contracts ensuring that the studio would keep control over the key elements necessary to create a sequel to a movie they produced based on material they owned—even after Warner Bros. passed on making that sequel—falls within such precautionary strategies: it was mostly protecting them from losing face if a competitor succeeded with the sequel to a film that was a box-office failure for Warner Bros.

At the beginning of the 2000s, this old model—in which studios produce a few blockbuster movies scheduled to come out for the holidays and a number of (big) independent films are released in between, with dates expected to be less favorable in terms of box-office revenue—was still in place. A star actor or director (such as George Clooney or Steven Spielberg) could get a studio movie made on his or her sole name and the subsequent anticipation that the film would attract sufficient audience interest. Even if such stars were always few and far between, and their power with the studios the exception in Hollywood, their existence led to the making of some of the most visible and memorable movies until the mid-2000s.

More recently, this type of star-driven film has tended to disappear and give way to another model for studio production: making fewer movies per year while focusing on franchises, sequels, and prequels of previous box-office successes—all of which are conceived as more likely to become lucrative tentpole productions. The new franchise-based model implies that studios focus on buying intellectual property (IP), allowing them to develop a series of movies from already popular books, comics, or stories without necessarily having to pay for costly A-list talent who will make the movie noticeable and familiar to the audience. Consequently, for a studio to produce an original, one-off movie such as *The Silence of the Lambs* becomes increasingly unlikely and is delegated to studios' "independent arms"—such as Fox Searchlight, Sony Pictures Classics, or Paramount Vantage (before it was shutdown in December 2013)—or it results from rarefied " first-look" deals.[11] In general, studios tend to outsource to partner production companies or independent producers (via "negative pickups" or similar distribution deals) the development of comparable projects, even when a deal is made for distribution by a studio.

The audience's "pre-awareness" to the stories and characters is deemed to make the fate of these movies more predictable and the huge financial investment that they represent for the studios less risky. Studio heads indeed describe being held responsible for the investment of $100 million or more,[12] and the subsequent potential loss, attached to such films (Rothman 2004). Owning the material that is at the foundation of any movie—be it a book, a script, a real-life story—gives studios more control over the filmmaking process and diminishes their dependence on writers or stars, and on agencies who represent and sell them. Focusing on film franchises, for a studio, means keeping as much creative and financial control as possible while reducing production costs:

And the biggest movies, the big, big movies, they are developed by studios alone, because they're based on underlying properties—you know, *Batman* and *X-Men* and *Spider-Man* and things like that—and then you own those things. [. . .] If you looked at the top ten movies of the year, basically none of them would be those packaged movies that would be coming from outside. Marvel, they're owned by Disney; *Lord of the Rings*, they're owned by Warner Brothers, they own the property. It's like all the animated films, they're all owned and developed, so yeah, you're going to get a movie, every once in a while, like a *Zero Dark Thirty* or a *Wolf of Wall Street*, there's a movie that was packaged and went out. No studio would have spent that money, because it was too expensive, it was stupid to spend that kind of money. [. . .] And there aren't any big properties left to buy really, but, you know, big books and stuff like that, true stories, studios *have* to buy all of that. They *have* to. Otherwise they will be entirely dependent on the agencies. [. . .] And you can survive a bidding war on some things, but not on everything. (Top studio executive, March 2014, his emphasis)

This new studio production strategy did not emerge in the mid-2000s from a sudden desire to be a profitable business—which, of course, was always there—or from purely rational new economic calculations. It was the result of a gradual perception shift that derived from various intertwined elements, jointly leading key players in major studios to believe that the market had irreversibly changed and that franchises were the answer to the new economic challenges. In this process, the long writers' strike of 2007/08 appeared to the participants as a "game changer" (Obst 2013).[13] At a time when studios were heavily relying on writers to create and develop material, this intense power struggle was a war of nerves challenging the logic of the majors. The strike paralyzed their activity for a while. But it also forced them to define another modus operandi that would make them less dependent on cooperative writers. When the strike finally ended, the studios had started successfully experimenting with such new manners of operating. Industry reporters, columnists, and bloggers covering the writers' strike—such as Nikki Finke, whose online publication, *Deadline Hollywood*, was already an essential landmark and was about to become even more influential—also played a decisive role by providing interpretation frames in reference to which the participants defined the situation and strategized their actions.[14] Studio moguls felt free to state publicly that the vocation of their company was to make film franchises that are internationally lucrative, preferably using studio owned material rather than external material brought in by writers. In a context of rapid decline of domestic film revenue and, conversely, of increased reliance on foreign markets, betting on world-famous superheroes rather than on stars whose international numbers weren't high, or on film genres that don't travel well,[15] appeared as a profitable choice. It also seemed to be a safe option in face of the challenges brought by the collapse of DVD sales and the rise of digital production/distribution. Such interconnected perception change resulted from tacit coordination in a situation of competition rather than from some conspiracy-like initiative on the part of studio heads.[16] Together, the events of 2007/08 gradually shaped this perception shift: the participants felt that the game was put to the test, redefining their anticipations in interdependent ways and eventually leading to the stabilization of a new collective interpretation of "the market reality."

The new studio practice came with various effects. The accent placed on owning IP mechanically made writers secondary. The pitching of ideas that could attract star talent also became less important. This process also went hand in hand with changes in what is valued (in terms of skills, best use of one's time, valued type of behavior), and therefore *who* is seen as an asset among studio executives and heads: the model of the creative entrepreneur recognized for his or her eye for promising original projects and his or her close relationships with star talent, whose success appeared to stem from a succession of risky bets, was being gradually supplanted by the figure of the top corporate executive who is an expert in conducting risk-controlled investment strategies by securing the rights to film franchises and "sequelizable" productions, and whose practice resembles that of certain professionals in the world of finance.[17]

Production professionals, when they have started in the industry before the 2000s and identify with the risk-taker profile rather than the risk-controlling one, frequently deplore what they describe as "more clinical" practices, less oriented toward the building of interpersonal, talent-oriented relationships (Obst 2013). As studios became part of large media conglomerates that don't place the making of movie at the center of their activity,[18] the very definition of what constitutes a "big project," a "profitable film," an "acceptable risk," and a "studio movie" itself changed accordingly. What the "market" was imagined to be took new dimensions. This former CAA agent recalls and recounts his experience of such changes:

The studios [. . .] all used to be privately owned, but now they're all parts of big companies. Look at the studio movies that have been made, two things have happened: when Universal released *Jaws* in 1975, Universal's stock went up seven points, from that one movie, which is tremendous. Warner Brothers owns arguably the largest, biggest franchises in the history of motion picture business: they have the Batman movie series, Lord of the Rings series, the Superman movie series, the Harry Potter movie series, and the AOL-Time Warner stock has dropped almost two hundred and fifty, three hundred points in the last five or six years. With all of those franchises, the movie business is maybe two, three, maybe four percent of the net income of the parent company. It's nothing, it's not even on the radar, it doesn't move the needle. [. . .] A hundred million dollars' gain or loss doesn't change their business. The studios need to make a billion dollars per film, seven hundred million dollars per film to make it profitable. So little movies, [. . .] an independent company movie, that kind of movies, the studios aren't making any more. If you're a writer, studios aren't buying your script, because the movies they're making are all based on source material that is familiar to people: Harry Potter, Spider-Man, Batman, Superman, The Avengers, Lord of the Rings. (April 2013)

The dominant position of the major studios allows them to "lead the dance" and defines what is left for other production entities—be it mini majors or smaller production companies—to do. Changes in studio practices thus induce the interdependent reshaping of activities in the whole production system. As studios increasingly withdraw from financing one-off movies, "big" independent films—even those involving top talent and made for an already fairly consequent budget—are financed through different channels, studios stepping in at the distribution stage (often to fill their less desirable distribution spots) at best. This also rearranges the relationship between studio production and critical/professional consecration, as the movies that get nominated for awards and acclaimed for their aesthetic quality tend to emerge from this pool of talent-driven independent films.

The reshaping of the production side and that of the representation side are also inseparable. After 2008, in what industry participants describe as a "tight market," the power of the buyers over those who sell talent was enhanced by fewer projects and job opportunities offered to artists. The traditional distinction between the "incoming-call business" of the biggest agencies, constantly receiving offers from the studios/producers, and the "outgoing-call business" of smaller companies, that need to be more proactive, becomes less relevant when the extremely lucrative deals once granted to the stars now rarely happen, and the status of stardom itself changes accordingly. Because the prominence of the young movie stars of the 1990s whose names seemed to open any production door is "gone"—in the words of a top talent agent—"so the [corresponding] money, for agents, is gone."[19]

The decline of star power from which the large agencies used to draw their own leverage affects the balance of power relations between studios and agencies, but it also gives rise to new agenting strategies by which sellers invest new domains of activity and restore their standing. The development of packaging has brought agenting in many ways closer to production practices, making it increasingly decisive for the orchestration of cultural production in various sectors. Now packaging different types of projects (studio movies and TV shows, as well as independent features or projects of shorter format) for various media (film, TV, digital), agents are involved in a form of meta-creative work. Packaging independent films with domestic and foreign artists, financiers, producers, and distributors is opposed to pure sales activities by the agent quoted below. It is also understood as the sign of an ongoing process that places the agent more and more at the heart as well as the starting point of the creative process. While, by law, agents are not supposed to produce and therefore cannot officially be credited in this capacity, interviewees repeatedly claimed such a producing role, expressing the pride they take in these production-like dimensions of agenting:

We, agents, are trying, even more so now than ever before, to *be the engine*, and the creative force, [. . .] the producerial power behind the packaging of film. Traditionally, you're really in the sales business, your bread and butter is selling clients into jobs that already exist, so it's less about involvement and more about sales. [. . .] There's more of a desire, because studios are making fewer and fewer movies, so there are fewer jobs for clients, and the jobs that exist are paying less money, so you have a lot of anxious clients who want to go to work and it's become imperative that you create work [for clients]. (Talent agent, big agency, November 2014, her emphasis)

Agencies also diversify their activities in other ways and toward other sectors, from the lucrative nonscripted television or brand representation businesses to the challenge of monetizing digital media. That film buyers have in time become fewer[20] and more "risk averse"[21] is a shared perception of industry transformation; it is also recounted in more personal stories that senior agents tell, evoking a significant shift in what was possible for projects and careers experienced over a relatively short period of time. At this individual level, the new state of the game leads a younger generation of agents to imagine their profile and specialization differently from that of their predecessors. For instance, a interviewed literary agent newly promoted at one of the major agencies described his career strategy: to build a strong list of writer-directors who would be key elements of independent film packages (and would therefore be in demand) first of all internally within the agency and with its department in charge of packaging indies/international productions, and ultimately in a market he anticipated would keep developing. Interdependent systemic changes thus tie together the fate of all the protagonists. I will now look more closely at the inseparable transformation of the agency system.

The New Reality of Agenting in Big Hollywood

Recent transformations of agenting in Big Hollywood are often referred to the new agency model that CAA represented from the late 1970s on, and to the shift from that to a "post-Ovitz" era. Through his success in building CAA into the most powerful agency in the 1980s and '90s, Michael Ovitz is commonly described as the demiurge responsible for shaping and leading the reconfiguration of the system linking together the main agencies and the major studios. Turning an agenting style into an organizational "culture," the group of five young dissidents[22] who left the reputable William Morris Agency (WMA) to create CAA in 1975 ushered in new practices in the talent representation business. These new professional repertoires were attached to an organizational model: building teams of agents that attract already high-end talent through the exhibition of ostensible signs of power and importance; that is, notably, through the staging of relationships with other key players. At an organizational level, this strategy intended to create a more collaborative type of structure encouraging the sharing of resources and assets internally, in contrast with the more individualistic and internally competitive model under which other agencies were organized—and that ICM, under the leadership of Jeff Berg, was especially known for.[23] The success of their endeavor put Ovitz and his collaborators in a position to systematize packaging practices, to attract some of their competitors' most successful clients, and oftentimes, because the stars that the studios wanted were massively represented by CAA, to impose their conditions to the buyers.

But the story of how CAA changed the industry is only one piece of the puzzle. In fact, a more collective and systemic process was in play. The modes of action and organization that made CAA successful circulated widely in the agency world and hybridized as they were appropriated by others in different contexts. All the leading agencies transformed on a relational level. The new ways of agenting born from the diffusion and the adaptations of the CAA model (focused on packaging, "poaching" competitors' clients, etc.) progressively became a professional norm in Big Hollywood. Veteran agents had to convert themselves to these new ways of doing the job that newcomers perceived as typical. Those who launched new agencies in the early 1990s—UTA (1991) and Endeavor (1995) in particular—had the precedent of CAA in mind, but they had already distanced themselves from this model. The collective reorganizing of the agency business, in a favorable economic context in which the studios had money to spend on hiring stars and developing projects, led to the constitution of a group of big agencies that had the critical mass of clients and agents necessary to develop the practice of packaging. By the start of the 2000s, agents had negotiated unprecedented salaries for their star clients, and star power inseparably meant agency power. But, as I just recounted, the balance of forces between studios and agencies, then in favor of the latter, was about to swing back.

At the same time, for agencies internally, growth translated into an increased division of labor, both in compartmentalization and specialization (see figures 2 and 3). The constitution of new roles and areas of expertise generated institutional boundaries within the structure of the agencies: the departments by which agencies were traditionally organized—(talent or literary) motion pictures and television, music, theater, commercials, books—were subdivided and supplemented with new divisions in charge of the yet-uncharted territories. These new agenting roles manifest the *extension of the domain of Hollywood* in new sectors such as nonscripted television, gaming, branding, sport, and digital media. They emerged from transformations in the economy of media, especially with the development of cable television and then the supplanting of DVDs by digital outlets for distribution. They were shaped interdependently with the transformation affecting the studios and the production side that I described above. The development of "alternative TV" agents into separate teams responded to the persistence over time of the type of television shows regarded at first as a passing fad; the importance of literary rights for the agencies changed with the new studio focus on IP; agency departments specializing in packaging independent films pulled even further ahead once the studios withdrew from that segment. At the same time, they decisively contributed to the development of such transformation process.

The development of these additional branches of activity has led to new areas of expertise: new subprofessions and career paths have emerged within the scope of talent representation.[24]

It used to be a high level of specialization back in the day, in the '60s and '70s. At William Morris when I worked for them, I was in the music department; I wanted to get

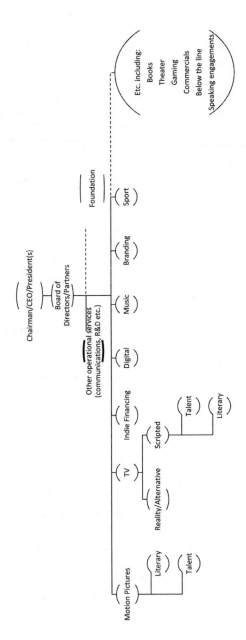

Chairman/CEO/President(s)

Board of Directors/Partners

Other operational services (communications, R&D etc.)

Foundation

Motion Pictures
Literary
Talent

TV
Reality/Alternative
Scripted
Talent
Literary

Indie Financing

Digital

Music

Branding

Sport

Etc. including:
Books
Theater
Gaming
Commercials
Below the line
Speaking engagements

2   Example of functional division in a large talent agency

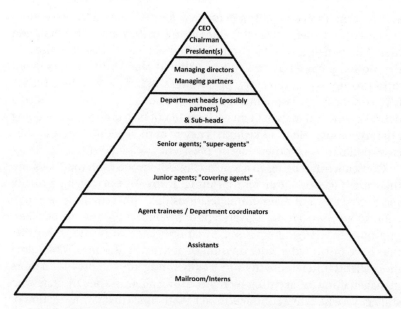

3   Example of hierarchical structure of positions in a large talent agency

out of it, I wanted to move in the actor's business . . . they said no. And I left. They were specialized. Then, they were like: "That's dumb because TV actors are movie actors, TV writers are movie writers! We want hyphening agents!" Now you are in [the] reality business or in [the] digital business, and these things really don't cross over as much. That's interesting. That creates more specialization, but not the old [way of specialization]. (Talent agent, big agency, September 2012)

These changes take the form of organizational dilemmas in the private bureaucracies that are the large agencies. Growth and increased specialization translate into the development of agency compartmentalization. The institutional functioning of the big agencies tends to reinforce the differentiation between departments, and so does the way in which agents are usually evaluated and compensated. At the same time, agency leaders know that they must institutionalize the necessary circulation of their artists between complementary sectors, and toward what they believe to be the most promising new areas. For instance, the boundary between film and television has become permeable, and the symbolic hierarchy between the two has been rearranged in favor of the latter. However, for the individual agent, crossing an artist over to a different media or area of practice without deferring to colleagues in the concerned department remains a risky subversion of organizational order, as this agent quoted describes; "crossover agents" remain the exception: "I started as a literary agent [representing writers and directors], and then I branched into talent [representing actors], I've always been in the motion picture business. When I started representing actors in addition to my writer-directors, people were like: "You're doing *both?!*" It's like shocking, blasphemy. And now it's not so unusual. I'm called a hybrid agent, and it's what I love—I would not be happy to just be doing lit[erary] or just talent. I like both. They're both very different, but they cross-pollinate each other" (agent, big agency, March 2013).

Consequently, "being an agent" in Big Hollywood from the 2000s and thereafter takes on a different meaning. It involves practicing a highly specialized job, and maintaining relationships with a small circle of pre-defined buyers regarding a given type of product and/or profile of client, in a quickly changing environment and in large corporate companies that have instituted a strict division of activity. It also means handling more clients, often more than 150. Only top agents can preserve a more managerial way of agenting by representing a few of the rare stars who still get very lucrative contracts from the studios. This transformation of agenting and agencies in Big Hollywood is directly related to the notable development of management companies since the late 1990s. Nowadays, actors and actresses commonly have both an agent and a manager, and this is more and more the case of directors and writers as well. Convergent mechanisms have made managers into an increasingly important professional group in Hollywood. First, agenting is a "numbers game": agents have to manage a very long client list, and the artists who are not generating enough revenue to the agency are likely to be forgotten or less diligently serviced, and tempted to look for the more personalized attention of a manager, who typically handles a lot less clients. Second, the profession of manager appears as an attractive alternative to agenting for agents in various positions. Agents from the big companies might be able to take one or two star clients with them and establish a more quiet practice, allowing them to also produce on the side. Another case is that of agency employees who are laid off and who find in managing an obvious professional reconversion.

The development of large talent agencies into such complex organizations has also generated a new class of agency leaders, who are more distant from the practice of agenting itself and closer to other types of powerful business leaders, and whose professional value is no longer exclusively or primarily derived from their client list. This big agency leader explained:

The major companies, each does something similar and each is engaged in things that are different. I think our core businesses are similar, but our emphasis may be different. Our sizes are different. Our method of capitalization is different. We have private equity partners in this company. [. . .] But the businesses are run, managed, and operated by professionals, each of whom has been in the business for an excess of twenty years. So there's an experienced professional class of executives who run these firms, but who are also agents. (April 2011)

In sum, agencies as organizations have radically changed shape as part of the more general process of corporatization and globalization of Hollywood (Curtin and Sanson 2016). Parallel to the studios, the big agency world is a shrinking oligopoly. From the "Big Five" agencies (CAA, WMA, ICM, UTA, Endeavor) made "Big Four" by the WMA-Endeavor merger in 2009, two giants have emerged as a result of the concentration and diversification process: CAA and WME. The latter now surpasses its competitor in size, thanks to the $2.4 billion deal wherein WME bought the sports marketing giant IMG Worldwide, announced in December 2013. WME and IMG combined then totaled more than 3,000 employees in cities around the world, compared with CAA's 1,500. Later acquisitions increased WME's number of employees to more than 5,000. The extraordinary growth of these companies is better measured when one considers that, in the mid-1990s, CAA totaled only approximately 500 employees. This former motion picture agent remembered the start of his career at CAA in the mid-1980s and the drastic changes the company underwent:

Likewise, the studios have changed—they're all owned by very large companies, they're making four, five, six movies a year, down from thirty or forty movies a year, and the agencies also have now large companies that have bought them. When I started at CAA, it was fifty people on half the floor in Century City. Now, it's probably three thousand people, seven or eight offices around the world, sixteen hundred people here in Century City, and they have another company that came in and purchased a percentage of it. So there's accountability across the board that there wasn't before. They're in the business of making money. (April 2013)

Both CAA and WME have relatively recently partnered up with a private equity investor as well as invested in outside companies.[25] They are expected to soon have an IPO and become public companies. By contrast, the still privately owned agencies UTA and ICM work at repositioning their image as more "artist-friendly" companies, while the industry press reveals that client representation was only 14 percent of WME's revenue in 2013, and certainly less thereafter (Waxman and Shaw 2014). The gap separating Little from Big Hollywood grows wider as bigger entities tend to focus less exclusively on representing artists. In fact, the meaning of talent representation itself changes. Agenting develops beyond what formed the core of the practice—that is, the brokerage of artists and projects, with identified film and TV buyers, for which the agency receives ten percent of the negotiated contracts, from which agents get their nickname of "tenpercenters." Agencies venture in new directions, distant from the mission of representing individual talent and even from a literal understanding of "show business": agents nowadays represent reality television performers, chefs, athletes, and web celebrities, as well as corporations and brands, as much as (and often more lucratively than) actors, directors, writers, and below-the-line personnel. "Talent" is also redefined in this very process.[26] In addition, as agencies have developed investments in tech companies and start-ups, they are increasingly drifting apart from the original definition of agenting, which placed the relationships with (successful) artists at its heart and defined the type of economic activities that are a priority for the agency accordingly. Such transformations have not made the reference to movies and stars and the activity around them completely irrelevant. The aura and "sexiness"[27] of Hollywood movie stars—and the symbolic capital attached to them— are precisely what investors acquire when they decide to put money in Hollywood rather than in a more predictable and stable type of business. However, "the end of the reliance on the ten percent" business, as a senior talent agent at one of the biggest company described it, is a shift in terms of economic model as much as it alters the significance of the relationship between agents and artists and the association between agenting and "being in the arts," therefore affecting the agent's professional identification.

The evolution of studios and big agencies into complex corporate entities, institutionalized and rationalized in their organization, and whose activities go way beyond talent representation and filmmaking, directly impacts the *experience of agenting*. Agents who have entered the profession before the 1990s, although they don't form a homogenous group, tend to manifest a vision of their professional mission that differs from that of younger generations, whose concept of what an agent is and does has been formed in a different context. When the former were socialized in this professional world and trained for the job, even the most powerful agencies were not the large corporate entities that they are nowadays, and the studios had not yet fully undertaken the transformation that their inclusion in today's media conglomerates implies; "having relationships" with the production side therefore meant something significantly different. Senior agents describe the physicality of agenting—going in person to a studio and physically standing in an executive's way, handing him or her a script or an artist's headshot and résumé in paper form, advocating in face-to-face interactions—that new technical devices and professional arrangements have partly eclipsed. They express the distance they feel toward increasingly bureaucratized structures, be they compartmentalized agencies or studios where anonymous committees seem to rule and executives are subject to a high turnover. The mentioned changes in the social definition of stardom inevitably affect their relationship to talent, and the impact it has on their own stature. Changes in the types and genres of the movies that major buyers are willing to buy also come with repercussions for an agent's career and self-concept. So does the fact that Big Hollywood agencies get increasingly involved with activities outside the realm of individual talent representation.

This comes with consequences that agents can anticipate, and which they describe as making them question their career perspectives and threatening the creative dimension of their professional identity (Roussel 2016): "If you are partially owned by an outside, non-entertainment company, they're kicking the tires to see their return on investment, and they're not always as knowledgeable as they need to be about really what's going on, aside from just what the bottom line is. And so WME and CAA both have P&L [profit and loss] statements that they have to really *manage*, and that means cutting clients, cutting agents, making choices not based necessarily on the artistry, but based on the bottom line" (talent agent, big agency, March 2013, her emphasis).

Agents who were trained at a time when agencies focused more exclusively on representing artists in the traditional areas (cinema, television, books, music, theater) are the first ones to point to such changes. A former agent with responsibilities high up at a big agency, later converted to management, confessed that agenting had become "not as fun as it used to be" with the growth of the major agencies whose leaders now "want to dominate the world" and "do not care as much," as opposed to a time when one didn't "sacrifice relationships in the business just for an extra buck" (April 2014). Indeed, as the agent quoted below suggested, agency owners and managers who are running large businesses and have to report to their shareholders cannot value what this talent agent called the "lost art of agenting," which is precisely at the heart of his worth as he sees it:

I feel like I'm an artist. My art is being able to craft an argument and leverage other artists and find collaborations that will work. And then get the money. That's the job, that's what I think is my art form. . . . I don't think that the executives today have a reason, nor are they cultivated, nor are they trained to think of it that way. And because frankly, art does not necessarily mean commerce. I think that it's the goal of the owners to create more corporate executives and agents who are more interested in turning a buck than they are relating to talent. (Big Hollywood, April 2012)

Indeed, agents are more or less explicitly invited to change their daily practice in ways that meet the extension of Hollywood professed by agency managers,[28] even though at this point of the process no one fully knows what this reinvention of agenting will mean exactly, or how it will precisely happen. This employee of one of the leading agencies described it like so: "You feel the intimidation that you have to evolve and adapt for the young agents; you feel the pressure from the competitors who call every one of our clients night and day to try to sign them as though we are no longer in that business; you feel the opportunity of [other] agencies offering agents jobs and trying to pull them out now that there's uncertainty at [this company]. So that's a real upheaval in emotion and structure" (January 2014).

In this context, top Hollywood players improvise just as much as smaller professionals do, paving the road as they go, by trial and error, and feeling their way according to gradual and interconnected shifts of perceptions. While the most experienced agents might be nostalgic for what agenting used to be, it is not completely gone, since the professionals who embody these perceptions and this definition of agenting are still at work. They adapt to present professional models, resisting them to a certain extent, tinkering with the old and the new, building forms of continuity in their identity and experience. Let's now turn to the concrete conditions in which it all happens: the process by which professional agents are made in organizations.

THREE

The Making of Professionals in Talent Agencies

Who are the agents?[1] Just by spending time at the agencies, it is easy to observe that agents form a predominantly white-male professional group.[2] The recent and fast feminization of the group is well illustrated by the case of Judy Hofflund, who was in 1982 the first woman to be hired at the entry level of CAA, its mailroom.[3] In the past thirty years, as women were increasingly getting access to the profession, they started populating the bottom and midlevels of the agencies. While the numbers of male and female agents are gradually evening out at the bottom level of the large organizations, and as women are sometimes reaching managerial positions at small agencies, female agents remain underrepresented as department heads, partners, and owners of the biggest companies.[4]

In terms of socioeconomic backgrounds, those who become agents are mostly from upper-middle-class origins when they operate in the major agencies (typically with a father in a liberal profession—often a doctor or lawyer—and a mother who stays at home) and more often from middle-class origins when they work at smaller companies (their parents being small business owners/storekeepers, or sometimes teachers, among the more intellectual and cultural professions). They thus tend to come from families that accumulate and retain cultural and economic resources in diverse proportions. The interviewed agents often insisted on having inherited from their parents their interest for and familiarity with the arts. However, against the idea of the prevalence of "Hollywood families," most of the agents I talked to initially had either an extremely loose connection or, often times, no connection at all with the entertainment industry.

Given such social backgrounds, it is not surprising that agents commonly hold a BA if not a higher level of diploma, from well-ranked schools and sometimes from Ivy League ones, especially when they end up working in a big agency. Agents with such profiles are the ones who have penetrated the profession since the 1980s and who are now in their fifties or younger. Among my interviewees, 38 percent hold degrees from art programs and schools (mostly in film or production studies, but also in other areas such as theater or dance, for instance), while 24 percent studied another discipline of the humanities or social sciences, and 33 percent come from a law or business school background. Among the latter are those who industry insiders themselves call the "Harvard kids"—graduates from prestigious schools holding MBAs or law degrees—who entered the agency business in the 1980s and '90s, during what is considered by the concerned as a golden age: studios' activity was flourishing and money was flowing. The entertainment industry was seen as one sector among others (such as finance or banking) that could offer job prospects to people who thought of themselves as future top executives in a lucrative business. Individuals who embraced agenting with such a perspective were usually comfortable with the idea of working in a corporate environment and as specialized experts in the manufacture and transaction of specific types of artistic product or practice.[5] In many cases, television became their area of expertise, since this is a sector from which the agencies make a lot of their profits. Some of them made their way to leading positions in the major agencies, which placed them in a position to weigh in on the current reconfiguration of the game, turning agenting into corporate entrepreneurship.

During the 1980s and '90s and thereafter, agents with much more "art-focused" educational paths and backgrounds also penetrated the industry. They formed a numerical majority—all the more so today, as Hollywood is no longer seen as "another Wall Street" and the profile of the "Harvard kid" has rarefied among the candidates to agencies mailrooms and assistant positions. The latter are now massively populated by graduates with diverse backgrounds in art, social sciences, humanities, psychology. Agents who studied art often initially envisioned their future to be on the "creative side" (as an actor, a filmmaker, or a producer), even though the cases of people who actually tried to make it as an artist before converting themselves to agenting are in fact rare. What remains, however, is their inclination to define themselves as film connoisseurs, who operate "in the arts" and aspire to participate in the creative process. Some of these agents have also climbed to the top of the agency game; they then tend to possess the type of power associated in Hollywood with the building of a strong talent list. This, of course, doesn't mean that the sales dimension is completely overlooked or not acted on by agents with such profiles. Nor are the ambition to be creative and the reference to talent absent in the case of agents with more business-oriented backgrounds. I will show below that both dimensions are continuously present and constitutive of agents' professional definition.

The formal requirement that new recruits at an agency hold at least a bachelor's degree and the fact that they often have an even higher degree in practice show the specialization and sophistication that have accompanied, in the recent decades, the growth of agencies as organizations and the diversification of agenting activities. By contrast, agents who started prior to the 1980s entered the profession at a time when no diploma was required to be hired at the bottom level of an agency and to make one's way up. Such "self-made agents" are now progressively disappearing from this professional group. They were trained at a time when the agency and studio world was far from being the complex and institutionalized space within which the perceptions of younger agents have been structured. This transformation has changed the morphology of this occupational group. While agenting was morphing into an increasingly professionalized and corporatized activity, the agencies were attracting new profiles that were, on one hand, increasingly similar to those characterizing other types of businesses and, on the other hand, more diversified than the stereotypical idea of the "Hollywood community" suggests. This observation contradicts the preconception—which I was repeatedly confronted with while I was writing this book, although usually not from Hollywood insiders—that religious affiliation directly matters for understanding agenting and agents' inclusion into professional circles, with the specific reference to Jewish networks in Hollywood.[6]

Indeed, when an agent is an executive performing a specialized activity, possibly working in a large corporate entity, often hired among graduates of top universities rather than on the basis of interpersonal connections, forms of solidarity based on belonging to the same religious community and to local interconnection networks cannot be or remain prevalent. However, once in their professional role, agents do work at getting/staying integrated into occupational networks, which is achieved—especially in Big Hollywood—on the basis of a shared life-style and the presence in common spaces of sociability: for instance, living in particular neighborhoods (Brentwood, Beverly Hills, Malibu), going to the same restaurants and vacation sites, belonging to certain country clubs, getting your children into a limited number of "elite" schools. Going to the same synagogue or hosting events on religious occasions—when someone is observant enough to do so, which is not always the case in a secularized professional world such as Hollywood—can be one of these mechanisms by which "the camaraderie" (as one of the agents I shadowed put it) gets built and maintained.

That said, in the spirit of Weber's approach to the Protestant ethic ([1905] 2002), we need to ask ourselves what exactly is *the way in which* religion matters in this case.[7] Rather than religious mental schemes shaping the professional, or Jewishness structuring agenting by way of cultural determination, what I have observed is mostly the opposite: professional dynamics frame the relevance of activating other types of affinities or proximities, as well as the ways and occasions whereby this activation happens. In other words, occupational logics preside over the formation of social groups. For instance, a former agent at a boutique agency explained how, at the start of her career, she used multiple mechanisms of identification—as a woman and/or as a Jew—to try triggering reactions of solidarity from other Hollywood professionals and opening certain doors in this way. Even if she described being somewhat successful in gaining support, she also highlighted her ability to learn the language of the industry, recognize key players, and know who was a trustworthy dealmaker as the determining elements that allowed her to establish herself professionally. Playing on multiple social affiliations and identifications was a tool among others to build occupational relationships. Such identifications gave substance to strategies aimed at creating ties and drawing inclusive boundaries, favorable to her professional endeavor, rather than an intrinsic source of mutual support or connection. Another illustration can be found in the endless time that assistants devote during their evenings and weekends to socializing over drinks and at events, so as to be included in circles of industry professionals (as the next sections explain in detail). Whatever dimension of one's "identity" is used and displayed to engage others in such contexts, what is at stake with this type of sociability work is to *belong to the industry*. The boundary between private life/identifications and professional ones gets blurred in the process, at the same time as the frontier separating Hollywood insiders from outsiders is fortified.

Indeed, in a city, Los Angeles, in which a considerable proportion of the population works in the entertainment industry, Hollywood should be approached as a professional world with "thick boundaries" separating insiders from outsiders. Agents have often started, from a young age, investing most of their energy into activities that relate directly to their professional practice and role in one way or another: activity in this world tends to transcend the usual definition of a "professional" space that could be kept clearly separate from "private life" and its particular scenes and times. Indeed, being an agent is usually a very absorbing activity that comes to pervade (almost) all of someone's life, including nights, weekends, and vacation time—all moments we are used to thinking of as "private" or "domestic" time and that define "professional life" apart from the "personal sphere." So, whereas the boundary between inside and outside Hollywood is thick, the boundary between the professional and the personal appears blurry. Success in agenting also comes at this price.

I'm guilty of, before I'm going to bed, checking my e-mail, you know? [. . .] In this business, because you want to be readily accessible to everyone, you're constantly on the phone. If we leave our office, our phone is forwarded to our cell phone, so if you dial my office, it rings my cell phone. I don't want to miss a call. It's kind of sad. I've even found myself in a movie theater, getting texts and quietly texting back an actor while watching a movie, taking myself out of the experience to do my job. So now, I think most agents and managers that are really in the know and working constantly are 24/7 on their phones. It's kind of bleak. [. . . There's never a time] at the end of the day [where] you close your shop and you go home and you spend time with your family. You start your next day. I don't ever have any family time. (Talent agent, Little Hollywood, September 2010)

This chapter and the following one examine how agents' professional identity[8] forms. They explore the relational making of trajectories in Hollywood, in the context of the configurations that agents inhabit successively as their career develops. Trajectories here do not simply refer to preexisting steps that one can take to progress in an objective hierarchy of positions; I will show that they have a lot to do with the more informal, interdependent perception of power relations tying small circles of participants together over long periods of time. This approach to trajectories leads us to elucidate how identifications are constructed in the same process. Newcomers to the agency business have to learn the inner workings of this relational game in order to make sense of it and become a player in it.

"Fulfilling Somebody Else's Dreams"

Contrary to the model of the professional vocation, starting at an agency is almost always depicted as accidental, the result of unforeseen circumstances. The profession "chooses you more than you choose it," to paraphrase one of the interviewees. This is because, as another agent stated, "as a little kid, nobody sets out and [says], 'I want to be an agent.' You sort of fall into it a little bit."[9] This perception is not typical of agents with modest careers or whose professional situation would seem likely to inspire resentment. Very successful professionals in this field express a similar perspective. An agent in his early fifties—one holding a powerful position in the agenting world, as he represents star talent at one of the biggest agencies—shared the disenchanted conviction that agenting is always something one ends up doing "by default": "I've never met anybody who grew up wanting to be an agent. That's an entire industry, and I've never met anybody who knew in high school that they were going to be an agent! [. . .] You don't want to come to Hollywood to fulfill somebody else's dream, and being a dream fulfiller of others becomes your dream. It's a little not real, it's a little bullshit" (October 2010).

Such a reference to initial (and lost) Hollywood dreams is especially present with agents who have first imagined pursuing an artistic career themselves (as an actor, a director, a writer, or a producer, or sometimes in the world of music), after completing a degree in arts or entertainment. Most of the time, working on the talent side remained a briefly entertained hope or a fleeting idea—often dissipating during college years—rather than a failed professional choice. In rare cases however, becoming an agent was a real professional shift, conceived at the same time as the continuation of the initial artistic vocation in terms of skills that the agent can reemploy: for instance, a former actor turned agent insisted on the fact that he "act[s] now more on the phone than [he] did as an actor [. . .], improvising constantly."[10] Other interviewees have underlined the analogy between the necessity of "hanging in there" and starting with demanding and underpaid internships and jobs only loosely connected to the agent's real professional practice, on one hand, and the situation experienced by actors-to-be when they arrive in LA and have to accept insecure and unwanted jobs to survive, on the other hand. Leaving behind an early "Hollywood dream" in which one was standing on the talent side and pursuing agenting as a career sometimes means making virtue of a necessity and reinterpreting, in retrospect, one's professional path as a lucky fate.[11]

At the same time, it certainly doesn't mean that disappointment and frustration are common modes of the profession. In fact, there is no reason to question what agents with this type of path say when they express the passion that they have developed for their activity, having fully embraced it as a *vicarious vocation*. In that sense, "fulfilling somebody else's dream" truly does become their dream. It is, however, important to understand the centrality of the creative component of their professional practice (versus its deal-making dimension) in their own eyes. Their connection with artists and what agents call their "sense of talent" are placed at the core of their professional self-definition:

I want to make sure, after my time is here, to be able to make as much of a difference as I can, potentially in as many different people, but do it in a meaningful way. [. . .] To me, it's much more important to touch people. If you really think about it, that's why so many people get into this business, not for the money or the fame. They got in it because either a movie or a TV show touched them. It made a profound effect. So, that's why I got in. [. . .] I'm never going to be a good writer, I have no desire to be a director or an actor, and I wouldn't be really any good at either those [things]. But I'm really good with talent, so this way, I can help the talent, in that sense, and have them make a difference. (Below-the-line agent, Big Hollywood, September 2010)

This "vocation by proxy" allows for the expression of forms of vicarious singularity—that is, being unique because your clients are, feeling like an artist by association with the talent you represent—and the use of the vocabulary of inspiration and creativity to define one's craft and identity. But it also manifests agents' ambiguous relation to their own role. Because they "fell into it" and often didn't imagine at first that they were going to spend a professional lifetime practicing it, many agents conduct their career with an eye toward other paths that they could possibly follow, one day, in the entertainment industry. A senior agent speaks about what he perceives to be the state of mind of the younger colleagues that he mentors during agency "retreats," the sessions organized in this context being, beyond their official focus on communicating agenting skills, an occasion to share personal impressions and experiences:

There's no intention of being agent in the first place. No one said: "I want to be an agent." Some of them fell in[to] it, and they love it. And even the ones that fell in[to] it and love it, if you gave them the opportunity to leave it, would leave it. [. . . They'd want to be] elsewhere in the business. Not necessarily elsewhere in the world—elsewhere in the business. They want to run studios, they want to run Steven Spielberg's company,

they want to partner with George Clooney, they want to open a management company, they want to produce *Modern Family*, they want to direct *Meet the Parents*, whatever it is, that's what they want; it isn't this. (Big Hollywood, February 2013)

Even if agents don't systematically turn to management and/or production, this is indeed a common transition to make after having spent
the first part of a career at an agency. This gives us an indication of
the symbolic (and sometimes, but not always, economic) hierarchy that
tends to keep agents' positions "below" those occupied by their counterparts on the production side. On the other hand, it also reveals another
characteristic of the agenting profession: it is, as insiders put it, "a young
person's job"—interviewees often referring to the intense and frenetic
pace of an agent's life and comparing it to the impossibility of remaining "an athlete" past a certain age. One can certainly have a career in
agenting and eventually become a mentor to junior colleagues and an
agency manager/owner, either in Big or in Little Hollywood. Nevertheless, the scarcity of such leadership positions and the aspiration to have
more control over their own time and activity often lead agents over
fifty to at least consider moving into talent management and production. In some cases, academic programs in production and film schools
also offer job prospects to former agents, whether they operated in Little
or Big Hollywood. This incentive for career change can take the form of
a late professional challenge for those who have practiced agenting from
a young age and have constructed their entire identity around it.

An Agent's Initiatory Path

There is no university curriculum in agenting,[12] no program or institution in charge of training these specialized professionals before they start
operating in Hollywood. So Hollywood is, in this sense, *integrally* where
agents are made. Agents' "schooling" is in fact internal to the agency
world itself. More precisely, the making of the agent's savoir faire and
interpersonal skills is, for the most part, delegated to the largest companies. Their mailrooms function as an entry point and a filter for access to
the profession as a whole and, in fact, to the business side of the industry, more generally speaking.[13] The many trainees and assistants of the
major agencies serve as a pool from which are hired not only those who
will be promoted to junior agents, but also future managers and production professionals. Many of the agents who end up working in a midsize
or small agency have started in the mailroom of one of the big agencies,

without always going successfully through the test and being selected to move one step forward in the hierarchy of a major agency.

The dependence of the young agent on the agency as a place of accreditation and professional socialization derives from an *initiatory process* followed by each newcomer within the largest companies. This path begins in the *mailroom*, where the intense work (as undervalued as it is badly paid) contrasts with the profiles of the candidates who oftentimes hold prestigious university degrees that usually give rise to other expectations. It then follows a succession of well-organized steps that allow those who were "nothing" to be made part of the game by the organization. To start in one of the famous agency mailrooms and spend from a few weeks to several years learning the ropes there belongs to the instituting experiences through which one becomes an industry insider.[14] It is invoked as the original moment in someone's professional history, and it also contributes to sustaining a shared professional mythology— among Hollywood insiders—defining possible and successful career paths and the qualities that one is required to possess to go through the journey and "become somebody" in this world. This is an egalitarian mythology adapting the Hollywood dream (and the American dream) to the professional space of agenting: it tells us that anyone can make it in the profession with sufficient ambition and hard work, regardless of social origin, education, or other resources or credentials acquired outside of the industry itself. Being a "self-starter" and a "forward thinker" are described as key qualities by agency managers and human resources heads who are in charge of hiring future agents. The invocation of the "self-made agent" is also omnipresent in this field. This female agent— who entered the agency world with a drama degree but professes that "you could do marine biology, it doesn't really matter"—confirmed:

Anyone can get into it. You don't necessarily have to be the smartest person on the planet; you don't have to have a certain amount of credentials, necessarily. So it's really about personality and drive and a variety of things. I do think that the exciting part is that you don't have to necessarily pass a certain test. But, it's easy to read out who legitimately knows how to conduct their business and who doesn't. And it's all based on how hard you work, you know. Connections—sure, they can affect how fast you progress or who you get in with, but, ultimately, for the most part, you could have graduated from Harvard and you still have to start in the mailroom to become an agent. (Manager, former agent at a big agency, November 2010, Paris)

Because starting in the mailroom characterizes a standard path and is almost always a prerequisite for a career in the agency business—with the exception of only a few side paths—all situations seem to be equalized and social inequalities erased as one enters the organizational framework of the agency. However, one's initial background and social resources do continue factor into the chances one has to rise faster out of the mailroom and to progress in the hierarchy of a large agency. Since agents' activity focuses on reading (scripts, projects) and writing (notes, coverage), as well as mastering the art of speech (to attract talent and to pitch)—all abilities that are known to depend on one's social background and education—it is not surprising that agents with prestigious university degrees and families likely to pass down such types of social dispositions tend to be the ones who occupy top positions in the agency system. This is also true of the ability to "network" and create the useful professional ties that are notoriously key to success in Hollywood. At the same time, such general remarks do not explain how agents acquire their *particular* skills, given the fact that "reading," "writing," and "speaking" take in this professional context very particular forms and meanings that translate into specific hierarchies and power relations.

While still in the mailroom, trainees face a domestication process: it involves understanding the agency's internal structure, divisions, and operations, plus its relationships to its surrounding world, and learning to adapt to it and to play *by the rules*. Agents-to-be are expected to show complete dedication and loyalty to the organization training them and making them who they are and will be so as to become part of this collective game. The interviewed agents depict their time in the mailroom as an unavoidable ego wound, a time when they had to kowtow to the system and its incarnations (that is, at this stage, potentially to anyone who isn't also a mailroom trainee), sometimes going as far as describing it as a self-inflicted humiliation:

[Becoming an agent] was a hard decision because it meant I had to step back and join the mailroom, the most feared place in Hollywood. And, you know, for me, I was a little bit older and I had experience, and I had an ego. And I knew that being in a mailroom wasn't . . . you had to park your ego at the door, and be completely selfless and full-serving to the agency—delivering mail, pushing the cart, making photocopies, the most demeaning stuff that you can do. It took me forever to be able to get past that and be like: "Okay, this is what I have to do to be an agent." (Agent, cofounder of a boutique agency, October 2010)

This experience—in some aspects similar to the hazing rituals that are familiar to other occupational groups—functions as a *rite of passage*. Following a few agency trainees and assistants throughout their journey to becoming an agent has allowed me to witness the transformation of their perceptions and expectations, and the process by which they increasingly bought into the agency system as a place where they envisioned their professional future to be (even when they entered it with the ambition of ending up on the production side). Doing their time in the mailroom is not the only "trial" wannabe agents have to successfully go through. Anyone who comes into the agency as an intern or mailroom trainee typically becomes a "floater" for a while—delegated to stand in for assistants who may be absent for a few hours or a few days—before being appointed as an assistant "on a desk" at the service of a specific agent, with a career path in this particular position consisting in progressing to the desk of a more powerful agent. Experienced assistants can become department "coordinators"[15] and/or be selected for the agency's training program, officially becoming "agent trainees."[16] This learning process is sometimes relatively formal, as with the "classes" and "exams" organized at UTA under the denomination of "UTA University." It can also be more loosely organized, and more about the crossing of a symbolic boundary manifesting (to the agency and to the industry) that one is now seriously considered for a future promotion. Being chosen and therefore validated by the agency matters more in this context than do the practical and social skills acquired in training programs, which don't significantly differ from what one learned as a regular assistant. This is what this talent agent evoked, recalling his recruitment into the ICM training program after six months as an assistant in the same agency: "About six months later, I was offered the training program, which involves a weekly meeting where you learn more about the departments in the firm, what else is going on within the firm, what other departments there are. You discuss how to pitch, how to sell a script, how to sell clients, through the entire industry. It's funny, because they say it's a training program, but I found it more of a fraternity. Once you were in the training program, it meant something, and the agency looked at you differently" (September 2010).

The selection of trainees draws a boundary that signifies, for the chosen ones and their counterparts, access to a professional world: their admission to the training program contributes to instituting them as Hollywood insiders. The metaphor of the "fraternity" refers here to the associated feeling of "belonging"—to Hollywood, to a given agency, but also to a group of peers, in relatively equal positions at the bottom level of the agency system. This initiation is also an access to a hierarchized world.

Overall, it is only after a period of about one to three years that one gets promoted to junior agent. But each stage of the process may lead to a possible exit, as it is clear that only a small proportion of assistants and mailroom trainees make it to becoming an agent. The above interviewee, for instance, for lack of being promoted internally, started as an agent at a small company, thus leaving Big for Little Hollywood. What makes all the difference at this stage is to be able to gain the support of one or several powerful mentors, first and foremost within the organizational framework of the agency.

Under the Wing of a Mentor

The making of an agent relies on a modern apprenticeship system encouraged and organized within the agencies. For the assistant who aspires to be promoted to junior agent, being noticed and accompanied by a mentor as highly placed within the organization as possible—ideally a company partner or department head[17]—is crucial.[18] These trajectories create commitment and dedication to the agency and to those who embody it, as one feels he or she owes them everything. The master/apprentice model implies building and maintaining close personal ties of solidarity and loyalty in an organizational context that is, at the same time, highly institutionalized and rationalized in the big agencies. The agent quoted below spoke in very strong terms of the long-lasting relationship of mutual support tying him to his mentor, which he now means to reproduce by training newcomers himself. Interviewees often express such an intense and unconditional loyalty to their mentor: "I definitely wouldn't be sitting here today if it weren't for [my mentor]. I owe pretty much everything I am as an agent to [him]. [. . .] He's like a brother to me. We're incredibly close. And I still go to him for advice. He comes to me sometimes for advice. And we work incredibly well together. I'd trust him with any client. I'd trust him with anybody in my life. I'd take a bullet for him" (agent, big agency, October 2010).

Getting sponsored by a mentor conditions the real insertion into the collective system formed by the agency that the trainees often then describe as "fraternity" or a "family" they feel like they belong to. Internal ties become all the more important, so that apprentices are expected to dedicate most of their time to earning their integration into the organization, and so that the professional realm that forms in this context develops extensively, at the expense of what is usually considered to be the sphere of private or leisure life. This process does not only determine the acquisition of the technical skills of agenting and the familiarization with the rules of the agency/industry game. The mentor is primarily re-

ferrer, accrediting entity, and facilitator of the inclusion into professional "networks" that are indispensable to the young agent.

I worked for the head of the talent department; he ended up becoming my mentor
and really guided me through my full career. I think the good thing is that you have
that person who is walking ahead of you, validating you along the way, singing your
praises, making those introductions for you, and really putting that stamp of approval
on you to the community. Which is key. And then from there, obviously you have to
have continuity of the relationships yourself, and live up to that. [. . .] That afforded me
those relationships, those client relationships, those manager relationships—and then
it was really figuring that part out. (Former talent agent, big agency, February 2013)

Aspiring agents cannot avoid going through such an apprenticeship
system, just as the ethnographer who tries to enter the agency world for
research purposes also needs, to an extent, to be taken under the wing
of established mentors in order to gain full access to the game. Assistants
and trainees' paths directly reflect the position of the sponsor(s) who
they are able to mobilize. They thus develop strategies of self-placement
in the game that rely on their understanding of the more or less formal hierarchies organizing the agency; on their recognition of the most
powerful players, but also those who are known to be the most sup-
portive of their "protégés"; and on their ability to map out the various
specialized areas forming the agency departments and subdivisions so as
to define their ideal place within it and appropriate tactics to reach it.

Assistants depict, in interviews, their evolving strategies (as they get a
better understanding of the game and as new opportunities seem to open
up) to win the support of this or that senior agent in order to get closer
to the specialized path they would ideally like to follow—for instance, to
be appointed to the desk of a motion picture literary agent, if they want
to be promoted in this domain themselves—or on the contrary, to avoid
being put on an unwanted track that they would have a hard time ex-
tracting themselves from. Because certain positions are more valued and
tend to arouse more interest among assistants, the competition to reach
them is also more intense. Typically, motion picture (especially talent)
and nowadays television divisions (scripted more than alternative/real-
ity TV) remain at the top of this hierarchy. Assistants know that their positions prefigure what their career in agenting might be, and that the positions they successively occupy tend to create a self-reinforcing process
in that regard. This "self-agenting" work is also a prelude to what junior
agents will have to do for their clients and is, in fact, explicitly referred
to as such by the concerned.

As much as assistants try to strategically decrypt and navigate the organizational and power system of the agencies, they are never really in control of the process of role reproduction and transformation that they are a part of. Whether they want it or not, the association with a master *situates* the apprentices *in the game* (within the agency, the agency system, and the industry as a whole) both in terms of functional specialization—the place they occupy with regard to division of labor and structure of the compartmentalized organizations that are the big agencies—and because the assistants are led to operate within the same informal circle of mutual recognition and affinity in which their mentor is located. In a professional world in which conflicts and divisions inseparably take a personal and emotional dimension, and knowing who one is "close to" is of primary importance, such associations make you instant allies and adversaries at once.

What agents-to-be learn through contact with a mentor is sometimes referred to as an elusive, natural ability that echoes the gift or talent attributed to the artists: "It's being smart, but it's not sheerly an intellect thing. It's getting it. *It*. [What *it* is] is a lot of intangibles. You either have people that can do it and do it well, or you don't."[19] However, "getting it" is the result of a socialization process that starts with understanding this world's specialized language and norms. As an assistant, one learns to read, write, and speak according to what this professional context requires. As in any specific occupational system, Hollywood professionals share somewhat of an esoteric language, specialized vocabularies and phrases that both bring insiders together in a common realm of meaning and keep outsiders at a distance. Newcomers have to decrypt what seem at first to be coded exchanges.[20] For instance, the constant reference to what happens "in the room," which also appears repeatedly in our interviews, is often mysterious to beginners. Several interviewees recalled their initial perplexity in face of the terms—which, as they quickly find out, designates the space in which transactions are conducted, be it the meeting room of an agency where agents present scripts and ideas to their colleagues trying to entice them into teaming up on a project, the venue where auditions take place when an agent gets an actor "in the room" with a casting director, or the office of a studio executive or head in which a project gets pitched, for example. Interviewees also underlined the time it took them to fully grasp how exactly one is supposed to behave "in the room"; in other words, what the code of conduct is that goes with these vocabularies (how much time you are likely to have "in the room," who are the players who will be there and what will be at stake for them, what are the most relevant and meaningful ways to present yourself and your expectations, and so on). As they acquire this new language, come to think in those terms, and use them as if they were natural, newcomers lose the estranging feeling that they first experienced, at the same time as they show signs of their progressive integration into a community of meaning and practice to other Hollywood professionals. This is also how their ability to pitch is formed and refined, and how they can prepare clients to be their own advocates when they are "in the room" with potential employers, from casting directors to producers or studio heads.

The multiple tasks that make up the responsibilities of an assistant—from answering calls to reading scripts and writing "coverage"—are occasions to learn by observation the various dimensions of the practice of agenting. Industry insiders all know that agency assistants and trainees systematically listen to the calls that the agent they work for gives and receives, as a powerful means of socialization and self-training. This allows them to discreetly witness the sometimes very personal exchanges that take place between an agent and an artist, as well as the steps and ways of negotiating with buyers. The protagonists practically forget the silent presence of the assistant and paradoxically do not consider this practice as a breach of privacy.[21] The assistant, just as the agent, becomes the protector of intimate secrets and learns what "confidentiality" really means in the context of an agency. This access to sensitive information and the associated dimension of information control have to do both with the relationship of (future) agents to the agency (as a repository for collective secrets) and with the power relation tying them to their clients (explored in chapter 5). The beginner gets acquainted with what "building relationships" means and what the proper way of making deals is, forming both practical and ethical abilities. Inseparably, they become familiar with the structure of power relations characterizing their agency, and with everyone's place within it: "You're learning who the clients are, which agents represent what clients. It's osmosis. You're watching, you're listening, you're seeing how people interact with each other, you're seeing how different agents are treated by employees, what's the difference between associates and partners, you're understanding that. Because if you walked in and were an agent on day one, you wouldn't understand the politics, and the biggest challenge [when] you wind up being an agent is understanding the political nature of the internal atmosphere of the company" (cofounder of a boutique agency, October 2010).

Learning how to read and judge a script, or any piece of material, and write about it in ways that are directly relevant to professional needs is also an element of this training process. This skill is acquired by trial and error as a result of long evening hours and entire weekends dedicated to reading and evaluating various pieces comparatively. Even if there aren't any objectified criteria or rationalized methodologies transmitted by the agency that the newcomer could use to assess the quality of a script or the value of a concept, in a world that cultivates the idea of innate taste and intrinsically personal talent of the participants, agents-to-be progressively infer what makes a "good" script thanks to their increased familiarization with successful and acclaimed work that they contrast with their other readings. In so doing, they form a specialized *professional taste*, which tends to dissociate from their "personal taste" in movies or entertainment.[22] To use the agents' words, this is how their "sense of talent" takes shape, tying together the capacity to evaluate quality and salability. The junior literary agent quoted below recalled how his "taste developed" when he was an assistant and over time, and how he acquired it on the job:

It doesn't work like school here. I think you learn through osmosis, really, looking at other people, and you just suddenly start picking it up. For example, you have to start reading great writing—an Aaron Sorkin, a Bill Monahan, or a Steve Zaillian—and you understand what they do, how they write their dialogues and how they write their descriptions, and how the flow of the script is, and how efficient the writing is. And then you read a lot of bad scripts too and you see the mistakes that these writers make. And suddenly, without being able to explain it, you're able to recognize good writing. (big agency, December 2013)[23]

These elements manifest an agent's professionalization, and they go hand in hand with an increasing specialization of agenting roles. This specialization also determines specific evaluation criteria that apply to projects and artists depending on the type of media, buyers, or genres involved. What matters and will be used to judge what something or someone is worth in television differs from what it is in motion pictures, for instance. The categorization of films and shows by genres also comes with differentiated emphases in terms of what a "good writer" will be in each case:

In television the most important thing is character, because you want to know: do I want to follow these characters for fifty to two hundred episodes, several seasons? So in television, it's fairly easy—it's all about character. I think in feature [. . .] it starts with good character writing, which is fairly tricky. I myself, just because it's easy to read, respond really well to dialogue. Especially in comedy, it's so incredibly important. [. . .] Then I think the second most important thing would be the plot, and with the plot comes the world, and it's especially important when it comes to science fiction or real genre piece like a western, a historical piece—for those you have to create a world. Some writers are better at one element than others: you have so-called world creators, big sci-fi writers; you also have great dialogue-creator writers, for great drama and thrillers. (literary agent, big agency, July 2014)

The transmission of the know-how of how to be an agent does not only happen through the somewhat intangible relationships between an apprentice and his or her mentor(s). It is mediated through more institutional channels too, as the future agent gets to participate in the many meetings organized within the largest agencies especially. Daily meetings—bringing together the entire agency, a department or a specialized segment or subgroup within it—make the structure and divisions of the company come to life; this is where one hears about the agency's clients, learns who "the buyers" are and what interests them, what the yearly calendar is like in television and film and what the best time is to sell a project, what packaging means in practical terms and its centrality to the activity of a big agency. The capital of professional recognition that the agent in training can mobilize is also that objectified in the three letters composing the acronym of the leading agencies (WME, CAA, UTA, ICM). Describing how he was able to use this symbolic capital of the institution to his benefit when he was an agent trainee at one of the biggest companies, this agent who ended up leaving for a very small company and pursuing his career as a talent agent in Little Hollywood—finding himself immersed in very different waters in terms of the clients and the buyers he was now confronted with—epitomizes one of the typical paths that agents can follow:

I think the thing that I got from the big agencies was the networking abilities, because when you're at ICM, those three little letters behind your name mean a lot. Even as a trainee, people mistook me for an agent all the time. [. . .] The big agency opened up a lot of doors for me as far as introductions. When I left—and I've seen this happen with the agents that leave big agencies—you realize how quickly, the minute that [those] three little letters are not behind your name when you're calling and saying, "Hey, it's [name] from ICM," how unneeded you are. All of a sudden, you're not as important. So, I had to get out there and create a name for myself, and a name that the people could trust when I'm calling. Because you really rely on the casting community at a smaller level. When you're not the Big Five,[24] you really are in bed with the casting directors, really getting to know them and building relationships with them, because that's how your actors are going to be seen. It's not always so with the big agencies. It's oftentimes: the casting directors are skipped over and I notice it goes straight to the division directors. So that was a huge learning curve for me. It took about six months to understand that difference, that I am by myself now in a small firm, and it's just me—it's not me with ICM behind me. And also, the roster changes. You don't have a million television and film stars. You have working actors. You don't have big stars on your roster. So that was kind of a culture shock for me. (October 2010)

Indeed, the big agencies do a lot more than just training their future agents. They operate like a "farm system" that produces professionals who will then populate smaller agencies, management companies, and production entities as well. They consequently preside over the transmission of professional norms and models—both embodied by their agents and institutionalized in agencies as organizations—that are reproduced but also altered as these organizations transform. This remark does not exclude, of course, the existence of career paths that start, for agents, at a boutique agency and develop from there, mostly within the space of representation in Little Hollywood. But the prevalence of trajectories that originate in one of the few large agencies has significant structuring effects that I will now highlight. It is consequential to understand not only the modes of professional definition that agents come to share, but also the formation of configurations that intertwine the trajectories of talent representatives with those of production professionals over long periods of time.

Forming "Generations" in Hollywood

Moving up from being an assistant happens in various ways and gives rise to diverse career paths. It can be lived as a natural evolution by those who get promoted "in-house"—a transition that is not always immediately formalized in legal terms.[25] It is more of a radical change for those who leave to pursue their career in talent representation at a small company, experiencing the "culture shock" mentioned by the interviewee quoted above and by those who get hired in a production company or a studio, thanks to connections they made as an assistant. This initial circulation between talent representation and production/distribution (and between Big and Little Hollywood) does not usually give birth to career paths that would be characterized by a high level of mobility between those spaces. On the contrary, specialized professional identities gradually strengthen and crystallize after a few years spent in a particular type of position, and the chances that such circulation would happen thereafter decrease. If agents commonly turn manager in the second half of their career, transitions to the production side become less likely as time goes by. Top agents who have successfully made it to the production/studio side are in fact rare entities. In addition, the boundary separating Big from Little Hollywood becomes thicker with time, in the agents' experience: after a few years, a Little Hollywood agent has very few chances to make the leap to Big Hollywood and pursue his or her career in one of the leading agencies, even when he or she was initially trained at a major agency, whereas his or her clients will on the contrary systematically leave to be represented by a bigger company if they meet with success (and possibly cross back to Little Hollywood when they are less "in demand"). The "glass ceiling" separating Little Hollywood from Big Hollywood tends to keep talent representatives from traveling to the other side, and agents whose career consists in moving up from a small company to one of the biggest are exceptions.[26] In most cases, trajectories remain internal to either Big or Little Hollywood, as well as to a given area of specialty (a certain type of category of clients, of media, and so on). Circulation spaces narrow down and stabilize with time; the "Hollywood" that different types of agent experience is a very small world made of long-lasting interrelations.

Those who were once part of the same cohort in a big agency's mailroom or training program thus progress on distinct but interdependent professional paths. As their careers develop simultaneously, they form peer groups that remain bound by this common socialization process. When they come to face each other on the talent representation side and the production side, they become obvious counterparts in professional transactions: their mutual identification and their affinities of perception emerge from the fact that they have been trained and *made professionals* in similar organizational contexts and at the same time in the history of the agency system and of Hollywood at large. In other words, similar *modes of generation* (Bourdieu 1984) form groups of mutual recognition made up of individuals whose careers have simultaneously unfolded and who share a common interpersonal history. Such groups take different shape depending on whether agents operate in Little Hollywood or Big Hollywood, as their relevant partners and counterparts are different in these two spheres of activity—for instance, the counterpart of the experienced Little Hollywood agent has become head of casting at a television network, while the talent agent at a one of the largest companies is now able to directly reach the head of studio. But, as the following quotes suggest, they all experience and express the feeling of belonging to a peer group that formed over time, delineating a "generation."[27] While the groups that form are specific to Little or Big

Hollywood, the generational mechanism that agents perceive characterizes the entire industry, up to its higher level. The evocation of the interconnected paths of top industry players also gets integrated into a more public narrative, communicated through the press in particular (and sometimes represented in movies or books), defining "Hollywood" at a given point in time. "A lot of what we do is a generational thing, which is fun because, you know, the producer of [this or] that is now the president of Disney, or the guy that I was an assistant with is now the president of Warner Brothers, or one of our good friends is now president of Paramount. And so it's a very relationship-based industry. So, all boats rise with the tide" (motion picture agent, Little Hollywood, September 2010).

Those who cannot rely on such systems of relationships built up over time have to compensate for it by mobilizing other types of resources, but social events and networking lunches never fully replace it.[28] Conversely, for those who have been made through such modes of generation, further interactions activate latent forms of solidarity that stem from mutual recognition and the feeling of belonging to a community with a shared destiny over time. This goes beyond the possible common experience of similar primary socialization in the mailroom or training program of a large agency and really emerges from the durable interdependences shaping professional trajectories. These ties are not established once and for all; they must be continually renewed in context and adjusted to the constant arrival of newcomers. This need for maintenance is the reason agents who have had to interrupt their career for several years struggle to get back in the game, relationships being a currency that demonetizes very fast.

Consequently, we face a relatively transparent world, as far as Hollywood insiders are concerned: everyone tends to know the career paths of his or her counterparts and, more important, the debts and obligations that one may have accumulated along the way, creating informal professional hierarchies, and hierarchies that sometimes differ from those defined by presently held titles and positions. This successful senior agent at one of the biggest agencies explains how he draws his credibility from his past, being known by his relationships, both through what others know of him as well as what they know they owe him:

I put him in jobs. And so when he was answering to [big producers' names], who loved me, he would come and get advice. So now, he's the head of the studio, and he and I both know that he sat in my office, you know, at the edge of his chair, getting my advice when I was running the agency, so that he can be the guy. But with me, he can only be so much the guy, and that's how the town works. He's more powerful than me; I'm way more powerful than him. [. . .] I'm more powerful because of my relationship with him. (Talent agent, big agency, February 2013)

Because agents put the requirement of managing strong ties and common futures first, they do not conceive their activities or their career as project driven, with the subsequent discontinuity between projects and exclusive focus on one main endeavor at a time. On the contrary, while agents simultaneously juggle a higher number of clients, projects, and tasks that they deal with at a fast pace, they also develop a vision of their activities as rooted in a more stable and lasting system of practices. This shows that—unlike what many studies of cultural industries have suggested—the various participants in the transaction of talent and projects do not all think of themselves as pursuing a project-based career.[29]

This leads us to approach the making of *trajectories* in ways that do not reduce it to the occupation of successive institutional positions, but underlines the importance of the systems of mutual recognition within which such paths take meaning and carry out social effects. Similar learning processes and common past experiences progressively lead to a form of shared "professional spirit" made up of converging representations and the sharing of a common language by agents and their counterparts. They allow for the internalization of shared conventions guiding action in a world where the protagonists often feel that "there are no rules."[30] Participants know how to behave, what to expect, and how to anticipate. They know how to play the game and are known players because they have a common history in the game.

There's still a relatively small group of agents and lawyers who do these deals, it's like a big fraternity, you know. You get to know the five hundred or one thousand people who are really important to know; and you trade phone calls and e-mails and we all work together, and sometimes people hop jobs and change agencies or change studios, or [TV] networks, it's the same group of people. I'm having lunch with a guy I've known for thirty-five years today—or thirty years—he's a lawyer I've been in business with forever. We just do a lot of business back and forth, and you know, you can pick up a conversation with somebody two, three, four years later, and it's like, you know [*snaps his fingers*], yesterday. [. . .] You know the shorthand, you know that they understand the language, that you're in the same mind-set of what it is deal-wise that you're trying to do, or representing a client or the steps that have to be made, and . . . everybody knows them. But, if you're not in that club, you don't; and it takes years to be involved in that, and to make those connections and have those relationships, so that you can get them on the phone, so when you call them, they don't ignore you, they call you back. (Scripted television agent, midsize agency, March 2013)

This agent suggests that what is professionally at stake is nothing less than to be acknowledged as a player, to be taken seriously—which often means in practice having one's calls taken or returned—so as to stay in the flow of work exchanges and to simply exist in this world. Staying "in that club" (as the interviewee put it)—that is, in the relational triangle tying together talent representatives, artists, and production professionals—implies, as I will now explain, the performance of specific *relationship work* on the part of agents.

FOUR

Agenting as Relationship Work

Existing and succeeding as an agent are often equated by the concerned with "having relationships." This is probably the most central element that these professionals identify as making up their value. The abundance of people in the milieu who have expressed that "an agent is only worth their relationships" is revealing. The constant mention of the fact that "an agent is only worth their client list" is only a variation on the same theme: "When I represent someone, one of the great [artists], when I'm sitting down with them to see if we should work together, they look at me not just as a smart guy, or a thoughtful guy, or a guy that has good taste, *they look at me as a set of existing relationships*. How all of my relationships can help them. That's a huge factor" (manager, former talent agent, big agency, March 2013, my emphasis).

In this chapter, I focus on what "having a relationship" means in this context, and on how such relationships are created and maintained. The specialized activity by which this is achieved is what I define as *relationship work*. Relationship work is the fundamental cornerstone of agenting. It is also the activity through which occupational configurations form in Hollywood—configurations from which emerges the economic and symbolic value of people and products, as the following chapters unveil. I explore below the forms and meaning of relationship work, as well as the organizational settings in which this apparently purely interpersonal activity is in fact ingrained.

The Meaning of Relationships

Although the exclusive and glamorous social events that make the head-lines of the specialized press and the public face of Hollywood do exist, there is not much mystery to them. "Forming relationships" does not simply derive from a few minutes of co-presence in the context of such social or public events. In that, the common preconception that roman-ticizes how one finds success in Hollywood—the unpredictable but life-changing encounter with a key player—is deceptive. If occasional co-presence alone meant "relationship," the frequency of interactions is such that this type of social capital would be flowing; in fact, it would be so generously distributed in Hollywood that it wouldn't be an opera-tional form of capital at all (that is, a valid resource whose holders can do things that others can't accomplish). In other words, there are social conditions to being in the "right room" with the "right people," and to knowing how to present oneself and one's projects so as to be recognized as full of promise and to stand out from the crowd of solicitors. What is at stake is to be admitted into a specialized professional system.

Superficial contacts with Hollywood professionals tend to be relatively easy to get for the newcomer, including for the ethnographer (Ortner 2010); and potential connections through a third party are even more common. But such "weak ties" (Granovetter 1983) do not have here the strength that this author famously identified in a different context; they do not translate into what agents call "having a relationship." The latter designates a more substantial and solid type of tie, formed over time. One skill consists precisely in agents' capacity to distinguish the two types of ties, and to build the second. This is not simply the result of the natu-ral ability of well-suited personalities. On the contrary, agents perform a genuine relationship *work*; that is, *an effort specifically oriented toward the binding of people*. The construction and maintenance of *personal* relation-ships with different counterparts is at the heart of agents' professional activity and is even described as the substance of what professionals do in Hollywood at large.

The absence of formal and explicit "rules" guiding this activity does not mean lack of identifiable patterns or rationales in play. Ethnography has allowed me to investigate agents' relationship work and its specific forms in ways that challenge analyses of Hollywood in terms of networks or network-made markets.[1] By methodological definition, network ap-proaches tend to leave out the questions of the meaning of relationships for the participants, the processes by which they emerge, and the work by which they are maintained. By contrast, the focus is here placed on the *practice* of relationship, the type of activity that "having" or "building a connection" covers, and what it means and implies for the concerned; in other words, the *work* of relating.

The process of becoming an agent—through the organizational and mentoring arrangements that the previous chapter describes—models the different facets of relationship work. Relationship work is a learned ability; it depends on accreditation mechanisms that allow the junior agent to be taken seriously and become a player in a given segment of the Hollywood game. Initial connections (with other talent representatives as well as production counterparts) and early clients that a beginner can get from more senior agents at the company where he or she is trained are crucial in a world in which word of mouth builds fast and in a self-reinforcing way. Hence the recommendation is made to young agents to "be nice to everyone" because one's status or stature can change quickly and seemingly unpredictably, and people are expected to base future decisions of cooperation on what they remember of initial interactions. For beginner agents, befriending people and creating a web of potentially relevant contacts to which they make themselves visible are imperative to professional growth. Additionally, this work manifests itself in conscious, systematic, and organized ways. From an early career stage on, the protagonists develop a strategic approach to this activity:

When you're young, you literally work seven days a week, going to dinner, going to breakfast, going to lunch, going to events, just interacting with people, meeting people—"Hey, you know, so-and-so is a friend of so-and-so," "Oh yeah, I guess I'll call them up and have a drink with them"—just kind of building those relationships. [. . .] And just building over time shared experiences: sometimes you go on vacation with them, or you see people in social settings, charity events, at industry events. (Scripted television agent, midsize agency, March 2013)

"Relationships" are often sought with the indirect goal of generating other connections, of getting the referrals and recommendations that are so central to ensure a young agent's professional existence. Such dynamics continue as one's career develops. Not only do established agents still have to "network," in the ordinary meaning of this word, but senior agents—especially when they are department heads or in a position of leadership—are also expected to show by example and to provide occasions for such physical interactions (for instance, hosting a party or organizing a screening). Indeed, relationship work takes multiple forms: it goes from knowing someone by voice and name and communicating through repeated telephone or e-mail conversations to building a connection through regular in-person encounters. The importance of materializing such ties in face-to-face interactions is denoted below by the reference to the participants' physical co-presence in Los Angeles and to Hollywood as a "town":

This town works totally on relationships. It's: who do you know, and who do you want to work with. [. . .] But it's also: you're always expanding your relationships, always looking out for new relationships, and you don't shut it off, you're always in this constant mode of growth. [. . .] And there are just people calling you [to] say: "Hey, would you meet this person?" And, "You should know that person," "Have you met that person?" You know, information is the lingua franca of what we do. It really is the money that flows that makes it work. But it's the relationships that are the real meat and potatoes of this business. And that's why you have to be in LA. (Agent, motion picture literary, midsize agency, March 2013)

The *preexistence* of interconnections and mutual recognition, especially with production professionals, is a condition of possibility for the practice of agenting. As this agent at a small talent agency explains, even if he can contact a casting executive at a studio or a network, for instance, he is not likely to get a professional response unless he has already established a relationship with this person—that is, unless he has worked at becoming part of his person's circle of potential work counterparts and credible partners in negotiation:

If you don't know an executive personally, the odds are you will not cold-call them. I've seen very little cold-calling in this business. In any other business, if you have a product to sell, you pick up the phone, you just [say]: "Hey, may I speak to the vice president of blah-blah-blah?" and you're in. Here, you'll be lucky to get a return phone call if the executive doesn't know who you are. And that's interesting. It's one of the few sales games out there where you literally don't know the marketplace and cold-calling is kind of frowned upon. (Manager, former agent, Little Hollywood, October 2010)

Legally, agents are responsible for selling talent to buyer-employers. In fact, an agent also needs to "sell" to the artists the idea that the agent has relationships with production professionals, as much as the agent builds his or her credibility with producers on privileged access to promising or successful talent. In this tri-faced mirror game, "having a relationship" does not just mean holding someone's contact information, being known in return and able to make an introduction.[2] Agents' relationships point to their ability to affect the behavior of other players and consequently to effect change in the relational system they belong to. On one hand, agents think of relationships as a capital, an asset that they possess and actively work at keeping. As an interviewee put it, "The agency doesn't own the clients, the agents own the clients." Indeed, when agents say that they "have relationships" with certain key people, it's about long-term bonds that they fight to protect and maintain. Accumulating this type of capital is an end in itself, because it makes up an agent's worth. On the other hand, creating ties can be a means to another end: a bargaining chip or currency that enables an agent to conduct transactions. What relationships allow for might then be an exchange of information (about job prospects and future projects, privileged access to material, etc.); it might also be the formation or maintenance of other ties (using a connection to reach and sign a new client, keep a current client satisfied, or form a relationship with a studio executive). The same connection can be both an end (part of an agent's capital) and a means used in the transaction of something else, depending on the situation. Agents are relationship dealers in that sense.

In addition, relationship work in Hollywood generates ties in specific ways. A senior talent agent at one of the major agencies explained how he finds new clients: "I use the network. [. . .] I know that [a star client] and others are special, so I have to listen to them. If you are a brilliant artist in my mind and you tell me that Sally is a brilliant artist, I'll believe you and I'll sign Sally" (October 2010). Beyond what this tells us about the relational building of one's client list, there are here two interesting lessons to learn. First, we can grasp *how* "the network" that this agent belongs to emerges from the activities that its participants deploy. Hollywood "clusters" or "networks" don't exist and subsist in nature; they are made and reshaped *through relationship work*. Relationship work forms networks with firm boundaries. Second, we can understand how such processes of co-opting "the close" and, in many ways, "the similar" into restricted relational systems create differentiated groups, and participate in the continual reshaping of the boundaries separating Little from Big Hollywood and delineating circles of specialty within each of them. Chances are, for instance, that an established agent who has gradually specialized in representing comedy actors with big commercial hits will attract and be referred to potential new clients with comparable profiles who are already operating at a comparable level of recognition. This informal making of specialized groups goes hand in hand with institutionalization mechanisms, as specialized subdivisions and teams are organized within the agencies (such as a "comedy group" or an "international group"), all the while management companies and production entities/studio divisions also tend to specialize internally. Agenting is thus *making* relationships in this way, and not just "having" them.

There are of course other social spheres in which the relational aspect of the professional definition and practice is important; Hollywood and the agency world are not radical exceptions in that regard. Relational economic sociologists have forged the concept of "relational work" to analyze the meaningful and continually negotiated interpersonal relations constituting economic activity, therefore substantiating the argument of the embeddedness of economic activities into social relations and grounding it in empirical evidence. In Zelizer's (2012) perspective, "relational work" is the activity by which people shape economic relations and, most important, by which they *distinguish* between various types of relationships that are associated with different categories of economic transactions and specific media: in Zelizer's terms,

Not any economic transaction is compatible with any intimate relation. [. . .] If you are my casual girlfriend but not my wife, we don't share a checking account; if you are my patient but also my friend, I won't charge you, but you might give me a gift. In the world of courtship, couples have historically differentiated among categories of relations: engagement, dating, treating, hooking up, and more; and they mark those relations apart from both marriage and prostitution. In each case, we see participants engaging in delicate, consequential relational work as they match each of those relations to specific sets of economic transactions (such as varied forms of payments and gift exchanges) and media (money, engagement rings, and more) (Zelizer 2012, 152).

This matching of meaningful relations, transactions, and media creates "relational packages" and contributes to shaping the boundaries that organize social and economic life. In that sense, we all perform "relational work" as part of our everyday lives, most of the time without noticing it or reflecting on it.

The type of *relationship work* that Hollywood agents perform is, however, different in several ways. It is not only that the types of "relational packages" that agents contribute to are specific. Firstly, we are talking about practices and processes that are both the source and the mechanism of one's professional existence. Indeed, being involved in personal relationships is *what makes the agent*. Being an agent is first and foremost being able to create and maintain close interpersonal ties with other Hollywood professionals. Secondly, unlike most of us when we do what Zelizer calls "relational work," agents and their counterparts who engage in relationship work are involved not just in a conscious activity, but also in a *reflexive* practice whose *purpose* is to generate, maintain, and strengthen attachment and loyalty. It's not just that personal or intimate ties shape meaningful economic transactions here: agents' binding effort *creates intimacy* in the same movement as the economic relation between the concerned is formed. This is why, as I will soon explain, the moral and emotional components of it are so crucial in the eyes of the protagonists.

There is another interesting difference distinguishing relational work in economic sociology from the agents' relationship work that we have observed. Relational work has to do with the fuzziness, the uncertainty, or the opacity of situations that participants play with and have disputes about. In our case study of *The Silence of the Lambs*, relationship work is not about negotiating unclear situations as much as it is about producing meaning and belief (in the economic/artistic value of professionals and projects) within professional configurations that are in fact relatively transparent to the participants but nevertheless subject to such activities. Associating negotiation activities with "fuzzy situations" would be misleading here. There is always a degree of indetermination and "drama" (as agents often put it) that surrounds the fate of a project in Hollywood; however, relationship work is possible in this context precisely because participants already share certain interpretations of identities and situations, at the same time as it affects them in turn and contributes to the stock of shared expectations and representations. The need for relationship work therefore does not emerge from the fact that this professional world is more marked by indetermination than others, as it has often been suggested, but rather from the fact that the forms of power structuring it are more *embodied* in people and less *objectified* in titles, positions, and other institutional means. In this context, the participants' belief in interpersonal relations is a precondition for the collective process that produces the belief in the value of art and artists in Hollywood.

Agents' relationship work is a two-faced activity: on one hand, it involves the creation and maintenance of a certain type of bond with other Hollywood professionals. This bond can be described in terms of moral feelings (such as "trust"), especially as far as production professionals are concerned; or it can take more emotional and affective forms, in particular with artists. On the other hand, relationship work also has an internal face: it's the constant molding of one's personal "agenting style," which is a relational style that each agent works with to distinguish him- or herself.

The Definition of an Agent's Style

Agents insist on the imperative of defining (for themselves) and displaying (for others) a specific "agenting style" distinguishing them from others according to the way they perform relationship work. In other words, an agent's "style" reflects the work on oneself that relationship work implies, as well as the singularizing effect attached to it. The attitude and mode of relating that define an agent are indeed expected to be a unique and sincere expression of who one is outside of the professional realm: "It's really believing in yourself as an agent, it's not putting on a suit pretending that you're somebody else. If you're a gangster outside, be a gangster agent; if you're a hipster outside, be a hipster agent; if you're in a suit outside, be in a suit inside. Because eventually it's going to leak out. This is who I am, not a version of myself, a profile for agenting. Because it's not banking" (talent agent, big agency, September 2012).

The need to "be your true self"[3] as an agent echoes what is expected of artists in a world that praises authenticity and approaches success as an expression of innate qualities (gift, genius, talent, drive). It expresses forms of identification of agents to artists; and it attaches the agent to the creative side of the industry: "It's not banking," the agent quoted above emphasized. At the same time, publicizing such professional styles is a way of differentiating oneself from competitors. Somewhat comparably to their clients, agents (especially top ones) have to "brand themselves" by establishing a personal and consistent manner of interacting, with which to attract and secure the loyalty of clients and partners, and to be identifiable in the agenting world. A senior agent at one of the leading agencies expressed it as follows:

The client is paying me, in my opinion, for me to feel his vulnerability, his concern, his squeaky wheel, his dream, his hope, his whatever—whether or not I agree with them—and to let him know that I am attentive, and on it. [. . .] Then my reputation is one [where] I am completely available. [. . .] So, when you look at my recent phone calls, and you see the missed calls, they are all taken care of immediately. And the e-mails are the same thing. That's what I'm selling. [. . .] I become immediately attentive during the workday and even beyond for certain people. Immediately. And it becomes a trademark. And every agent has got their way of doing that. Sometimes it's established; sometimes it's too low-key to ever be established but it still exists. And the style of our phone sheets, the style of the way we file paper and push paper, and everything. It's a way of approaching. You've got to approach these things any way you want. [. . .] It's a different posture. (May 2012).

Building such a profile and signaling it[4] to other Hollywood professionals is not an optional matter for agents. Saying that "every successful agent has, or *should* have their own style," in the words of a former big agency manager (October 2013), is more than the testimony of a personal experience—it reveals what is required to establish oneself in the profession. This is also distinct from the mere acquisition of technical competences or forms of expertise in agenting, in a specialized area of this business. Crafting a singular profile comes with profits of distinction: "If there's one thing that anyone in the industry seeks to do, other than insure credibility, it's to separate yourself from the queue and become unique!"[5] This singularity, however, is never radical difference: there are paths and models that an agent's style has to remain a variant of. If distinction is rewarded, extreme differentiation becomes costly.

"Becoming yourself as an agent" is a relational process. At the start of a career, it is also closely tied to the insertion of the young agent into the organizational framework of an agency. The agent-to-be defines and gradually makes visible to the milieu his or her own way of relating to talent, colleagues, and buyers, by choosing and extrapolating from a range of preexisting possible professional attitudes observable in the industry, and especially at the agency where this agent's training takes place:

What you have to quickly understand is: every agent has a different relationship with their clients. And when you're a first-year agent, you don't have any clients. You're put on teams to service other people's clients. So you have to understand instantly how that senior agent deals with their clients, what that relationship is like. That's what helps you define how to build your own relationships with these clients. You have to follow their lead, right? [. . .] You've got to follow that model. Understand their approach when they give them material. Understand their relationship, you know. And everyone is so different with their clients. And, at the same time as you're doing this, you're learning about what type of agent you want to be. Some agents, every time a client calls, they talk to them for one hour. Some talk to them for one minute. And you've got to define yourself, *who you are*, as an agent. (Motion picture agent, Little Hollywood, September 2010, his emphasis)

Therefore, the construction of a profile is not pure invention; nor does it simply reflect differences in personalities. More accurately, it is the inflection of preexisting styles offered—and sometimes prescribed—by agencies, and often the hybridization of diverse manners of performing relationship work incarnated by mentors. The modes of mutual choice/recognition between a mentor and an apprentice stem simultaneously from strategies and from elective affinities. Shaping one's style derives from embedded strategies of imitation and distinction. Hence the importance of considering the organizational spaces within which this process occurs. The agency sets up the framework for individual identification. Each agency offers a number of different styles, always embodied in "personalities,"[6] as potential models. One's style crystalizes through successive adjustments, in context: it is first constructed by trial and error and then strengthens, marking someone's identity in a long-lasting way. Through the organizations an agent has belonged to, as well as through relationships with mentor(s), he or she has learned how *to be* an agent as much as how *to do* the job. The earlier a young agent's style is shaped and publicly displayed in the industry, the earlier his or her career is ready to start.

In Little Hollywood and at small agencies, the building of individual profiles and the construction of a *group style* (Eliasoph and Lichterman 2003) distinguishing the company refer to two closely intricate processes, even though one is thought of as a question of personal identity or reputation, while the other is often expressed in the language of business management and marketing strategy.[7] Agencies—through the activity of their owners/managers and communication departments—promote distinctive "cultures" that define a collective brand and can be used diversely in individual strategies of self-branding. The folk category of "agency culture" (especially when applied to the biggest agencies) refers to the images associated with a company—with the style of its visible leaders and with the history that the organization claims to have inherited. The major agencies have well-known public "personalities" of this sort, and these shared representations serve as cognitive landmarks with which one makes sense of situations in Hollywood. For instance, WME's image, following the merger that gave birth to this organization, borrows both from the "tradition" that the older William Morris Agency represented and from the "modernity" of the young up-and-coming agency Endeavor—modernity personified by the energetic personality of Ari Emanuel, who became the CEO of WME as well as its public face. When referring to the contrasted cultures of WME, CAA, UTA, and ICM, interviewees anthropomorphize these organizations, often describing them according to the agenting style of their leaders (for instance, Mike Ovitz and his successors, Bryan Lourd and Kevin Huvane, at CAA; Jeff Berg and his successors at ICM):

I think all of the agencies have very distinct personalities. I think that CAA is looked at as the very glitzy red carpet/parties/star agency. [. . .] The personality is really the people at the top, so the WME personality really stems from Ari [Emanuel] and Patrick [Whitesell], and the CAA personality really stems from Lourd and Huvane, that style. And I think there's not a lot of individuation at CAA, it's sort of this: "Everyone's the same, and we don't speak of any sort of individual," it's a very "we, we, we, we, we this, we, CAA, CAA, CAA, CAA," and it's not individualized. And I think that UTA has very much more of a little boutique kind of feel, individuals, very strong personalities of people that work there, a lot of egos, and so it became very segregated in that sense, and about the agent, and not the agency. And, I think Endeavor did a good job of balancing that. But it's [*snapping her fingers repeatedly*] fast paced, and it's about "getting the deal done, getting the deal done, getting the deal done." You know, that's always personality. (Former talent agent, big agency, March 2013)[8]

Indeed, the five WMA agents who cofounded CAA in 1975 strove to personify a different manner of agenting and to create a new type of organization in the agency landscape: one that would be less focused on the exclusive connection between artist and agent and on individual client lists, and instead based on teams of agents around shared clients, generating less internal competition between agents and more loyalty to the organization, as well as multiple connections tying each client to the agency (so that, if an agent were to leave, the risk that the client would follow would be reduced). In spite of what the heroic story about Ovitz's charismatic personality suggests, CAA's "culture" did not simply emerge from the influence of individual leaders; it was inscribed into the structure of the organization and institutionalized in ways that incentivized agents to pull together and present a united front. Such incentives were both positive ones, such as modes of compensation that encourage cooperative behaviors on the part of agency employees, and negative, in the form of top-down control mechanisms (which led some of our interviewees to describe CAA as characterized by a "culture of fear"). Conversely, the organizational structure of other very large agencies—with stricter departmentalization and a compensation system that follows the "eat what you kill" principle—tended to encourage competitive individualization and distinction within the agency itself. As this literary agent explained, when "you're being paid for what you've done [that is, the clients and contracts you have individually brought in], then you're not going to want to collaborate with someone else because you're going to have to share it with them," and "at ICM, you had to protect your clients that could be stolen from someone inside. You didn't have to worry about outside as much as inside" (March 2013).

Because all agents in Big Hollywood perceive differences between specific "agency cultures" that they can describe and that organize their

understanding of their professional environment, and because they sometimes make career choices according to these differences, they all participate in the existence of these distinctions and in their reproduction.
Distinct group cultures characterizing agencies as organizations exist in
that sense. However, seen from Little Hollywood or from the perspective of
producers or managers, the few major agencies appear to have many more
similarities than differences. In addition, in recent years, the specificity of
agency "brands" has tended to correspond less with contrasted experiences of agenting: leaving CAA to go work at WME or UTA, for instance,
is less described by agents as "culture shock" both because the team-
oriented organizational model initially launched by CAA has proven
successful enough to be adopted and adapted by all the big companies
in a context of general growth and corporatization of the largest agencies, and because it gradually loosened up at CAA itself, under new
management.

In the meantime, the dominance that CAA achieved in its glory years
produced a typical image of the successful agent that pervaded the entire profession and beyond. It was built and disseminated through the
sustained strategy of CAA leaders to have "packs of agents at events" so
that they would be "seen out in force"—in the words of a former CAA
agent (October 2013)—thus displaying a new and unified representation
of what success in agenting looks like and of how top "tenpercenters"
are supposed to behave. These groups of agents, all spruced up in dark
suits at events and showing their powerful acquaintances at dinners,
came to personify "modern" ways of practicing relationship work and
socializing, delineating a dominant frame for the creation of one's agenting style: "At CAA, they all look like it's banking, so a lot of clients and
stars were conditioned to think that the agents should look like Wall
Street types. It's like a legitimacy that makes [clients] think like they're
with big business, and that's going to protect them and serve them. I
never understood it."[9] Defining oneself by distinction, against this model,
although still possible, might come at a professional cost, and the concerned agents have attested during our interviews to being repeatedly reminded of what was expected of them by their hierarchy.

However, in a world in which embodied forms of power prevail, the
existence of such agency "brands" and collective identifiers still leaves
room for the shaping of individualized styles. Whatever the strength of
an agency's image and the power of its managers and owners may be,
a unique style is never imposed, even though the agency management
can create incentives to bring their employees to adopt certain styles
rather than others. The formation of individualized agenting styles is

also embedded into the organizational structure of the agencies in an-other sense: the shaping of a style depends on specialization mechanisms as well. Agents' professionalization espouses lines of specialization that materialize in the functional divisions organizing the big companies—in departments (motion picture, television, gaming, books, etc.), de-partmental subdivisions (talent, literary, etc.), transdepartmental groups (comedy, international, etc.)—and all the more so when top agencies have become large compartmentalized corporations. Agents sometimes point to it negatively, deploring the narrowing effects of the high level of division of labor characterizing "factory-like" agencies containing one's self-definition within preset and institutionalized categorizations: "There's a label. You're a literary agent, you're a feature talent agent, you're a video game agent, you're a digital agent, you're a publishing agent, and you have all these very specific brands. Now, it's great for the people on top, because they have all these assets. But when you're a factory worker, you're stuck in one little box" (agent, cofounder of a boutique, October 2010).

In any case, agenting styles are not just *individualized*; they also have to be *specialized* in a way that directly derives from the position one oc-cupies in a given agency, especially at the start of a career. For instance, a first-year motion picture literary agency at a major agency described how he had to "build his brand"—at the center of which he placed the rep-resentation of emerging directors known for "genre movies," defining himself as a specialist of this particular type of client—under the con-straint of covering certain studios assigned to him by the agency, which therefore constituted the buyers he was "organically" inclined to sell his clients primarily to. The position that an agent occupies in the structure of an agency, which is conducive to the development of relationships with certain production professionals who themselves tend to look for certain types of talent according to the segment of cultural production they specialize in, frames and gears the shaping of the agent's style: he has to define himself within the parameters that are organizationally given to him.

These mechanisms of professional self-definition are also self-reinforcing, as one's style has to be coherent to be recognizable and distinctive. This coherence often has to do with the perceived homo-geneity of a client list. As a former agent turned producer put it, "good agents" are the ones whose client list has "connective tissue"; that is, who can be identified in relation to the specific type of successful art-ists that they represent (for example, several up-and-coming indie film directors who recently received awards at festivals); "otherwise, who are you as an agent?"[10] That is to say that the building of an agent's style also has to do with the identification and classification by others, both within the organizational framework of an agency and outside of it, in the interrelation circles in which agents meet other types of Hollywood professionals: one motion picture agent recalled how this style and his area of specialty formed in interconnected ways when the perceptions of his counterparts converged to categorize him as "the guy who sells a lot of spec scripts and crosses people over from television to motion pictures."[11]

The style an agent has initially shaped in the context of an organization and a given professional configuration adjusts, though mostly strengthens and develops in the course of one's career, as the agent may move from one company to another. This inertia of individual styles that crystalize early on and have turned into a matrix of perceptions and practices—that is, a professional habitus—partly explains the difficulty for agents who have sometimes achieved a high level of recognition to successfully change paths and reinvent themselves as studio heads or producers: it is because their "style" (their manners of thinking, behaving, talking, and relating that have over time inscribed them into specific relational systems) is maladjusted to the new context. In the end, if relationship work and the building of an agent's style have to do with the signaling of one's professional existence and the constitution of one's credibility, they go beyond what Zafirau (2008) has characterized as interactional "reputation work." They shape identities, both felt by the concerned and recognized by others.[12] They also contribute to forming groups and structuring activities through which artistic careers and products get made.

"Trust" between Agents and Production Professionals

In the agents' experience, forming relationships with the production side and building their reputation mean creating "trust relationships" from which their credibility as counterparts in negotiation arises. The vocabulary of moral feelings—trust, integrity, honesty—that is recurrently used by the agents is not simply covering a more Machiavellian reality. It points to an informal but effective system of ethical and pragmatic norms that rule the interactions and transactions between agents and production professionals. The equation that the agent quoted below suggested between "making relationships" with the production side and inspiring "trust" and "honesty" sheds light on the relational process of reputation building: one's reputation shouldn't be thought of as the attribute of a given professional as much as an *attribute of the relations* tying this person to a professional system. "You network, you make relationships [with] people that like dealing with you, people that know that they can trust what you're saying, that you're not dishonest in your dealings. And that's how you build your career and you build trust" (manager, former agent, big agency, March 2010).

Similarly, other agents repeatedly stated that their career is built on the recurrent display of honest and trustworthy behavior. But what does this "trustworthy" way of conducting oneself—that is, a condition of possibility for professional exchanges—refer to? What does "being honest" mean, exactly, in this professional context? How is the boundary between an acceptable lie and unethical behavior negotiated in practice? In the absence of a code of ethics, knowing how to negotiate "by the rules" and "honestly" is not self-evident, even if some elements of professional regulation are in place. The meaning of "dealing honestly" is also not exempt from ambiguity, as selling talent often requires that agents embellish the facts in order to protect their client's best interest, as well as their own:

There are rules of ethics. Everybody has got their ethical standards. I'm a believer that you deal honestly, and nobody can fault you for talking the truth, you know. Even if it's your perception of the truth. There is that in deal-making. There is honesty. There is also . . . almost like a poker game, there's a level of bullshit. If I'm selling a script, I might not say that you're the only one who's interested, who wants to buy it; I might say there are other interests out there. You see that happening. So there's a level of kind of positioning, and it's almost like poker play, you know. So it's like, you don't know what I have in my hand, or you want what I have, so you try to get some leverage in your negotiation from kind of saying everybody wants it. [. . .] You have to figure out a way to protect your client, to make sure that they're getting what the other people are getting, or they're getting better, and so there's ways to do that. (Manager, former talent agent, big agency, March 2010)

The definition of a *pragmatic work ethic*,[13] of the principles and values to observe and the boundaries to respect, is part of what assistants and trainees acquire by observation in the organization where they are trained, and what they learn on the job, by trial and error, when they are made junior agents. It is about understanding Hollywood's "proper etiquette" in one agent's words; that is, what is allowed and doable, beyond legal provisions, and which limits shouldn't be transgressed in order to stay in the game. Because the art of negotiation consists in "maintain[ing] your integrity *while playing the game*,"[14] it implies knowing the structure of the game well enough to recognize who the players are, and which positions and situations might give one enough power to slightly bend the rules or renegotiate the limits of the acceptable (typically, access to the most in-demand star talent does), notwithstanding others' judgment of such behaviors as ethically questionable.[15] It is primarily by anticipating the perceptions of their counterparts on the production side that agents identify tenable behaviors and draw the limit between justified embellishment of reality and professional dishonesty:

I try to be direct and honest with the people that I make deals with. I don't play games with people, I don't lie—I never lie about whether somebody has another job offer. I don't lie about what their salary history is. Some people utilize that, on occasion, I guess, as a negotiation tool. [. . .] Then people know what you are. And I think that it's too difficult to tell too many lies, because, as the old saying goes, to be a good liar, you have to have a good memory! And I would rather just be honest with people, and straightforward, and cut to the chase, you know. If we're negotiating for a contract, I will let the producer know what's important for my client, and if it's not important, we won't have unnecessary fights over it. [. . .] We always rely on honesty because, sure enough, as soon as you get caught being dishonest, that's what you will be known for. And people will never trust the information that you give them. You can't be dishonest with producers, because one of them will figure you out." (Below-the-line agent, Little Hollywood, April 2011)

But what this reveals is more than just the pragmatic ethics of deal-making. Transactions around projects and contracts for clients constitute only a limited dimension of the practice of agenting. The informal rules governing the relationships between agents and production professionals go far beyond them, and are here at stake. The constitution and regular use of exchange channels tying agents to production counterparts are consubstantial to agenting practices. At the start of a career, they greatly depend on organizational mechanisms by which a young agent is assigned specific buyers to "cover," depending on the position he or she occupies at a given agency:

At CAA, just as an example, if you're a young agent and you are assigned to cover Warner Brothers, your job is to own the studio. You want to give as much information about what the clients are doing to the producers and the executives so they rely on you and they need you. And at a certain point, if they trust you or they like you, they might say, "Hey! I read a script over the weekend that I really liked and it's a new writer who doesn't have an agent. You should look at it." So that's the way you start. (Talent agent, Big Hollywood, March 2013)

In this way, through means that are both institutionally guided and highly interpersonal in their form, the beginner agent gets integrated into a "give-and-take" system, which consists in the reciprocal—often deferred rather than immediate—exchange of services and favors. What is here at stake, and named by the participants in terms of "access" and "information" issues, has mostly to do with the management of ties with artists, the third party always present—even when imperceptibly—at the heart of the relationship between talent representatives and production professionals. Agents and their production counterparts competitively work at developing preferential bonds with successful artists, which, as a studio head put it, consists in "courting" them on social occasions and, importantly, happens "through working with them" (February 2014). If producers as well as studio and network heads often confess that their ideal situation is not to have to go through an agent for access to (top) talent, they also know that they remain inevitably tied to the agents in the relational triangle holding together artists, talent representatives, and production professionals. Both agents and producers are aware of being caught in interdependences that are destined to last. The materialization of these exchanges in the form of actual collaborations on projects and around artists is decisive. As an interviewee pointed out: "The best way to network is to work on something [and to work] at making things happen," and, "until you've done that, *you haven't really had that connection.*"[16] When the cooperation on a project has begun, the management of relationships remains focused on anticipating the needs and constraints of important long-term partners. It also entails not putting them in inextricable situations, so that the possibility of future transactions is preserved:

I've got a client right now that is in rehab for alcoholism, and he's supposed to be in a really big movie—I mean really big—they'll start shooting probably in August. My job is to be able to call an executive at the studio that oversees that project, maybe even a top-level executive, and make sure that they know that we're working very hard to get this client in good shape. I'll make that plan available so they can see that he is not going to cost them money when he gets on [to] production. So, there's a lot of that, and I wouldn't have those relationships and the people, the executives wouldn't pick up my call if I had not treated them well in other situations, or they didn't just like me. [. . .] And a career is building a reputation. I've been doing this for thirty-five years, so it's been a long, long time. (Manager, former agent, big agency, March 2010)

The economy of mutual favors between talent representatives and production professionals is perpetuated through such experiences. It is also sustained by repeated gestures of courtesy pertaining to the management of information (such as letting a counterpart be the first to know about a project or a piece of material) or the acknowledgment of the other's arguments and imperatives that manifests as a form of professional collegiality.[17] All of this contributes to the constitution of *strong ties* that are meaningful and consequential in the eyes of the participants, and clearly distinct from the weak ties that superficial encounters at social events can generate. The making of generations in Hollywood and the parallel career paths of interdependent categories of professionals that chapter 3 has described appear to be directly connected with the experience of such relationships as "trust":

You start out with this broad base of people that are assistants that are agent trainees, that are agents, that are development executives, creative executives, or just newborn lawyers. Whatever they are, they sort of all network together and as you go up, people fall by the wayside and [are] fewer and fewer as you go up, and people who you met at the bottom are your friends forever, because they knew you when you were nobody. I trust people that I've known for a long time far more than people that I feel want to be my friend because of what I do, rather than me personally. So you always have to be on your guard. (Literary agent, Big Hollywood, March 2013)

In this perspective, "trust" emerges from long-lasting ties at the same time as it allows for their perpetuation. Trust and time are inseparable:[18] the practice of agenting is oriented toward the building of long-term relations with production counterparts who are likely to be around for a long time and, consequently, who are not only current buyers but also potential future ones. Trust implies not just immediate anticipation, but the projection into a distant future. Being seen as "honest in your dealings" is important far beyond any specific financial negotiation, any project, or any short-term goal: in Little Hollywood or Big Hollywood—both being narrow games whose players know and recognize one another easily—the *memory* of interactions is vivid and conditions the continued inclusion of the participants in the game. This memorial dimension does not only concern the individuals who have been personally and directly involved in a relationship. In small and specialized professional circles, reproved behaviors leave visible markings on the concerned. The *history of relationships* disseminates and becomes common knowledge, providing all players with benchmarks for action:

If you don't deal with people in a fair way, or perhaps reveal confidential information for your own benefit, you probably will not last in the business for too long [because] people won't think you're a respectable person. Over time, that stuff gets weeded out—I mean, the people that are here a long time are all pretty ethical people. [. . .] You can't be an unbearable asshole in this business and expect to survive a long time. [. . .] You have to work with all these people, you know. And the actors come and go all the time, the movies come and go all the time, the television shows come and go all the time. It's your relationships with these people that stay. (Talent agent, Big Hollywood, April 2011)

The above remark suggests that "trust" should not be approached here as a moral substitute for rational action in cultural markets that are supposedly marked by opacity and uncertainty as far as competence and price are concerned—which is often the way in which studies of the film and entertainment industries have seized it.[19] The perceived need for trust and the way in which Hollywood professionals execute the corresponding relationships are rather the product of the longer history of this professional system; and they are reproduced over time via the day-to-day activities that professionals in such configurations carry out, in a path-dependent way. The history of relationships refers to a systemic process of which the experience of trust is the expression at the micro-level of interpersonal relations.

"I am trusted. People believe what I say, I guess. They must. It's all I've got!"[20] By saying this, a super-agent at one of the major agencies accounts for what makes the performativity of his utterances (Austin 1962): what his counterparts come to "trust" is not exclusively, and maybe not primarily, the (moral and/or rational[21]) attribute of not being "dishonest" in financial negotiations; it is his judgment and evaluation of something or someone's worth—in indigenous terms, his "taste."[22] It is what he says of someone's "talent," "quality," or "bankability," his tried and true ability to make "good matches" (between artists, with projects) and spot "promising" talent and projects. This "trust" that Hollywood professionals grant to one another refers to their inclination—progressively formed over time—to rely preferentially on certain counterparts. In this way, repeated shared experiences involving talent representatives and production professionals over long periods of time lead to the formation of a *game of mutual reliance* where "collegial currency" is produced and attributed to relationships. This process of mutual evaluation based on recurring cooperation is expressively described by this senior talent agent: "When I say that the relationship is everything, it does not mean that it has to be deep and best friends. It has to be one of *collegial currency*, where you've got enough in their bank and they've got enough in your bank—not leverage, *history*. There's enough experiences [with me] at Paramount Pictures for them to appreciate my power with the client, my power with the agency, the leverage, the validity of my arguments, my intellect" (big agency, December 2013, his emphasis).

The agents' vocabulary expresses in suggestive ways that inspiring trust and trusting others is not a choice or a matter of moral satisfaction but a necessity and a condition of professional existence. This contrasts with professional worlds in which participants believe that their inclusion in the game and their legitimacy depend on more institutionalized attributes and guarantees (such as title, diploma, position). Hollywood professionals navigate a space that is explicitly governed through the shaping, framing, and norming of interpersonal relations rather than one in which possible and legitimate action is primarily referred to general and formal rules. Here, "all you have is your credibility, [. . .] people need to believe you," and once you are known as someone who "lies conveniently to get what [you] want done and people can't trust you, [. . .] that never goes away."[23] The expression of moral feelings ("I trust you") has to do with the definition of durable identities within stable mutual reliance systems. These interrelation systems linking talent representatives and production professionals thus function as *spaces of informal control* regulated by peers through mechanisms of collective sanction toward those who transgress its norms more than through legal means. But the forms taken by these mechanisms of social control are never limited to one-on-one interactions, just as relationships are never purely dyadic. One-on-one interpersonal connections are always inscribed in the larger professional systems of interrelations (that form in either Big or Little Hollywood). Hence the comment that a senior talent agent at a big agency made about his relationship with a studio head: "He will never betray me overtly, because then he would get crushed by someone who is more powerful than him who also loves me" (February 2013).

The value of one's word garners all its importance in light of the surprisingly low level of legal formalization of relationships and transactions, taking into account amounts of money often at stake. It is worth noting that many super-agents do not ask their star clients to sign an agency contract that would protect the agents' own economic interests, given the huge financial stakes at hand, in case these clients defect. Comparably, when such agents and their counterparts at studios or production companies reach a verbal agreement—most of the time on the phone—defining the terms of an artist's involvement in a project, both usually consider that they "have a deal" that is final and binding enough (although not yet legally enforceable) for the production of the movie or show to begin and for expenses to be made, before the corresponding contract has been fully formalized and signed. Cases in which a studio tried to prevent the making of a movie from materially starting before the lawyers' work was complete and the formal contracts signed are mentioned as rare exceptions and "incidents." Agents explain that they "do everything by a handshake and by [the] words" they exchange with their counterparts, as opposed to relying on written formats. Requiring that paper precedes and conditions the effectiveness of commitments is described by this talent agent in Little Hollywood as an anomaly as well:

This is one of the few industries where paperwork is kind of an afterthought. So much of my business is done over the phone. [. . .] We do the deal over the telephone, we agree on the deal points. Often the client is off on a plane and shooting the movie before pen has even been set to paper. So that's all about relationship and trust. So to cement that, we're all constantly . . . you're having drinks with people, you're going to dinner with people. You are cementing those relationships. You're making sure that you can trust this person. [. . .] I think they have a greater accountability to you. You know, just as a human being, it's kind of hard to spend an hour talking about how you both have kids going into kindergarten and what have you, and then the next day get on the telephone to do something a little sneaky with someone. [. . .] And if you had drinks with them and they seemed like a jerk, then you also think, "Okay, so, I want [paper] for this deal before . . ." you know. (September 2010)

An agent's power to do things with words—often by the technical means of phone conversations—therefore appears to be a highly individualized, personal attribute of the concerned Hollywood professionals. It seems all the more magical because it does not present itself as derived from the institutional power of the agencies. However, organizations matter for the constitution of agents' capacity to act performatively. Let's get back to our previous remark regarding the strength of the verbal agreement between an agent and a studio head: if it is considered binding enough by the parties to readily act on it, it is not merely by virtue of the intrinsic personal power or commitment of counterparts in negotiation who are presumed to have spoken in "good faith," but it is because their word also engages organizations—a large talent agency and a major studio, in this case—and because involved individuals embody forms of institutional power that these organizations hold.

Moreover, talent agencies provide formats and tools on which performative action depends. Individualized styles, relationships, and transactions are *institutionally and technically equipped*. Considering this technical equipment of the daily practice of agenting guards us against the temptation of fetishizing the personal and subjective nature of relationships. On the contrary, observing agents at work led me to notice how relationship work is instrumented, what the consequences are on the modes of interaction and the types of ties that ensue. Walking into an agency generally feels like penetrating a busy hive of activity where energy is palpable. The architecture and the design of the place contribute to this effect. The structure and physical organization of the agents' work space—for instance, the horizontally oriented building that CAA occupied until 2007 conducive to the permanent intermingling of agency employees, or the glass walls that have characterized UTA from its creation—make the speed, the intensity, and the interactional dimension of their practice visible, reinforcing the experience of this activity in such terms.[24] The lobby of the big and midsize agencies typically opens onto one or several vast office suites organized around a central open space shared by the pool of assistants whose desks are lined up parallel to the agents' offices. In the offices that surround this central area, one can catch sight of the agents engaged in loud phone conversations, wearing hands-free devices and gesticulating expressively, and sometimes clearly multitasking.

The agencies are vibrant places where agents constantly have their eye on the cell phone and the computer that instrument (through calls, text messages, and e-mails) the intense and permanent circulation of information characterizing their activity. The repeated sound of incoming e-mails and text messages gave a particular tempo to the days I spent shadowing agents at various companies, revealing the fast pace of the exchanges that agents have to manage, especially in the large agencies. This is all the more true since new digital technologies and platforms, as well as the use of social networks, have multiplied and accelerated all types of communication, including the transfer of materials such as scripts and artists' promotional tapes or videos.

The formats, tones, and rhythms that mark relationships depend directly on the equipment of interactions. It is also what allows the agents to build a distinctive agenting style. However, agents are collectively equipped with devices that limit the possible dissonance between individualized styles, such as software programs designed for agencies and used to follow up on projects and with clients, one of their functionalities being to remind the agents of who (clients, production professionals, other talent representatives) they should get back in touch with, in the context of a particular project or simply to set up meetings in order to maintain ties. Such software programs—custom made in the biggest agencies and more standardized in the others—equip and rationalize the daily, routine relationship work.[25] These programs may also be used to store information regarding relevant counterparts—what happens in their personal life, what they like and relate to, for instance—which will be reused strategically in later interactions in order to make good matches (between people and with projects) or simply to give a more personal tone to a conversation.[26]

The agents who entered the profession several decades ago are able to describe how much new technologies and tools have transformed their daily experience of the job, which used to be characterized more by physical interactions, by the need to deliver material and information (scripts, clients' resumes) in person and in paper format, and by face-to-face meetings. The systematic use of online interfaces such as Breakdown Services to submit actors for roles in response to casting professionals who advertise them simultaneously to the entire agency world has standardized the forms that the exchanges between talent agents and casting professionals take. It has changed the modes of operation that agents follow as well as the pace of communications and the temporalities of agenting. In Little Hollywood, because the same information is delivered to all talent agents at once, what distinguishes the successful agents is no longer their ability to be the first to know about a job or a project by virtue of their preexisting connections with casting executives or directors. What makes a difference becomes one's capacity to mobilize such a relationship *after* having submitted all potential client matches for a job through the preset electronic format of the Breakdown advertisements. Pitching an actor to a casting director thus means selecting among the submitted clients who is worth the activation of this relationship and personalizing what started as a more standardized process. The timing and shaping of the "good pitch" are therefore transformed. The importance of cultivating direct relationships with casting professionals is not undermined, but it is reorganized. Picking up one's phone to call a casting director also takes on a different meaning.

More generally speaking, phone conversations tend to have a greater impact when short and sketchy e-mails or text messages have become the norm and a constantly open channel of communication. The generalized use of e-mail and electronic devices to send scripts (which used to be delivered physically to artists) or information regarding a client or a project (which, in the past, would have justified that the agent physically go to a studio) has rarefied the occasions for direct interaction and co-presence. It is often described by agents as a shift in their professional experience. For instance, this senior talent agent highlights the physical dimension that an agent's job had and partly lost, pointing to what contributes to the agent's power: the ability to impress, influence, convince, inspire; that is, the use of all corporeal means of domination involved in face-to-face interactions: "In the talent management business, it used to be very combative physically: you get up and move, you don't hit people, but you get up and step in, you sit in front of them, in the front of the table, you push a picture over, you put a tape in, and you were very interactive. Now it's much more clinical, digital, and clean, and the agents aren't as good" (big agency, March 2010).

It is revealing that, like the interviewee quoted above, agents who deplore the "clinical" turn taken in their work also connect it to a judgment on the current quality of the agents and their agenting. Indeed, new technologies such as digital devices are never a matter of pure technology or pure form: technical and technological changes manifest, and in fact contribute to generate, a rearrangement of existing hierarchies among agents and between the agency and the production sides. The new skills that the manipulation of digital tools and the practice of the associated modes of agenting require get gradually inscribed into what henceforth makes a promotable trainee, partly complementing and partly conflicting with the attributes that used to distinguish the "good agent" (more attached to in-person closeness, to the physicality of exchanges, to the corporeal expression of passion and aggressiveness). This goes hand in hand with the access to the profession of new generations who learn the job according to these new models. As comparable mutations happen on the production side—marked as much as the agencies by organizational growth and corporatization—it also develops in sync with new manners of relating and selling to the buyers. The agents' judgment on these transformations therefore expresses the objective competition between different definitions of excellence in agenting. It directly connects to how agents evaluate the artistry of their own activity and to the perception that agenting has become "less of a creative experience":

Training is not the same, by virtue of the fact that you're not selling in the same world. When I was trained, I pulled the picture, I pulled the résumé, I stapled it, I updated the résumé, I did it by handwriting, I called the buyer, we sent the actors for reading, there was no digital file, you sent the tape, you recorded the tape, you cut the tape . . . television, the movies, everything has changed; the nature of what the assistants listen to and audit, and hear their bosses doing, as far as selling and packaging, is far diminished from the way it used to be. What they are hearing now is more how to turn a buck in this way and that way, and not necessarily the more artful and creative side of agenting. (Talent agent, big agency, September 2010)

However, the mediation of technical tools does not dematerialize the exchanges as much as it reframes and refocuses them. Remote practices of agenting combine with the continued use of agents' mastery in the management of face-to-face interactions. Agents' professional repertoire of action now forms at the intersection of these two dimensions. Consequently, being physically close to the geographical center of "Hollywood" (that is, mostly in or around Beverly Hills and Century City, as far as the agency business is concerned) still matters greatly. Moreover, the new technical equipment of agenting not only coexists with the persistence of decisive physical interactions, it elevates them to a higher level of importance. When physical co-presence is no longer a material necessity (to deliver a piece of material or information for instance), it becomes of greater significance. Face-to-face interactions—prepared by technically mediated exchanges—*put a relationship to the test* and are often a prerequisite to further formalizing professional collaborations. Agents then use specific skills to evaluate a person,[27] as is evoked by this interviewee: "I don't think there's anything that replaces being in a room with somebody, looking them in the eye. I think it's a unique experience that cannot be replaced. [. . .] I want to look in somebody's eyes! And again, it's not the same when they're on Skype or on the screen—it's just not. I want to see their body language, I want to see who they are, I want to get a sense of them as people" (motion picture literary agent, midsize agency, March 2013).

The places where agents most often work and socialize (the agencies and studios, but also the restaurants or bars where the maintenance of relationships takes place) constitute the physical space where interpersonal ties form and stabilize over time,[28] delimiting small milieus of long-lasting acquaintances, in which word of mouth is crucial and categorizations are durably attached to individuals. Relationships thus form in very small circles in which reputations stick (to borrow Gary Alan Fine's [2012] terms), trajectories and histories are known, and ties are expected to last.

In conclusion, analyzing how agents perform relationship work sheds light on the constitution of a *professional social capital* that is specific to this occupational space and central to its functioning. We are used to thinking of social capital as an inherited form of power, mostly transmitted by virtue of its embodiment into family relations, which, especially in the Bourdieusian approach, has to do with the reproduction of class domination (Bourdieu 1986). However, the present case illustrates how social capital can be acquired in professional settings.[29] It also draws our attention to the differentiation of *specialized* forms of social capital:

the particular capital of relationship and mutual recognition that agents build and maintain is proper to Hollywood's occupational system; it is (re)produced and effective within its boundaries. This derives, in our view, from the structural differentiation of contemporary societies into relatively autonomous spheres of activity: while social differentiation has been often observed, all its implications (for understanding the specialization of power relations and social action) have not yet been fully elucidated. What it means to possess this professional social capital, how to accumulate it, how to use it, what one can do by virtue of holding it—all of this is specific to the configurations that make up Hollywood. In other words, "Hollywood" is the space within which this professional social capital is relevant and effective, and within which it is the *primary form* of resource that one needs to hold in order to exist. This social capital consists in the transformation of superficial acquaintances into long-term bonds that are relevant to professional transactions. When agents or producers say that, in Hollywood, "relationship means commerce,"[30] this is what they refer to, not only in the restrictive sense of enabling them to conduct financial negotiation, but in the more inclusive sense of allowing for professional exchanges to happen and be sustained over time.

Relationship work is precisely the activity through which this professional social capital is constituted as a form of embodied power. As I will show next, it allows an agent to make statements that matter regarding an artist's talent or price. Relationship work both is an activity constantly in need of renewal, and generates a cumulative dynamics as a result of which this capital strengthens: as a talent agent in Big Hollywood recounted, "there were a lot of people that wanted to help me because I had relationships" (March 2013).

This activity obviously pertains to the realm of personal interactions, but forms of power also get objectified as a result of their occurrence. This capital partly takes organizational forms: talent agencies are repositories of this specific professional social capital. In other words, they are places where mechanisms and arrangements that further the effectiveness, the solidity, and the durability of relationships get *institutionalized*. In particular, the major agencies may metaphorically be thought of as reservoirs for this type of capital. One of the WME agents whom I interviewed insisted on the importance of belonging to one of the top agencies for his power to "convert" pure access to information regarding potential acting jobs for clients into actual chances of getting his clients hired (the buyer committing to professional cooperation based on his "trust" in the organization, not just in the person of the agent). He was thus pointing to the difference it makes to be able to access and use the type of institutionalized social capital that this agency retains.[31]

There is always a certain amount of tension between such institutionalized forms of social capital and the ones that are individualized and embodied in the agents. The exclusiveness of personal ties between the agents of their counterparts sometimes diverge from what the agency requires from its employees: loyalty to the organization, teamwork around clients and buyers, and institutionalized specialization in compartmentalized structures. Regardless, agents' capacity to act effectively and legitimately in Hollywood emerges from the *circulation between embodied and institutionalized forms of this professional social capital*. The combined or alternate use of both forms—depending on the situation—allows for agents' performative action and, collectively, in the configurations they form with artists and production professionals, for the constitution of the commercial and the artistic value of people in Hollywood. Let's now go one step further in examining how, by focusing first on the relationships that agents develop with artists.

FIVE

Agents and Artists: Enchanted Bonds and Power Relations

Interviewed agents often described their relationships with talent as *enchanted bonds* deriving from elective affinity. Shared "creative inspiration" is mentioned as the source of the association an agent seeks with an artist.[1] Agents constantly refer to their belief in someone's artistic value ("talent") and, inseparably, in the aesthetic emotion they felt ("that person is magic") in order to make sense of the bet on the future that signing a client always represents. Conversely, several interviewees spontaneously told a story about actors or directors whom they decided *not to represent*, even though the artist had already reached some commercial success, because they had no admiration for the artist's work, "did not get it," or thought that the artist was not talented enough. Such a reference to inspiration is omnipresent in this world. It is at the foundation of the intimate tie that the agent wants to create with a client. There is no contradiction there with the belief an agent also needs to have, when signing a client, that he or she will be able to monetize this person's talent. Neither is there contradiction with it being a power relation which holds agents and artists together in parallel professional hierarchies.

Agents' Emotional Competence

In addition to this creative tie, when agents evoke the connection they feel with their clients, they also refer to a more affective dimension, an intimate bond—a source of emotional communion and empathy—that can be described by analogy with family ties: "You're not only a business handler for [your client], you're also part psychiatrist, probably part family member, whether it's a father, mother, brother, sister—that sort of thing—wife, husband, not in a physical sense, but certainly in an emotional and in an intellectual sense."[2] This partly corresponds to the image of insecure artists in need of affective support and emotional reassurance. However, this mutual tie (by which the agent's emotional commitment responds to the fact that the artist trusts the agent with his or her career) that takes the appearances of a friendship is not just a matter of feelings. For the agents, this emotional experience is in fact inseparable from very practical requirements that are directly attached to their professional practice. Creating and maintaining emotional connections with their clients is a prerequisite for the existence and success of the agents, especially when financial stakes are high and the clients are not legally bound by an agency contract. "Having strong relationships" includes creating ties that the agent hopes will resist the unexpected turns a career might take. This talent agent, who had to move to an established midsize agency when he was let go in the context of the merger of WMA and Endeavor, explained: "A lot of it is very personal, you know: it's who you connect with, who you trust. The majority of my clients followed me because they had worked with me, they trusted me, they liked me. They didn't care whether I was going to be at William Morris Endeavor or elsewhere, they wanted to be with me" (March 2010).

Agents consequently define their relationships with artists in ambiguous terms: oscillating between "business friendship"—an association that remains circumscribed to the professional world and its commercial stakes—and the unconditional affection that goes far beyond this sphere. For agents, the tension between professionality and intimacy leads to the need to draw and manage the boundary between "being friendly" and "being friends." This boundary work (Lamont 2000) is carried out through constant adjustments, both in context and according to what the agents perceive to be the risks and benefits of getting closer or distancing themselves from each client. The negotiation of this boundary has to do with the management of time and the effort to resist the complete absorption of what is ordinarily considered to be private time (weekends and late evenings) into professional time. The fact that an agent might have to justify not always being available for a client after 11 p.m. and on weekends reveals the pervasive effect of the intimate tie formed with artists.[3] So is the fact that agents, especially when they handle stars, often explain that they need to be potentially "on duty" at all times, nights and weekend included—a form of uninterrupted care for clients that they sometimes make into an attribute distinguishing "great agents."[4] Technological innovations, from cell phones to e-mail and all associated tools allowing for uninterrupted connection and permanent potential reachability (through instant messaging, etc.) have unquestionably extended, in the recent years, the imperative for agents to be available 24/7 for (important) clients and pushed back the limits of their "private sphere," thus requiring on their part the management of such invasive dynamics and an effort to set up new boundaries. However, agents usually don't talk about the acceleration process attached to technological change as a frustrating experience of "time famine"—to borrow the expression that Leslie Perlow (1999) forged to characterize the destructive effects of fast-paced, high-pressure, crisis-filled work environments. This has to do both with the fact that the pursuit of constant innovation in a frantic environment is at the heart of agents' professional ideology and with the importance of "closeness" with clients for the practice of agenting.

This type of necessary intimacy is a source of tension. This motion picture literary agent expressed the ambivalent nature of long-term relationships with artists that waver between friendship and service, inevitable intimacy and necessary distancing:

There are a couple [of client relationships] that have seeped into friendship, but I personally try to keep an honest line between them, because so many times you get fired. It's the worst thing about my job, being fired. [. . .] It's a very thin line, because everybody thinks they're your friend, because you get very intimate. You're really talking with these people about their wives and family and their children, and you're having very intimate conversations with them, but that's not the same as friendship . . . it's not. Friendship is people who are there for you, period. And what you find in Hollywood is: you're there for them. Very few are ever there for you. [. . .] I had a client who was, I thought, a friend. I mean, I'd been with him a decade, I'd built his career, I'd made his movie happen for him, and I got him on the map as an earnest writer, and a year and a half ago, on my birthday, he calls me at home, at seven-thirty at night to say: "I thought I should tell you I just left [your agency] and signed with [someone else]." (Big Hollywood, March 2013)

Indeed, agents are subject to a double bind: on the one hand, the risk of losing successful clients who do not feel "bound by trust" encourages the development of intimate connections.[5] On the other hand, the experience of being betrayed when a client "leaves you" causes one to learn the need to adopt a friendly distanced positioning throughout one's career. In any case, losing a client—especially one an agent has known for a long time and sometimes with whom he or she has been in daily contact—always comes at a cost that is both professional and emotional. Managing relationships with clients therefore means playing on the engagement of and detachment toward personal connections that sometimes closely tie the fates of the concerned, as the client's success is intrinsically linked to that of the agent's. This is why this attachment can rarely be purely superficial. A well-respected and successful agent I interviewed illustrated this fact. He brought up the decision of a star client whose career he had helped launch and whom he had represented for more than fifteen years to leave his agency for another big company, and confessed the dimension of personal turmoil that came with this professional loss: "just because you know it's the game, it does not mean that it hurts less." The vocabulary that is associated with a romantic breakup is sometimes present in the accounts that agents give of losing clients they invested a lot in:

They fire you, correct. And I've been there. And those things really hurt. You get this thing in your stomach: "What the fuck? Did I just get hit by a truck?" [. . .] That's also why I don't get that close; I never know when that's coming. So I can't expose myself emotionally to that kind of harm. Because when you really think you're close to somebody, it really is hard to pick yourself up. There was a client, I built his career, and I was getting him three and a half million dollars a film as a director, and he was a very hot, A list director and [. . .] he sent his then-manager in to fire me in his place, because he didn't have the fuckin' balls—excuse my French—to come and look me in the eye. [. . .] That was a guy, I was at his wedding, you know, I was his first call when his wife was pregnant, I mean, it's somebody I felt that I was very close to. (Motion picture literary agent, midsize agency, March 2013)

Such situations reveal the constitution and performance, in this professional sphere, of a specific *emotional competence*, made up of a subtle combination of involvement and restraint, and attached to the performance of relationship work.[6] Agents have to figure out through experience, and "by feel," what this distinction between "being friendly" and "being friends" exactly means in context and how to execute it, in a professional world that blurs the line between the personal and the professional and values the exhibition of emotional attachment. Being able to make this distinction and to keep themselves from crossing this line is described by agents as a gradual learning process through which they toughen up at an emotional cost: having been disappointed and having felt betrayed when losing a client they mistook for a friend. During our conversation, this senior agent at a major agency immediately disabused me of the idea that he had always been able to not take the defection of a client personally: "I did! I did! I took it very personally at times. I learned not to. And you know what? Taking it personally, getting hurt, feeling bad, makes you not take it personally. Then you disconnect a little bit, then it all starts to become a little more clinical, and eventually it is [easier]."[7] What agents also acquire is the ability to manage appearances and master discursive conventions that allow them to "save face" in interaction with a client who leaves: "A client will say, 'We can still be friends,' and the fact is, you can't. But they say it all the time. And, you know, you try to take the high road: 'Of course, if you need anything, let me know, I understand.' But it's always very painful."[8]

The formation of this emotional competence concerns both the agent's feelings and the client's: it includes the management of an artist's emotional ups and downs attached to the success or failure of projects. If these relationships are "rubbed with emotions," in one agent's words, it is also because talent representatives feel entrusted with their clients' dreams. The idea of being a dream keeper and a dream fulfiller—"somebody's dreams may be the most intimate thing that you can express to somebody [else]"[9]—is not just rhetoric used by agents in instrumental ways; it is at the heart of the symbolic transfer that ties the agent to the artist and gives creative value to the practice of agenting. I mentioned earlier the revealing expression an interviewee employed, saying that, as an agent, "fulfilling somebody else's dream becomes your dream." Another dimension of this emotional interconnection is conveyed by the saying according to which "the artists pay [their agent] ten percent to take the blame" if their career or a project does not meet the expected success. Managing artists' emotions means preserving the mutual belief in the "dream"; that is, the horizon of a future success, which is the foundation of the agent-client relationship.[10] For instance, a female talent agent at one of the biggest companies explained to me that it implies anticipating a client's reaction when producers or studios reject a project or their submission for a role, and translating this rejection in terms that won't undermine the artist's self-confidence (and therefore be detrimental to future chances of success). In such cases, a talent agent [. . .] wants to *pretend* that all doors are open. You're always juggling reality; you want to present a *certain* reality to the client that will make them happy, even if it's not a hundred percent accurate, [. . .] because they're looking to you to make them feel like their dreams *can* come true. And so you don't want to be the person who's saying yes or no. [. . .] You're trying to sort of dance around the client to make sure they feel like: "If not this job, then another job, and here's how we're going to get there." (November 2014)

This example illustrates that emotion management, just as other dimensions of relationship work analyzed in the previous chapter, is always both sincere and strategic. This was also observed by Laura Grindstaff and Vicki Mayer regarding the activities of the talk-show producer and the reality television caster, and the emotion work that such talent brokers have to do (Grindstaff 2002; Grindstaff and Mayer 2015; see also Wei 2012). Comparably, agenting is a reflective profession in which emotions that are truly felt need, at the same time, to be visibly performed. A revealing story evoking the legendary figure of industry mogul David Geffen was narrated to me several times: it pictures Geffen yelling at the top of his lungs on the phone, apparently beside himself, before hanging up and turning to his colleagues in the room, as calm and cold as one can be, asking: "Too much?" Whether true or not, this story tells us that acting is part of agenting and that being a showman is also required behind the scenes of *show* business (what colorful agency leaders such as Ari Emanuel, known for having rants, illustrates just as well). Hollywood is thus a multilevel emotional game in which the agent's worth derives more or less from processes of commodification of feelings (Hochschild 2009).

But this certainly does not mean that the emotional involvement professed by agents is nothing more than an act. The stereotype usually attached to the phony Hollywood agent must give way to a more complex reality. Agents' emotional competence does not simply reflect their capacity to perform a dual role or the formation of a "false self"[11] that dissimulates the true (economic) interest driving their behaviors. Looking closely at agents' emotional labor allows us to grasp its real and consequential nature. This also leads us to take some distance with the distinction between "deep acting" and "surface acting," following which Hochschild (1983) confines the practices of self-presentation in public that Goffman (1959) describes to the realm of "inauthentic" strategic activities.[12] On the contrary, in the agents' experience, "being friendly" does not contrast with "being friends" as the inauthentic contrasts with the sincere. The interviewed agents manifest genuine feelings of closeness generated by a long-term personal investment alongside artists that the agents' expertise in the management of emotions never enables them to fully avoid. Drawing a line between keeping this relationship purely professional and feeling bound by friendship is a constant challenge, as this limit has to be repeatedly reestablished over time; agents' experience of drawing this line remains full of contradictions.[13]

In fact, when differentiating "being friendly" from "being friends," agents refer to two separate repertoires of experience. These two repertoires manifest the coexistence, in our society, of two distinct spheres of relationships that have simultaneously emerged with the development of a market economy. This historical process has led to the constitution of a specialized sphere of commercial relations that separates itself from the sphere of pure friendship and disinterested intimate ties, the latter also becoming possible by virtue of this differentiation (Silver 1990). Friendship as a disinterested feeling has therefore been defined in opposition to the category of interested exchanges (including emotional ones) into which "business friendship" falls. When they talk about the mutual "trust" that they have established with production professionals, talent representatives refer to interested personal relations that have stood the test of time, and not to disinterested "friendship." Because their day-to-day interactions with artists are much more intimate and ambivalent, the boundary delimiting these two emotional repertoires also becomes fuzzier and more problematic in the agents' experience. The tension characterizing their perceptions, actions, and justification practices in that regard emerges from the dual cognitive frame that these two repertoires form. The professional system that Hollywood constitutes offers here a paradigmatic case study of the ways in which the spheres of the personal and the professional are socially constructed, the boundary separating them worked and redefined in practice, strategic bridges between these spheres built and crossed by individuals. Indeed, agents and their counterparts are able to "work" this boundary—be it to try keeping it in place or moving it—in interaction.

This also means that agents' emotion work does not pertain to the realm of irrational activity as opposed to that of rational action. The experience and expression of emotions, which is part of the practice of relationship work, is intrinsically connected to the selection of clients and projects, to the development of activities that get inscribed into economic transactions and legally formalized in contracts. It contributes to constructing Hollywood as an "industry" and a "market." The *emotional economy* of relationships in Hollywood—that is, the structure of emotional exchanges through which careers and projects are collectively shaped—directly forms economic as well as artistic divisions, as the final chapters of this book demonstrate.

Controlling Talent?

Variations in Power Relations: Agents and Artists in Little or Big Hollywood

The bond tying an agent and an artist—although sometimes described as "enchanted" by the concerned—is a power relationship. In addition, it is not simply a one-way domination mechanism but rather an inter- dependent relationship. The enchanted notion of the agent-client con- nection suggests the notion of mutual commitment: the agent's belief in the artist and the risky bet that signing new (especially "developmen- tal") talent always implies correspond to the faith of the artists who trust an agent with their hopes and dreams, and to the loyalty that the super-agent expects from the star who is often represented without be- ing legally bound by any contract. However, interdependence does not mean symmetry. If the agent and the client both invest in the relation- ship, they don't find themselves in equal positions. Generally speaking, the structure of this power relation depends on whether one operates in Little Hollywood or in Big Hollywood. In simple words, agents have the upper hand in Little Hollywood, whereas, in an apparent paradox, they are in a more subordinate position when working in Big Hollywood. Let's examine each case successively.

It all starts with how agents find their clients. Agenting differs in that regards in Little and in Big Hollywood. In Little Hollywood, agents chose their clients by singling them out among countless wannabe art- ists; they accredit them as professional as they "spot" and "sign" them. By contrast, in Big Hollywood, smaller numbers of successful artists are courted and "poached" by agents who compete for their attention. In other words, in Big Hollywood, attractive clients are able to pick their agent and their agency; in Little Hollywood, a mass of unknown artists rival to spark the interest of a representative. Signing with an agency is not an easy quest for newcomers in Hollywood. Agents mostly meet new clients through recommendations, which come from inside their professional system: a manager, a casting director, or a producer, or an- other client who has proven successful enough to be considered able to recognize salable talent. Agents also never sign absolute beginners: they look for early signs of professionalization. Such signs—objectified in an artist's résumé—consist of small contracts and job offers from respected buyers that artists have already accumulated (even if the job and the pay were minimal), and in ties with well-respected mentors or an established manager, all of which attest that the artist is already connected to a professional system. Such indications that professionalization has started allow the agent's bet on the client to materialize without being exclusively based on aesthetic affinity, and without being based on numbers or backed with institutional guarantees (similar to those attached to titles or diplomas in other professions).

This being a precondition to find an agent means that even beginner artists are never completely clueless. They have been capable of reaching small production or casting professionals by their own means to book their very first jobs. They are already able to make sense of the world surrounding them, decrypt the rules of the game, and identify relevant counterparts, to a certain extent. Unlike the image drawn by some studies of cultural networks and markets, artists cannot simply be thought of as disconnected units incapable of navigating an opaque market.[14] In addition, new electronic tools and platforms have recently offered them access to more systematic information about useful connections and potential jobs. This may be the case in ways that are in compliance with the platform's official mission—like with Actors Access, an online service where some casting directors release breakdowns directly to the actors who have subscribed. This allows actors, who now have the technical means to make their own videos, to submit their material, although this tends to involve very small parts and marginal projects. Oftentimes, artists also get hold of the job offers publicized to their representative through the platform Breakdown Express, which is the main system used by agents to submit their clients' profiles (résumés, photos, and videos) to potential buyers. Actors may have access to such data thanks to the indiscretion of a manager-friend or through another actor. Although actors cannot interfere with this submission process directly—as only agents can be officially registered and send a submission—clients use their early knowledge of what has been released to try to control what their agent does and restore some balance in the power relation in this way. The actors' goal is usually to maximize the number of roles for which their profile will be submitted, given that they often fear that their agent forgets about them or gets caught up in a conflict of interest, be it with the service of another artist, with the agent's own interest, or with that of the agency as a whole. Agents, on the other end, consider such "intrusions" as a dysfunctional behavior on the part of clients who are not always able to evaluate what jobs they have a real chance to be selected for and might have a distorted perception of their own profile.

Thus the changes brought by new devices and technologies have empowered the clients in their relationship with the agents, to an extent. In the 2000s and very early 2010s, agents at small companies sometimes wondered if they would eventually become "dispensable" (as a Little Hollywood talent agent that I shadowed put it), in a professional segment—that of small boutique agencies—in which organizations are fragile in the face of economic uncertainties and employee turnover is high. However, this preoccupation dissipated soon after, as the new instrumentation of client-agent relations stabilized. The agents' fear of becoming unnecessary didn't come true. On the contrary, artists need representation just as much as they used to in order to become fully professionalized and emerge from the crowd of (semi-)amateurs that exists at the margins of Little Hollywood: the "Very Little Hollywood" of wannabe-professionals, let alone amateurs who are just happy to be so. The artists' need to rely on agents' relationships does not derive from the fact that artists would be isolated in social vacuum or wouldn't have the possibility to make professionally relevant acquaintances. Artists need agents in order to emerge from the mass of aspiring talent because the process of identifying and therefore accrediting *professionals* in Little Hollywood takes place within the system of long-term interconnections tying agents to production professionals. The interconnection between artists, production professionals, and talent representatives cannot be reduced to objective economic transactions between collective forces in play on a market. The fact that it is made of *personal interactions* maintained in the long run is what gives shape and strength to the elements that are usually thought to be natural components of the market: talent "demand" (the definition of the key criteria for hiring an artist or creating a project around one, as far as name talent is concerned) and talent "supply" (the mechanisms of distinguishing promising talent and defining artists' profiles) are negotiated in face-to-face encounters in which specific projects may be at stake, but which always contribute at the same time to the more general mutual adjustment of perceptions and expectations.

New technical means have also transformed agents' practice into a more volume-oriented activity, since talent agents who handle 150 or 200 clients are now technically able to submit dozens of them electronically within a few seconds for job offers delivered directly to the agents' inbox several times a day. This mass management process is experienced by agents as a degradation of their work, where spending time on one-on-one interactions is so crucial. Inseparably, these new conditions require the creation of a drastic order of priority within an agent's client list. On the artists' side, evaluating their "rank and place" in the agent's priority list becomes all the more important. This also makes the precariousness of their situation even more palpable, and they can feel the power that their agent holds. Some artists talk about their effort to "mobilize" their agent and reactivate the affective and creative ties at the source of their relationship, to avoid losing their attention and falling to the bottom of a long client list. On the contrary, clients who feel neglected and abandoned by their agent (whether this be an accurate perception of reality or not) have a tendency to repeatedly move from one agency to another, which in the end makes them even more vulnerable, in a world in which building long-term relationships is key. On the other hand, when a client meets with sudden success (typically with a hit television show), the relationship between agent and artist is immediately transformed: the representative knows that the client is likely to leave now that he or she has become of interesting standing to a bigger agency. The client transitions to Big Hollywood.

In Big Hollywood, by contrast, the structure of power relations tends to be reversed: successful clients are in a position of ascendance over their representative, as powerful as the latter may be. It might seem paradoxical that the very thing that makes super-agents powerful in Hollywood is also what subjects them to the stars they draw their success from: this is how agents "are dominated by their own domination."[15] Of course, there is here also a hierarchy organizing clients within a client list, and some artists have more resources than others. Generally speaking, clients at a major agency are already known and recognized as professionally "competent" and "salable" in Hollywood (although their value varies with time and projects). However, this does not mean that they do not depend on an agent to be and remain in the game. There isn't any level at which the interdependence system tying agents, buyers, and artists would be avoidable. In other words, the biggest stars cannot do without being represented, because this is the occupational game by which projects and careers are made, not to mention that successful artists need assistance to manage the numerous solicitations and offers that they receive. Because star talent is courted by competitors from other agencies (if not by colleagues from the same company) and by studio executives and producers who look to create direct connections with name talent, agents in Big Hollywood are always fighting to protect the exclusiveness of their relationships with their clients. Their historical monopoly of intermediation is challenged in practice by such competition, to which should be added the presence of managers on the artist's side, which also plays a role in the definition of the power balance that the agent works at creating with the client.[16]

Even if agents depend highly on the loyalty of their biggest clients for their own professional existence and success, they are able to challenge and counterbalance their structural subordination in context by establishing specific modes of interpersonal relation with these artists. They craft and use personalized techniques for managing interactions and emotions in that sense. For instance, in situations that are contentious or emotionally challenging for the artist, this may mean placing the client in a position *to ask* for the agent's help or advice, and—as when one asks for a favor—to be *as if in debt* in the interpersonal relation. This senior agent at one of the major agencies described his response strategy after he received a text message from one of his star clients who was saying he had just come out of a "crazy meeting" at one of the major studios: "I just write: 'Call me.' I put it back in his court. So I don't chase him. [. . .] I don't want to reach into it too hard and chase him, because I don't want to show him that kind of service and not be able to maintain it, and it's not my style, and it's not how I want to be with him" (February 2013).

The power of the agent *in relationship* with the artist—despite the structural imbalance with star clients—is that of a personal advisor, a confidant entrusted with intimate (and sometime embarrassing) secrets as well as with other types of confidential information. It is also centrally attached to the creative influence that the agent holds over the client. Defining oneself as creative in this occupational space has to do with obtaining and keeping forms of power—and saying this is, of course, not to question the sincerity of such a professional definition on the part of Hollywood agents. Agents' "creative power" manifests itself in various ways, depending on the area of specialty in which the concerned operate. This talent agent at one of the biggest companies explained what differentiates how she contributes to the creative process with her actor clients from what her colleagues on the literary ("lit") side do with directors and writers:

On the lit side, clients who are pitching movies or clients who are pitching television shows will come in and talk to their agents and *practice* the pitch, and then the agent will give them notes: "Why don't you tweak it like this? Tweak it like that, change this, focus more on that, and otherwise it's great," and then send them off to do it. There's a little bit more coaching that goes on on the lit side than on the talent side. [. . . As an talent agent,] where your creativity does come in [is] advising them on what projects to do or not to do, and why. Telling them why *you* think a script is good or why it isn't, because they are paying you for your creative opinion on material, for sure. [. . .] Your knowledge of what's good and what isn't in terms of how things are perceived in the marketplace. What directors [are good to work with], definitely. To say: "This is an unknown director, but he's done three shorts that are really cool—I'm going to send them to you—and people like them, you know, Steven Spielberg saw two of them and said that he loves these shorts, so you should take this seriously." Or: "There's an unknown person who no one's ever heard of, first-time writer, first-time director, there are no merits on which to go." [. . .] Or: "Seriously well-accomplished director, really accomplished writer, excellent rest of the cast, strong script, do it." Or: "None of the above, but the script is fabulous because I love good material and I read the script and I think it's great, you should seriously look at it." So they are paying you for those kinds of opinions. (November 2014, her emphasis)

With these words, this agent ties her professional value to the importance of her creative opinion, placed at the heart of her professional mission. The role agents assign to themselves thus goes beyond just responding to their clients' needs; in the words of several interviewees, it is about anticipating these needs and knowing them "better than the artists themselves" or even "shaping them." From evaluating material (knowing what scripts are "good" or "bad") to recognizing "good matches" with other artists, this activity inseparably involves economic and aesthetic judgments. More generally speaking, the ability to conceive and express reliable aesthetic judgments is what agents define as their own talent, if not their "gift" or "specific art form,"[17] establishing a perfect parallel with the qualities of the artists they represent. In so doing, they include their own practices among the activities contributing to the social magic of creation. This self-conception potentially places them at a similar level of worth and dignity as the most acclaimed artists, by defining them as contributors to the artistic value of the projects, against an apprehension of their role as an auxiliary and subordinate activity: "I wanted to work *with and not for* people that I admired, people that had a talent I didn't have. [. . .] And it was also a match for my goal of being able to add value to great writers and great directors and great actors, or whatever it may be" (agent at a boutique agency, October 2010, my emphasis).

It's also through the "creative conversations" that agents have with their clients—as a former super-agent put it—that talent representatives work at establishing their influence in interaction and regain some ascendency in the structurally unbalanced relationship with successful clients. The same agent insisted on the importance of "giving [his clients] creative advice" and defending his views when he believed a job was "right for them," to the point of "really fighting with clients over what they should do," even at the risk of "losing them."[18] Similarly, this former talent agent at one of the major companies evoked her self-conception as an "authority figure" who has to impress clients in order to impose herself:

I think if you're too close to [your clients], they may not take your advice anymore; they may be too comfortable with you, you know. In other words, it's like when I have an as-sistant, we can be friendly, we can get along in many respects, but ultimately, they still have to view me as an authority figure. It's not different with a client. But inevitably, you speak sometimes on a daily basis, and a lot of them become your friends, so, I think, some people choose to only make it business, and some people also make the mistake of getting too close, because they work out of fear. Some people work out of fear in this business, which I think is the most dangerous thing to do, where you're constantly so scared of losing your clients. (Paris, November 2010)

These interviewees express the tension between fostering an intimate connection conducive to emotional bonding and imposing oneself as an authority figure who dictates creative choices, and the "dance" they constantly perform between the two dimensions. But ultimately, these are the two faces of the agent's power in the relationship with the artists they represent. Most of the time, the clients follow their agent's advice, and conflicts over projects and job offers that clients should consider, accept, or reject are ultimately very rare.[19] The agent's authority in such contexts does not simply derive from a psychological mechanism in play in a one-on-one interaction: rather, it has to do with the client's perception of the agent's (and the agency's) power with potential buyers and other key players. The belief in the agent's ability to obtain some-thing from production professionals and stars that they are uniquely acquainted with—but also to close these doors to a client if things go bad—is at the source of the fear of displeasing their agent or "stepping on the wrong toes" at their agency and "losing it all"[20] that many artists, even successful ones, express.

In sum, the question "who dominates, the agent or the client?" does not receive a simple and unilateral response. In the agent-artist rela-tionship, the domination structure varies with the agent's position: in Little Hollywood, being represented is a condition of professionaliza-tion for artists, and their dependence on the agent who accepts to sign them is complete in that sense. In Big Hollywood, successful clients can pick and choose their agent, change agencies, and put representatives in competition. However, power relations are more complex and are partly rearranged *in interaction*: in other words, the agent's "authority" is never only positional; it is generated and shaped by the agent's *work*. The production of authority is an activity, and it's inseparable from participation in the creation process. Consequently, this "authority" is not so much an attribute that preexists and conditions the practice of agenting; rather, it *forms in relationships*. It emerges from them and is reinvested in them. An agent works relationships in interaction so that the artist's *situated reliance* (on emotional and creative levels) counterbalances the agent's *structural dependence* on a successful client. The relational mechanism tying the agent and the client together is also never restricted to these two protagonists; it depends on their inclusion into the larger triangular system that organizes Hollywood (talent representatives/production professionals/artists).

Power Mechanisms and Mental Repertoires

The forms of power held by agents, as well as by other professionals who operate "behind the scenes" in Hollywood, depend on both the positional and the interactional systems within which they are located. On one hand, an agent's *institutional position* is given by his or her placement in interconnected hierarchies: in the structure of Big versus Little Hollywood and in the hierarchy attached to the functional division of labor that exists within a given agency. On the other hand, the same agent is situated within an *interactional system* which is attached to the history of interpersonal relations that cross over organizational boundaries and tie together representation professionals, production professionals, and artists. Repeated exchanges create lasting ties and, importantly, a *memory of relationships* shared in a group of peers. By describing how agents work relationships, including their emotional dimensions, I have documented how the *interactional system* that participants form over time affects the *positional structure* in which agents can be placed by the analyst.

As a result, to understand agents' power, a purely interactionist focus on relationships wouldn't be sufficient; nor would it be enough to consider the structure of positions constituting Hollywood as a social field. Interactions do not contrast with positions like situation opposes structure. Instead, we face two distinct but coexisting structural arrangements—a positional *structure* and an interactional *structure*—that co-produce the participants' ability to act and influence others' behaviors. Rather than approaching interactions as intrinsically fleeting ties subject to constant change by opposition to more stable power arrangements, we grasp here their lasting and systemic nature and their structuring effects:

"positional mechanisms" are challenged and reshaped *in relationships*. However, the complexity of past experiences, give-and-takes, and favors and debts can never fully translate into the logic of organizational resources and into the hierarchy of institutional positions. For this reason, the memory of relationships coexists with the more formal hierarchy of positions in Hollywood; it can alter it and interfere with it in the shaping of perceptions and anticipations. In the end, *what agents can do and make others do*—their influence, or what they themselves call their "authority"—*emerges from the interplay of positional and interactional structures*. In other words, agents' authority derives from combined forms of positional power (that gets objectified in organizations) and of relational power (built via face-to-face interactions).

Besides referring to the "authority" they should display in interactions with clients, agents talk about the "charisma" they need to manifest in relationships, and sometimes the "mystique" they built around themselves, their name, and their image. Because charisma is something that is actively and reflexively expressed in this context, it is part of the relationship work that agents accomplish. For instance, a senior talent agent described with a vocabulary almost similar to that of romantic passion the form of captivation that draws top talent to him, revealing the dimension of labor involved in the making of his "charisma": "I get emotional. I'm emotional right here. I live on emotion. I'm always conveying *passion*. Intensity. And that's what I'm selling. And that's what people want from me, and they get their rides from me. They can get excited and they want to be with me and close to me, because that's my charisma, right? My energy is *that*. [. . .] I don't think of that consciously, but I see reactions and I understand the power of it, so I use it!" (talent agent, Big Hollywood, December 2013, his emphasis).

Indeed, the existence of the "super-agent" emerges from this ability to evoke from the artists the personal loyalty and attachment allowing the agent to create a portfolio of star clients and to make him- or herself indispensable to the top agency that employs him or her and doesn't want to risk losing such lucrative clients. But the construction of an agent's charisma in professional relationships is also always a more collective product:[21] it emerges from the activities of various types of Hollywood professionals that attest to the personal ability of an agent to inspire beliefs and actions (the loyalty of a star, the commitment of a studio executive to a project, etc.) in ways that cannot visibly and directly be attributed to one's institutional resources and position. Such collective attribution of charisma dissimulates that organizational affiliations matter for one's ability to inspire or generate actions; as well, it attaches relational skills to intrinsically individual qualities similar to those used to characterize artists: "charisma" is a figure of "talent" applied to the agent.

Charisma and personal ascendance are in fact rooted in organizations; they are shaped in highly institutionalized and professionalized environments. Big agencies and studios especially are complex and compartmentalized corporatized structures, private bureaucracies governed through what could be described as legal-rational mechanisms. As I showed earlier, it is in the organizational framework of the agency that agents learn to "be charismatic" (in a specialized way, one that is operational and relevant to Hollywood) and to maintain relationships accordingly. In that sense, charisma is institutionally structured.[22] This case study incites us to subvert Weber's division between charismatic and legal-rational modes of legitimate domination (Weber 1978),[23] not simply by observing the combination of such mechanisms in practice but rather by approaching the construction of charisma in highly rationalized organizations.[24] Modes of domination are therefore shaped in the institutional setting that characterizes this specialized, formally organized, and hierarchized professional world, at the same time as they are structured by interactional dynamics that form ties across organizational boundaries and with which agents make sense of their experience, *first and foremost*.

This last remark drawing attention to agents' perceptions requires further elaboration. When I say that agents' authority, charisma, or general ability to do and make do stems from the interplay of positional and interactional mechanisms, I describe such intertwined structures from the position of the observer analyzing Hollywood. Agents, on the other hand, perceive their activity and talk about it primarily as relationship driven. The constant reference to Hollywood's "relational game" reveals *the mental repertoire* that prevails for agents and their counterparts. In other words, even though institutional positions and resources matter, the interpretative and argumentative frames that agents use are primarily attached to *the experience of relationships*. The system of personal ties in which agents place themselves in relation to others is what makes their activity meaningful and evaluable to them. Their repertoires of action and justification are associated with belonging to the relational systems that crosses over organizational boundaries and ties talent representatives, artists, and production professionals together. Agents' professional definition primarily refers to the realm of relationships.

More precisely, within the realm of relationships, the reference to "talent" is the central element of this mental repertoire. All interviewed agents have spontaneously placed at the heart of the abilities they con-

sider indispensable for the practice of/success in the profession the possession of a "sense of talent," a capacity to discriminate between "good"
and "bad taste," an aesthetic vision allowing them to evaluate artists and
artworks and sort them out, separating the ones they want to bet on and
associate their name with from the ones they want to keep at a distance.
If the belief in "talent" is so essential for the agents, it is because the
legitimacy of their creative mandate comes from their alleged ability to
"recognize talent." By taking on certain clients, agents in fact *make talent*
understood as an attribute that has professional value, manifests itself
in performances and products, and can therefore appear to a much larger
crowd. Agents thus "represent talent" in the double sense of speaking in
the name of their clients and of (participating in) giving them visibility
and artistic status. The *power of naming talent* is part of the social magic
of agenting, although it is not exclusive to talent representatives.[25] The
identification of talent presents itself as an inexplicable, immediate, and
permanent mechanism: agents talk about the obvious and unwavering
conviction that someone has talent as something that will supersede the
ups and downs of Hollywood careers. The belief that the agent will not
give up on the client if success is not immediately at hand is a condition
of possibility of the agenting relationship, on both ends. The designation
by the agent of those who have "talent" is also presented as a unilateral
mechanism. In fact, the magical act of attributing talent always comes
with a "counter-gift": the refracted attribution to the agent of a "sense
of talent" and of "good taste." The agents' own greatness or "gift" is a re-
flection of the talent recognized in the artists that they represent. Far
from being instituted once and for all, these mutual attributions of worth
are in fact constantly re-created and reassigned in relationships.

This reference to talent works like a *founding myth* from which agenting stories stem. Greatness in agenting is not primarily attached to the
repertoire of entrepreneurship or economic success. It first involves creativity, what Boltanski and Thévenot (2006) call an "inspired order of
worth." Of course, I don't mean to suggest that economic transactions
wouldn't be essential to the practice of agenting. What I point to is
that the primary basis for agents' *legitimacy* is not there. The symbolic
logic of talent comes first and gives meaning and relevance to the economic gamble taken by the agent on the beginner or the "cold" client. Talent and sense of talent—indivisible attributes of the artist-agent
relationship—operate as resources and means of action as soon as they
are mutually recognized and enter into a circle of recognition that includes some of the agent's counterparts on the production side. The
buyers' belief in the agents' sense of talent determines the agents' ability

to make things happen (to get the client "in the room" with a casting director, or to convince a studio executive to commit to a project starring a client) and to convert the symbolic recognition of talent into (potential) economic transactions. By insisting on the aesthetic and taste-related dimension of their job, agents also underline the practical dimension that the evaluation of talent takes in their day-to-day activity and the know-how that they have to develop in that regard. They need to gauge and decide, for instance, which scripts they will present favorably to an actor or director client, to try to get the client involved in what they perceive as "good projects": "The other thing I would say is, for agents, it *is* a job that requires an aesthetic, and what I mean by that [is . . .] a certain sense of, or a certain amount of taste—a taste level. So, for me, I need to be able to look at a DP's [director of photography's] work and decide whether it's good or bad. A literary agent needs to be able to read a script and know whether it's good or bad" (Owner of a below-the-line boutique, October 2010, his emphasis).

Like the artists, the agents commonly express their belief in the importance and the intrinsic value of art/aesthetics as something to promote and work for, and in the social power of artworks. This belief is in fact often what has led them to aspire to work in Hollywood in the first place. This is why we have no reason to question the sincerity of what they say in that regard, like this literary agent who insists on his intention to "make a difference" through his professional accomplishments:

We can reexamine from this angle the words of the Big Hollywood agent quoted in chapter 3, who insisted on his intention to "make a difference" through his professional accomplishments. The meaning of such a statement is inseparable from his identification with "the people who don't get into [Hollywood] for the money or the fame" but "because either a movie or a TV show touched them," and from the belief that "it's much more important to touch people." The recognition that he is "never going to be a good writer'" and has "no desire to be a director or an actor, and [that he] wouldn't be really any good at either those things," is immediately counterweighted by the assertion that, because he is "really good with talent," he can "have [the artists] make a difference": "I realize I can really make more of a difference by working with these people, in a sense" (September 2010).

These words are revealing of the type of "social libido"—that is, in Bourdieu's terms, the specific *illusio* that nourishes the activities within this social world. Bourdieu defines *illusio* as "the fact of attributing importance to a social game, the fact that what happens matters to those who are engaged in it, who are in the game" (Bourdieu [1994] 1998, 77).[26]

The agents' *illusio* is the type of belief they share about the relevance of the game they are in, and the meaningful nature of their contribution to it. In this specific professional sphere, believing in gift, talent, or "good work"—both your own and your clients', relationally—is essential to the definition of the value of people and the meaning of practice. The recognition of creative value is omnipresent and often associated with the expression of intense affection. This is why artists look for an agent they would *personally* relate to and *like* (and vice versa). This perpetual quest for the good match, the right person, is to some extent comparable to a romantic quest (and to the belief in great love in the realm of domestic relations), and similarly exposes the concerned to the risk of being disappointed. I have already insisted on the emotional forms taken by professional ties: liking and being liked, impressing and admiring, getting personally involved and crossing the blurred boundary between the private and the professional are constantly at stake in the agent-client relationship.

At the same time, it would be extremely naïve to imagine that enchanted bonds and feelings, and the common service of art, are purely and simply pervading the entire professional system of Hollywood. This is obviously not what I mean here. The *illusio* shared in this space refers to a *horizon* toward which activity is oriented. It is the common foundation of professional ideals specific to the various occupational groups at work in Hollywood. At the same time, in each of these groups, the experience of working in Hollywood is more ambivalent: agents both sincerely believe in true talent and claim that *they* make stars and artists through transactions that are far from being based only on creative preoccupations. Daily relationships with clients are sometimes lived as difficult partnerships and tinged with apprehension or fear that the artists are susceptible to heeding the siren song of competitors and likely to leave even a dedicated agent. On the artists' end, the perception of what agents do is also more ambiguous than the enchanted scenario suggests: on one hand, agents are sometimes described as a "necessary evil," suspected of favoring other interests and priorities (their own, their agency's, other clients') and of being commerce oriented at the expense of creative choices. On the other hand, the aspiration to being under the protective wing of a powerful agent who "gets you" on an artistic level is also expressed. Artists know that they organically depend on their tie with an agent/agency for their professional existence and credibility, and for the identification of viable counterparts among financiers and producers.

In addition, different occupational groups in interplay in Hollywood (artists of various types, various categories of talent representatives and production professionals, financiers, etc.) have distinct ways of perceiving their own contribution and that of others, their raison d'être, their relationships with other players. Agents' interest and commitment to the game is therefore not exactly of the same nature as the ones that artists or producers express, even though all of them participate in collectively fueling the belief that the game is worth playing. In other words, the *illusio* that forms in this space, rather than expressing identical beliefs on the part of the different occupational groups in interaction, is the product of *convergent beliefs*. This convergence process consists in the alignment of legitimization repertoires around the rhetoric of and belief in talent, while *strategic interdependence* between the groups that make up the Hollywood professional system (at both positional and interactional levels) is what ensures the stability of the game. In sum, power mechanisms—as far as agenting is concerned, but beyond this particular case study as well—must be seized at two levels combined: that of the interplay between positional and interactional interdependence structures (which forms particular professional configurations in Hollywood), and that of the mental frame that gives its primary meaning to activity in this context.

Embedded Identities and Hierarchies

What makes up agents' power, the logic of their practice, their self-definition—all of this is inseparable from how agents "make artists" and shape artistic profiles and careers, which in turn retroacts on agents' paths and agenting activities. This dynamic is what I will now examine.

Agenting and Typecasting

For agents, ensuring the recognition of the people they represent as unquestionable talent and "good artists" means, in fact, preserving their own professional identity and their own worth, directly evaluated by the yardstick of their clients'. If the social status and standing stemming from someone's labeling as a (great) artist affect, by contagion, the agent who speaks in this person's name, the contrary is also true, and the agents expose themselves to the risk of losing professional credit if their clients do. Some sectors of the representation business are of course more vulnerable than others to this type of disrepute: representing below-the-line personnel (who can be qualified as "technicians" versus "artists") or the new celebrities of reality television or digital media presents this type of challenge. The agents often have to battle to impose the idea that their clients are also full-fledged artists—although they might recognize the specificities of managing a different category of "talent"[27]—since the concerned clients don't (yet) enjoy full social and professional recognition of artistic status. In the quote below, the owner of a below-the-line agency illustrates this mechanism: he asserts the artistic qualities of directors of photography as well as the aesthetic dimensions involved in the activity of line producers whom he also represents, such recognition being the basis of his own creative contribution.

I want to be a part of the creative process. But, I guess the way I would describe it is, if you read the script and then you can ask the producer: "What kind of an aesthetic are you looking for? What kind of style? How are you going to shoot the film? Are you going to shoot digitally? What's your director like?" [. . .] So, take a look at this person's body of work—you'll see, I think, similar references that will appeal to your director. With the cinematographers, I think you get into that. [. . .] I will also say this: some people think that line producing doesn't really have an aesthetic, and I think it does. I think that you can see in a producer's body of work their ability to put the money on the screen, if you look at it carefully. And that's what you really want. (October 2010, Hollywood)

Similarly to defining below-the-line activities as art (make-up *artist*, visual effects *artist*, etc.), nonscripted television or digital media agents work at moving the boundaries of recognition and worth, by extending the realm of "art" and "talent" so as to include their clients' activities. They contribute to the continual process of redefining what is legitimately considered to be art and granted more or less aesthetic recognition in a given time and society. They participate in *classification struggles* that, in turn, contribute to shaping their own professional standing and legitimacy. Consequently, even if agents seem to follow only preexisting categorization mechanisms, they are at the same time, imperceptibly, engaged in the progressive and collective rearrangement of such division and hierarchies.

Artists' classifications are also at stake in the creative matchmaking that agents accomplish. Looking for good matches among talent and with producers is a valued element of agents' job definition, by which they clearly position themselves on the creative side. This pairing process consists in playing with existing connections and affinities between artists (who ideally are clients in the same agency, but not exclusively), to identify them, exploit them, and ultimately orchestrate the development of new creative relationships. The agent's skill is therefore to know "how to network [clients] into collaborative relationships that are going to inspire them creatively" and to consequently create "artistically incestuous" relationships between artists.[28] In practice, this may include "making introductions" between artists with complementary profiles, usually at comparable levels of career and success. For instance, during a session of in situ observation, a Big Hollywood talent agent explained how, in the context of packaging his client—a famous television writer and actor—in a film project he was about to sell to a TV network, he was helping bringing in an established film director who would make the project "a little more cinematic." By connecting the two artists, both known for successes in the same artistic genre, he was working at assembling the right talent team according to his vision of the film project and of the expectations of the buyer. Creative pairing also often means reactivating preexisting ties between artists who have worked together in previous projects when the time comes, at the beginning of the packaging process, to discuss with a star client the names of potential partners. Organizing meetings between the client and such possible co-stars is aimed at "seeing what they think of the script, and seeing how the project might come together, long before [the star client] controls it, or we make a deal, or we know when or for how much"; it is about bringing together "like-minded creative partners."[29]

Several studies have already noted the importance of recurrent work ties between consecrated creators and their effects in terms of cumulative probability of success in Hollywood (Faulkner 1983; Rossman, Esparza, and Bonacich 2010; attempting to predict which performances will be nominated for an Academy Award, these authors conclude that actors working with elite collaborators are more likely to be consecrated with an Oscar nomination). Such associations between high-status artists who repeatedly work together are in fact easy to illustrate: Martin Scorsese and Leonardo DiCaprio, Christoph Waltz and Quentin Tarantino, Ben Stiller and Owen Wilson, for instance, come to mind. But what we can grasp here is *how* this matching process concretely takes place. Agents who handle a star and who are therefore involved in packaging projects play an active role in shaping and steering collaborations, in line with their own perception of the particular type of project in question or with a client's specific profile. Matching operations always mean choosing between limited options depending on the category and genre to which a project belongs; on the status, career situation, and specific profile of an artist; as well as on the position of the concerned agent. The recurrence of similar creative associations in the past reinforces in return the closure and self-referential nature of such specialized collaboration circles.[30] Creative matchmaking is a valued activity in the eyes of the agents—an activity that has to come first, in terms of priority as well as chronology, before convincing a buyer and negotiating a deal even comes into question: "How do you find the like-minded guy? Who is not going to ruffle [the client]'s creative comedic feathers, but who is going to be able to add something? Who is not going to be a pushover, but who is also not going to be a buffoon? How is it going to work? And the job of getting [this creative partner] is the key to that transaction. Not getting [the studio] to do it, or not getting [the client]'s deal done" (talent agent, big agency, April 2013).

The interviewee quoted below similarly insisted on the fundamental impact that agents have through this process of forming teams attached to a given project, even when their activity does not affect the definition of the key elements of a film or a television show but consists only, at a more modest level, in establishing a connection that might benefit a client in the future. This co-owner of an up-and-coming boutique agency who represents mostly directors and writers described this pairing process as personality driven, the selection of a client's "good match" making the agent into an improvised psychologist and expert in human nature:

You're a writer. You have an idea. We then figure out how to take that idea and turn it into a TV show, a movie, a video game, whatever it may be, whatever it is. So, first, you have to figure out what it is, right? Which is a ton of fun. And then, part of that is matching up, it's a DNA match of your client and the producer, your client and the studio executive, people that would have similar personalities, DNA, whatever it may be, that would work well together. And sometimes it's not people that are similar. Sometimes it's people who are opposite. Because you know that this client needs a kick in the ass, and needs deadlines, and needs structure, because they don't have it in their lives, so I'm going to find a producer that will provide it. Or an executive that will provide it. So it's all about creating these kinds of creative marriages. (October 2010)

Despite the naturalization or even the biologization of this process in this agent's words, the competences that agents here put into practice have first to do with their knowledge of the divisions and hierarchies organizing the industry, and especially those directly relevant to their clients' areas of specialty; this often means finding, among the professionals who operate in a particular media and genre, the most recognized or promising potential counterparts who are within a client's reach in terms of success and career level. Prompting a client to engage into a "profitable" creative partnership always means classifying and hierarchizing: what makes matching practices possible is an evaluation process and the measurement of people's current or potential value (artistically, commercially, and in terms of popularity). Pairing activities thus rely on a shared and preexisting classification system that all the team-making activities contribute, in return, to maintaining and strengthening. What agents also do through all agenting activities—be it advising clients about job choices, packaging, pairing their clients with other artists, and so on—is attaching an identifiable and distinctive genre and profile to each client, participating in the making of *specialized identities* in Hollywood.

As other work has already demonstrated (Zuckerman et al. 2003, Faulkner 1983), a simple and generic "typecast" identity is beneficial for gaining visibility and recognition in the film labor market, and in the entertainment industry at large. This is the case not only because a generic identity of this sort is more easily recognizable and interpretable to audiences, but primarily because it is recognizable to the professionals in charge of selecting and hiring talent—casting professionals in the first place. It becomes even truer at a time when studios and television networks are reluctant to take risks with projects (and subsequently with talent profiles) that don't benefit from some "pre-awareness" on the part of the targeted audience. We can go as far as saying that being typecast is a *condition of professional existence and success*, even beyond the case of beginners who need to emerge from the mass and establish themselves at the start of a career; the idea that deploying a "generalist identity" would become the most profitable strategy once a career has started also needs to be nuanced.[31] In fact, even though artists aspire to show range and do diverse projects, the dynamics of typecasting by which artists get recognition in Hollywood make the building of a more "versatile brand" difficult, even for well-established talent. The observation of conversations between a talent agent and his successful actor client illustrated the efforts that they were jointly making to diversify the image of this actor, mostly known for family comedies, and have him achieve more professional recognition as a serious film director, inflecting this artist's general profile. But having become a "critical element" around which film projects are built and whose presence is enough to get a studio on board does not hinder the inertia of typecast identity. On the contrary, such artists are both visible contributors to what defines a cinematic genre (their name evokes a certain type of movie), and they are at the same time *assigned to it*, whether they embrace it or not. Breaking out of a typecast and broadening one's repertoire remains an ongoing struggle:

even Big Hollywood stars depend on a specialized identification and are subject to classification mechanisms. The successful building of a generalist profile is an extremely rare situation, even at that level.

In Little Hollywood, typecasting mechanisms take even more systematic forms. Artists—and especially actors and actresses—know and, for the most part, accept that their profile needs to fall into clear-cut categories, allowing for fast classification by talent representatives and casting professionals who face huge numbers of aspirants and screen out candidates who are not immediately identifiable. The formation of such specialized identities is not necessarily associated with a specialized technical competence (for instance, in the performance of a certain type of job or role), but it does not make it less effective. The generalized use of rationalizing tools such as Breakdown Services shapes the forms that this typecasting process takes. The job offers that are electronically distributed to the agencies through this system are already formatted according to the preset categories with which candidates will be evaluated. Agents are thus strongly incited to approach potential new clients with such a classification system in mind, both to sign the ones they perceive to be "in demand" and to work with them at inflecting their image so that it fits as closely as possible such classification requirements. The following extracts are revealing examples of the form that job offers circulated through the Breakdowns concretely take. The first one presented the parts available in a low-budget movie, whereas the second offered nonrecurring roles in an episode of the hit television show *How I Met Your Mother*:

HARDFLIP 2

Feature Film

SAG ULB Pending

Producer: Johnny Remo SkipStone Pictures

Director: Johnny Remo

Writers: Daniel Backman and Johnny Remo

Casting Director: Chris Williams

Interview Dates: TBA

Callback Dates: TBA

Shoot/Start Date: TBA

Pay Rate: $110 Day SAG ultra low budget scale

Location: Los Angeles—San Diego

SUBMIT ELECTRONICALLY.

IF POSSIBLE, PLEASE SUBMIT ACTOR'S ONLINE DEMO CLIPS ALONG WITH EACH ACTOR SUBMISSION.

[RYDER] Caucasian. 6'2" Blonde hair, brown eyes. He's cocky and a bit of a bully. Athletic, pro skateboarder. Skateboarding a plus. 22 to 24 years old Actor must be able to play wide emotional range. LEAD Replacing actor who played Ryder in the first movie.

[STAN] Caucasian, weathered but attractive mid to late 40s. Ryder's Father. Actor must be able to play wide emotional range. LEAD

[MIA] Caucasian, very attractive female mid-40s. Ryder's mother. She carries a burden from her past. Actor must be able to play wide emotional range. LEAD

[REBEKAH] Ryder's love interest. Very attractive, in shape. Perky but smart. Good girl next store. 19 to 21 years old. Actor must be able to play wide emotional range. LEAD

[BRYANNA] Rebekah's friend. Attractive, in shape. Has a wild side but still is a good girl. 19 to 21 years old.

[NORMAN] Mia's husband. Very successful. Attractive and athletic. Mid to late 40s. Arrogant.

———

HOW I MET YOUR MOTHER, Episode 723, "Trilogy Time"
Episodic
CBS / 20th Century Fox
½ Hour
SAG
Draft: 3/12/12
Executive Producers: Carter Bays, Craig Thomas, Chris Harris, Stephen Lloyd, Kourtney Kang
Exec. Producer & Director: Pamela Fryman
Co-Exec. Producers: Suzy Greenberg, Chuck Tatham, Jamie Rhonheimer, Joe Kelley
Director: Pamela Fryman
Writer: Kourtney Kang
Casting Director: Marisa Ross
Casting Associate: Jessica Ross
Location: Los Angeles
Shoot Dates: 3/19—3/23
SUBMIT ELECTRONICALLY ONLY.

PLEASE SUBMIT ALL ETHNICITIES UNLESS OTHERWISE NOTED.

[RHIANNON] Mid 20s, a beautiful hippie chick, hot and dirty, she appears in one of Ted's fantasies about his exciting future romantic life . . . 1 speech & 1 line, 2 scenes

[CHESTER] Late 30s, an upscale urban guy, apparently married to Veronica, he lives across the street from Barney, and is utterly baffled and fascinated by Barney's eccentric behavior . . . 1 speech & 4 lines, 1 scene

[VERONICA] Late 30s, an upscale urban woman, apparently married to Chester, she's trying to have a serious conversation with him—but Chester is completely distracted . . . 2 lines, 1 scene

[ADARA] Mid 20s, a hot Iranian girl, who likes it dirty, she is dating Barney in 2003 . . .
  3 lines, 1 scene
(Source: Breakdowns LA, March 14, 2012)

Physical appearance and characteristics are the primary basis for typecasting. It goes from ethnic looks ("African American or Latina"), age range, height and size ("muscular"), or hair color to other types of characteristics, which are also depicted as visual ones: "Jewish-looking," "looking intelligent and professional" or like a "distinguished business-man," "rocker type," and so on. Acting jobs are only very briefly outlined, with a few lines using mostly evocative adjectives and not telling much regarding the role itself or the story line of the project. Agents have thus to develop an ability to read between the lines what casting directors and television casters are really looking for. For the most part, agents work at anticipating and satisfying buyers' expectations without challenging the categories they use to express them: they feel like they have no other choice than slipping their clients' profiles into such constraining molds, which are narrowing a potential repertoire and fragmenting the elements of a profile, thus reinforcing this typecasting system by playing along with it. The use of such tools and of the associated preformed categories by all involved protagonists (casting/production professionals, talent representatives, and artists) is the practical and systemic way in which typecasting mechanisms occur.

This particular process of getting a job certainly affects the types of profiles that end up being the most represented on screen and retroacts on those that are preferably selected by the agents. It is therefore not absurd to imagine that the underrepresentation of women and minorities in front of the camera, repeatedly deplored by studies dedicated to the question of diversity in Hollywood, has to do with it (Smith et al. 2014, Hunt and Ramón 2015). However, if the collective use of preset systems of categorization embedded with professional routines can have discriminatory effects, this does not signal discriminatory intentions: agents—and probably their counterparts on the production side—can perceive such mechanisms (like a female below-the-line agent who was explaining during our interview how heartbreaking it was for her to observe that her female clients were fewer and had to struggle more, especially in certain areas of specialty), without feeling that they have any real power to redress or transform this situation. The high level of division of labor in this professional world partly disembodies the processes by which typecast identities are created, and certain characteristics (age, gender, or ethnicity) become more advantageous than others.

Some profiles would just be "in demand" and this would be "the law of the market." However, for the agents, the market often takes the face of the "buyers"—in an economic context in which "buyers are above sellers" (as a top talent agent put it)—the buyers being casting directors, producers, or studio executives or heads, depending on an agent's position and situation. The heads of studios and networks remain for the most part at a distance from the casting process, delegating the everyday typecasting work to an army of invisible employees. Casting professionals, on the other hand, feel that they have no other choice than to hire talent according to the expectations of their employers or superiors in a given project (that is, the director, the producer, the studio, the TV network). The modes of categorization they use in their hiring practices are, in their view, constitutive of the mandate they received from their employer; the categorizations are the basis their common understanding of what the film or the show at hand is about—the common language of a project.

Agents are in a position to perceive the limitations that sketchy ready-made categorizations such as those distributed through the job breakdowns involve for their clients, and "pitching" and "selling" artists precisely means using their connection with a casting director or a TV caster to try challenging these preconceived ideas of what a character may look like. Agents evaluate how much room for maneuvering they have depending on the "fuzziness" of a job description, allowing for more or less interpretation of what the right fit in terms of artistic profile might be, as well as depending on the relationships they have previously established with their counterparts on the production side, who will be more or less inclined to "trust the agent's taste" and meet with an actor who is not the most obvious choice a priori. For the female agent quoted below who represents mostly actors at a well-respected but small boutique, this is also what "being creative" in agenting means in Little Hollywood:

Every so often, I'll get into a conversation with a buyer, a casting director, a director, a writer, and I'll be able to convince them why a person's right for the role, when maybe originally they think that they're not. I like to kind of do an outside-the-box idea and say, "You're looking for this, but what about this person, what do you think?" And that's fun when they kind of go for it. And that's when you get to be creative. Especially if it pays off and the client gets the job, you're like: "Wow, I was being creative one day and I got to be." But nine times out of ten, it's, you know: "I need a pretty blonde girl in her twenties. Who do you have?" And I just go through the list and pick. (May 2012)

While working at marginally subverting categorizations and slowly moving the boundaries defining talent, the agents keep operating *within* a categorization system that organizes their everyday activities and exchanges with the production side—a system that they globally contribute to sustaining and reproducing, together with their professional counterparts. It's also in such a collective process—involving artists, talent representatives, production and distribution professionals, journalists and critics—that artistic profiles and "personalities" are constructed, and this goes far beyond the simple management of an artist's public image (which is mostly performed by publicists). By shaping an artist's profile and aligning it with preformed categories and traits, agents contribute to a typecasting process as well as to the *objectification of typecast identities* in tools and measuring devices such as artists' résumés, demo reels and audition videos, quotes, rankings, and other instruments of evaluation and classification (based on tweets, online views, popularity scores, box-office numbers, etc.). The collective making and management of specialized identities on the talent side correlates directly with the categorization and hierarchization of agents.

Parallel Hierarchies and Legitimacy Transfer

The categorization work that agents perform does not only consist of identifying, differentiating, and specializing talent: by doing so, agents inseparably place themselves in hierarchies that are parallel to the ones organizing their clients. Relationship work is also the activity through which clients' professional definition and recognition *reflects back onto* their agents. The homology of the repertoires with which agents and artists are evaluated leads to the shaping of the figure of the gifted agent. In many ways, agents and clients pursue *coupled careers:*[32] an artist's success directly impacts the agent's path and credit, not just on an economic level—of course it does, since the agency receives 10 percent of the client's contract earnings—but symbolically and emotionally speaking as well. The disappointment that agents experience when a client's project fails, the emotion and empathy that they can then manifest—stating, for instance, that "the clients' rejections are your rejections"[33]—also reveal the fact that the agent's reputation and credibility are closely tied to the client's:

I think the most difficult thing in my job is experiencing along with the client the rejection that they sometimes get when they test for a pilot, or they're up for a movie. I had one client that, literally I was told by the director she was getting the female lead in this movie, and it ended up not happening for a set of circumstances, but, you know, for me, I feel her emotion with that. I really do. I always have, always will. That's the most difficult thing for me. [. . .] When you ask what the most difficult thing is, it really is going along the emotional roller coaster sometimes with these clients. (Little Hollywood, April 2011)

I have already suggested that the building of an agent's "style" and reputation implies early forms of specialization: representing certain identifiable categories of clients gives a specific tone to one's agenting and makes up a distinctive positioning that others—be it other talent representatives, production professionals, and, most important, artists who are potential clients—are able to recognize. Such a specialization process is a condition of professional establishment, especially in Big Hollywood. It starts from the beginning of an agent's career and reinforces itself as the representative becomes increasingly known to work with a certain profile of artists. This talent agent at one of the major agencies describes how "like begets like" in the formation of an agent's client, which reflects the particular "business" that this agent has specialized into:

I think that ultimately you want your clients to be reflective of your taste; you want it to be clear what's the kind of client you represent. It's a hundred percent true—everyone's list is reflective of their taste, what they value. You can have some colleagues who represent a bunch of random, maybe talented, maybe not talented people who make a lot of money, and then that agent is really focused on: how do I generate revenue? That agent is really interested in the business side of it, you know. Then you have agents who are really interested in artists. [. . .] I like to pick actors whose work I really admire. Some of them make money, some of them don't, but all of them are *known to be talented*, and that for me came out of loving good acting, so I'm always really interested in good actors. Then there's another group of agents who tend very much to sign very young, beautiful people; smart business, because the young, beautiful people become movie stars, and if you really have an eye for who has the right look and the right quality, sometimes it really is just about look and quality. And I tend to sign older people, always, because you *admire* their body of work. So, how do you make a *business* out of your personal taste, you know? [. . .] I also think the clients you want to sign will look at your other clients and say, "Do I want to be represented by *that* person? Who else do they represent?" So, like begets like. Chances are, if you're pursuing the same kind of people for the right reason, everything matches up. You're pursuing people that will look at your list and say: "I like those clients because they reflect what I love too," which is why you're going after them in the first place. (November 2014, her emphasis)

Such mechanisms of specialization are in fact not only a matter of what the concerned agents like and value across media and genres. Agents specialize in a much narrower way, placing themselves in a hierarchy of media, creative formats, genres and subgenres, and levels of recognition—all of which get partly objectified in the organizational structure of talent agencies, and all of which correspond to particular circles of relevant professional counterparts (talent and buyers). Agents' specialized expertise builds up in the same movement, as they contribute to the recognition (and therefore to the labelling/typecasting) of their clients in a particular area of creative practice. This process is often desired by agents and clients, and it forms a constraining dynamic that the participants cannot usually escape. They become assigned to a (sub) genre and, at the same time, their practices directly participate in the definition of this (sub)genre and its constant reshaping. What the agent quoted below explained to be especially well illustrated by the "comedy business" remains generally true of specialization in other genres and client profiles:

The comedy business is its own business, and so yes, you can kind of be an agent who has a couple of comedians, but more likely than not, if you're interested in comedy, your list will be primarily comedic, because it's very relationship driven, so one comedian knows another, knows another, knows another, they all talk to each other, they all talk about what agents they like, what agents they don't—there's a real fraternity, particularly in the comedy world. So if you end up being an agent who works in that world, it's not really a world you can kind of have one foot in, one foot out. You really sort of have to be in it and have those relationships with those people who are at the center of that business. (Talent agent, big agency, November 2014)

If the division in genres and types of content are sometimes objectified in the organization of the agencies in the form of dedicated groups, the divisions according to medium, format, and type of creative practice always translate into the functional structure of the agencies and in the difference in prestige attached to their specialized departments: motion picture departments remain at the top of this symbolic scale in spite of the fact that films are a lot less lucrative than television products. The aesthetic criteria of evaluation show here their prevalence even in what is often considered the commercial heart of Hollywood: the agencies. Within this hierarchy, "talent" is more valued than "literary," in parallel with the symbolic and economic dominance of star actors[34] over top directors and writers. For the agents, it means that their domains of specialty are not equally valued: working in motion picture talent is still known for bringing more symbolic credit than any other specialization, despite the higher financial rewards and the greatest stability that television or other media procure.[35] What this former television agent described during our interview still stands today as far as the hierarchy of prestige is concerned, as many other agents have confirmed to us:

> There's no question the motion picture business is king. The television business, which brings in many times as much money, is put down here. But that's the attitude. I don't understand it, but okay, I'm not going to be able to change it. [. . .] I wanted to become a member of the Academy. And the two leading members who almost ran the Academy recommended me. And somebody on the committee said, "No, he's only in television." Which I really was, mostly in television. So they wouldn't accept me. (Former WMA agent who arrived in the profession in the mid-1960s, October 2010)

Of course, hierarchies between media are in constant reshaping. In particular, the segment of scripted television programs and the corresponding professional groups have benefited—in terms of symbolic revaluation—from the recent emergence and institutionalization (as specific divisions in the agencies and production entities) of the less valued field of reality television, combined with the decrease of job opportunities in the feature film world. The aesthetic dignity and the professional value attached to specialized sectors are gradually changing. Despite the quality now recognized in certain television networks and shows, the difficulty that agents sometimes still experience when they have to convince a client who is used to working in film to take a job in television illustrates the strength and inertia of symbolic hierarchies, which come not just from their existence in people's minds, but also from their many forms of institutionalization (in the structure of agencies, studios, and networks; the organization and the categories promoted by the Academy of Motion Picture Arts and Sciences; specialized journalistic work and sections, etc.).[36]

Besides the central division and hierarchy between film and television, other classification principles are also operating. The newer areas of practice that are distant from the motion picture business (such as digital media or gaming)—even though they can be financially significant and are not devoid of importance—tend to remain symbolically less valued, especially when they are not oriented toward the representation of artists (sports) or individual talent (corporate consulting). Another division at play in the unequal allocation of professional worth is attached to the opposition between above-the-line and below-the-line personnel in the entertainment industry: it distinguishes those whose artistic qualities and economic value are jointly recognized (above the line) from those whose consecration as talent remains uncertain as long as they are considered in charge of the "technical," less visible, and less lucrative aspects of cinematic production (below the line). Even if the biggest agencies can have dedicated production departments, most of the below-the-line activity is left to Little Hollywood's agents and companies to handle.

In addition, the joint categorization of agents and clients is not always associated with organizational or functional hierarchies. It takes more informal and elusive avenues when agents tend to specialize in representing specific social groups (women or Latino/a clients, for instance), or in categories that have to do with the expression of artistic quality. For instance, by suggesting that he has made a specialty of representing "classy film actors," this established talent representative in his midforties, a former talent agent at one of the biggest agencies turned manager, plays on the parallel repertoires of evaluation tying agents and clients: implicitly, the labels and categories ("classy," "chic," with "cachet") that express professional judgment about his clients translate into what makes the agent's distinctive style, positioning him in an homologous position among his own peers. "There are, within departments, people that develop reputations for being really good at representing women. And then they just expect [these agents] to do that. [. . .] There is a lot of that internal branding. [. . .] I represented what they call actor's actors. People that were very well respected by their peers and everyone wanted to work with. They maybe didn't make the most money, but they were very chic and they had a cachet amongst their peers. That is sort of what I did. Classy actors" (Big Hollywood, March 2013).

We observe here how some of the elements that make up artists' type-cast identities convert into the manner in which agents define themselves professionally and get "branded." The agents can never simply avoid such categorization transfers or fully control them, even though they actively work at specializing themselves and crafting their own "style." These (il)legitimacy transfers are reciprocal only to an extent: being known to be represented by one of the most visible and powerful agency matters even for the most successful artists. But, for the most part, it's the scales of worth used to measure artistic value in Hollywood that become relevant to make an agent's worth. Artistic recognition by one's peers, and especially the Academy and other award-granting institutions, is one such principle of worth: an interviewed below-the-line agent evoked, for instance, the Oscars that his agency (one of the largest companies in Hollywood) and himself "have won" repeatedly, aggrandizing himself by the association with such signs of recognition.[37] Popularity with audiences is another one. The "capital of extended renown" (Roussel 2013) that some actors and directors—but also celebrities of other types—have accumulated, which is often closely associated with economic success, affects informal hierarchies among agents (and sometimes formal ones too, when the concerned agents are subsequently promoted to partner, department head, or even agency manager).

In sum, "in a world where people are obsessed by your client list because that gives you stature, respect, power,"[38] the combined criteria that make up artistic hierarchies directly translate into those ordering agents. They are evaluated depending on (1) the recognition they get from their peers and the critics; (2) the differentiated value of various artistic media, genres, and formats; (3) the popularity of their associated work with a wide audience; (4) the economic resources that someone or something generates.

In practice, these professionals are ranked following hybrid principles of hierarchization, which do not separate the retention of "purely artistic" capital from the possession of economic resources. Playing the professional game means strategizing to try progressing in such composite hierarchies; but agents can also try to subvert established logics of hierarchization, or to combine them differently. I have mentioned above the efforts that some agents develop to obtain the recognition of artistic status for their less valued clients, and to increase consequently the credit, both commercial and aesthetic, attached to their activity. The fact that makeup specialists, technicians, executive producers, and new celebrities of reality television can also be defined as authentic "talent" illustrates such mechanisms.

In the end, the homology of the evaluation scales applying to artists and agents produces parallel hierarchies: "high-end" talent and stars symbolically generate the "super-agents" who, in many ways, have contributed in practical terms to make them. These representatives form a small aristocracy among agents in that they are the ones who have the most control over their own time, being in the unique position to be able to reduce their roster to a few clients whom they service because they represent big-name stars around whom the agency can package projects. In addition, those who stand at this pinnacle are well identified in the business, since, in this occupational world, everybody knows who represents which A-list artists, without for these agents to need to voice it in interactions. Mapping Hollywood in this way is precisely part of the training that future agents initially receive; this is also covered by the Hollywood trade press, allowing even those who are distant from the top of the game to stay current in those matters. Over the map of entertainment celebrities, one could thus superimpose the figures of a few "star agents" who operate in the shadow in a small world, but whose visibility behind the scenes makes *models of professional success*:

We all want to rise to the top and be the star agent of that firm. We all want to be Julia Roberts's agent. We all want to be Denzel Washington's agent or Richard Gere's or Mel Gibson's. [. . .] Every agent is trying to get their A game out, and be a face in the business, you know. They all want to be a Bryan Lourd, a Kevin Huvane, an Ed Limato—God rest his soul—you know.[39] They all want to be at that level, where the A-list stars, the millionaire stars are calling for representation. (Manager, former agent at a boutique agency, October 2010)

However, the level of success that an agent can aim at and potentially reach is delimited in practice by the occupational system within which he or she is operating, which is never "Hollywood" as a whole. I have already mentioned the thick boundary separating Little from Big Hollywood and keeping the players apart on both sides. Rarely do clients meet with big-scale success and cross that boundary; it is even more unlikely that their agent will follow. Once one has established him- or herself either in Little or in Big Hollywood *and* in a specialized area of the business, agenting careers typically stay confined within this space in which the relationships that define the agent have formed and are perpetuating. A Little Hollywood agent whose client suddenly jumps to a much higher professional status and visibility/recognition/salary level is immediately at risk of losing this artist to a bigger agency. The following interviewed talent agent at one of the major companies gave the example of a client she was actively trying to poach from the established midsize agency Gersh. By speaking very openly about it, she not only reveals that building a client list by poaching is the norm in Big Hollywood, but she also, more indirectly, signals the existence of the invisible yet effective boundary separating various professional interrelation circles that place talent representatives in front of their "social equivalent" on the production and talent sides and delineate an agent's reasonable career expectations: "Unless you're CAA or William Morris, when something's successful, it makes you vulnerable. Because people then *want* what you have, like: 'Well, that's shiny, I want that.' And then they're trying to poach in front of you. For sure! Absolutely. I mean, Gersh has a client right now that I'm trying to sign, because she was in a successful movie! They did a great job with her, so *I* want to represent her, you know, so a hundred percent" (November 2014).

If, in that sense, the agent's situation appears to be more precarious than the client's, the agent holds at the same time a more stable position. Because agents depend on organizational and transorganizational *long-term* circles of relationships, they are less vulnerable than artists to the fate of projects and to the effect of their possible failure. Artists (or producers) are often said to be "only as good as their last hit": what makes their worth is indeed directly project related. This converts *partly* into the modes of valuation of an agent because, if the client loses credit, the agent's capital consequently demonetizes. But such (il)legitimacy transfers are always *only partial* because agents' professional value is constituted in more *lasting* interconnection systems. There is therefore more inertia and foreseeability to an agent's situation.

This chapter has established that, in the realm of the symbolic, the client-agent relationship is at the heart of agenting. It's now time to come back to the wider relational system that *practically* makes the power of the agent and through which the manufacture of talent and projects happens: such relational systems are what I call *evaluation communities*, and they are the real core of the Hollywood game.

SIX

Naming Quality and Pricing Talent

The relationships that agents develop are situated in *(e)valuation communities*[1] that pertain to either Big Hollywood or Little Hollywood. Evaluation communities are interactive and interdependence systems that bring together different categories of Hollywood professionals who are collectively engaged in defining the worth—both the quality (evaluation) and the economic value (valuation) of projects and people. Agents' counterparts in evaluation communities are the other talent representatives, the artists, and the various types of production professionals whom they deal with on a regular basis, for the most part. Evaluation communities are thus relatively narrow, self-referential circles of people, and they materialize long-lasting acquaintanceship across organizational boundaries. They are interrelation and transaction circles where "everybody knows everybody"[2] and where professionals who specialize in the same area of the business become and stay interconnected. Evaluation communities are the systems of mutual reliance in which "collegial currency" forms and ties together agents and production professionals, which I referred to earlier when I focused on how agents build "trust" with these counterparts. This chapter looks at what agents do in evaluation communities at large, what comes out of this, and how.

Agents in Hollywood's Evaluation Communities

Before further analyzing how action in evaluation communities shapes the making of projects and leads to defining the value of people in Hollywood, I would like to sum up the elements of the approach that I have outlined throughout the previous chapters in order to clarify what we know, at this point, of agents in evaluation communities.

Evaluation communities exist at different levels of the hierarchy of Little and Big Hollywood. They may gather top talent representatives and artists, studio heads and top executives, and successful producers and financiers, who are all in a position to make a film or television project happen in Big Hollywood; or they may refer to different circles of interconnection tying Little Hollywood agents, their clients, and their counterparts in the casting community. It appears that, even if artists are fully part of evaluation communities,[3] the approach in such terms guards us from the illusion of all-powerful star actors or directors when it comes to understanding how entertainment and artistic products come to existence. As far as putting clients into jobs and casting are concerned, for agents at all levels, the primary mechanism of exchanges and transactions in evaluation communities derives from the ties they have consistently been building with production counterparts:

You call the casting director, the producer, the studio executive if it's set up at a studio, and the director: "What do you think about Joe Schmo for this? Here's what he's been doing, it was kind of the same script. How familiar are you with him or her? Have you been watching X, Y, or Z? Can I send you material? Would you take a look at it?" Then if you're still sort of not getting what you want: "Then can you at least get him or her in the room with your director? If you could [meet with him or her], that would be incredibly helpful." And then, your effectiveness at doing that is [based on], one: how good the client is for the job, and just in general; and two: what's your *relationship* with the person you're talking to? The relationship ends up being *everything*, because if they know *you* and they like *you*, they're more inclined to do a favor for you. They're more inclined to be more receptive to you, which already opens the door wider, but then they're also more inclined to be more helpful to you if you're asking them something; they might be more willing to do it. (Talent agent, big agency, November 2014, her emphasis)

The accumulation of such *capital of relationships* through activity in evaluation communities constitutes a means (to get a client "in the room" with a director or a casting director, engage a studio executive into a project, etc.), but is also its own end: specific interactions regarding particular projects in which agents participate are at the same time oriented toward the maintenance of the long-term relationships that make them possible. These interactions contribute to making and maintaining the relational system of an evaluation community, and the particular outcomes that are produced occasionally in this process—a job contract, or even a film, an episode of a TV show, or the like—are, to a certain extent, only secondary to it.

In each of these evaluation communities, the participants acquire and develop a "sense of the game" enabling them to identify the counterparts who have "good taste" and can be "trusted"; that is, those whose professional history and past successes have proven their ability to "guess right," whose judgments have passed the test and received validation (be it through commercial and/or artistic success). In the words of this interviewee, identification of valuable artistic projects derives from what he understands of the perceptions of his counterparts on the production side:

[You] see who the producers are. If it's Ron Howard, it's probably not going to suck. So I'll look at the players first, Who is attached? And then I'll also know the taste of a lot of the casting directors. If Mary Vernieu is doing a project over at Betty Mae,[4] or Mary Jo Slater's doing a project, these aren't casting directors that attach themselves to crap. Yes, they're all out there looking for a paycheck, but I know their taste, and I'll ask the casting director next: "What do you think of this project? Do you like this script?" And I could hear the enthusiasm. (Former talent agent, Little Hollywood, October 2010)

Conversely, I have shown that an agent's competence and legitimacy are *constituted* by the "trust" granted by production counterparts and artists in evaluation communities. Success and professional authority emerge from mutual adherence and attachment to interpersonal relations. This is the reason agents define their professional sphere as a "perception game"[5] in which "you're only as good as the perception that people have of you."[6] This does not mean that it does not matter what agents concretely do and practically have to trade in the context of specific transactions around projects, of course; but it does mean that an agent's professional worth ("importance," "influence," "leverage," "credibility") stems from the dynamics of recurrent exchanges that go beyond any particular client or project.

It's in these circles that artistic existence and greatness are collectively granted or borne out. One can empirically follow the ways in which the protagonists define such boundaries of recognition (Lamont and Thévenot 2000) by relying on their perception of what professionally consecrated partners believe, or on what they foresee of their strategies.

Agents' recognition within the system of an evaluation community enables them to say, in a consequential and effective manner, who and what is "real" (in the word used by these professionals themselves)—that is, who and what is creatively worthy of becoming an element of a project and the object of an economic transaction.[7] This eventually leads to making people and projects "real" when it is translated into commercial and artistic value, through transactions that are later formalized in legal ways. What is here in play is the *realization* of agents' capital of relationships. In other words, the social capital that forms and is maintained in organizations and in evaluation communities is the *primary currency* that gets converted into economic and symbolic forms of capital in the course of the activities that participants conduct together.

All three species of capital—social capital (the power to activate relationships), economic capital (the power attached to commercial success), and symbolic capital (the direct or indirect association with art and talent)—combine to make up the specific type of professional capital proper to this social sphere, which, in other words, allows for existence, action, and success in the agency business. When one's contribution to the production of economic and symbolic value becomes visible in the circles in which one usually operates in Hollywood—for instance, when an agent is known to have negotiated an particularly lucrative deal and/or to handle a critically acclaimed artist—this reinforces, in turn, the strength of this person's specialized social capital both in its embodied forms (that is, the "influence" and "trustworthiness" of the concerned individual agent) and in its institutionalized forms (that is, the power of the corresponding agency to accredit).

Together, and combined in the agents' experience, organizational games and evaluation communities form the *professional configurations* in which projects and careers are made in Hollywood (see figure 4). Agents are therefore simultaneously dealing with institutional structures and strong crosscutting ties that transcend organizational settings. In these crosscutting circles, the practices of various professionals driven by different specialized logics of action converge without ever destroying the boundaries separating them. Clients, producers, studio executives, managers, lawyers: "Everyone has their own agenda," as an interviewed agent pointed out. The rest of this chapter is dedicated to understanding *how* projects practically emerge from the context of such evaluation communities, and *how* the structure of professional configurations in general determines what gets made and who gets consecrated in Hollywood.

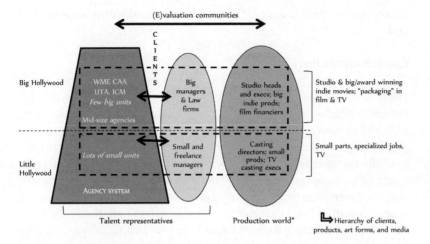

*Distribution and publicity entities are not represented here. Generally speaking, their work is more removed from the agents', taking place at a later stage of the process.

4   Agents in a dual system of cultural production

"What It Takes to Get a Movie Made"

I think it would be easier to find what it takes to get a movie made, as opposed to what it takes to get a successful movie made. [. . . The difficulty of getting a movie made] comes out of the collaborative aspect and the corporate aspect, and it's just amazing that, kind of like grass growing through concrete sidewalks, there are these miraculous things that happen.
—LITERARY AGENT, MIDSIZE AGENCY, JULY 2014

Industry professionals talk about the unlikelihood of movies being made, let alone the question of knowing if such projects will later meet with box-office success. The complex tensions structuring evaluation communities are what can reasonably make participants cautious as regards the fate of each individual project that they decide to champion or hope to put their clients in. However, as I will now demonstrate, the interrelations that compose Hollywood's evaluation communities are precisely what give shape to the making of movies. Examining how evaluation communities work at the granular level of day-to-day activities and exchanges allows us to grasp how entertainment products and careers happen in Hollywood. Even though this book looks at it from the particular perspective of what agents do, this is a paradigmatic case study for understanding how art emerges from complex interdependence systems (forming a "cultural industry"), as well as the embeddedness of economic and creative activities.

Chain Anticipations

When it comes to understanding how a film goes into production, the common pitfall—other than the illusion of the all-powerful star whose idea and charisma make it all happen as if by magic—is to imagine the just-as-magical moment when an identified authority (a studio person, a producer) "green-lights" a project: in this version of the fantasy, the figure of producer becomes the solitary hero who seals a project's fate, and the green-lighting process is approached as a well-defined turning point. In reality, things are not so clear-cut. First of all, the pivotal moment for the success of a project does not always coincide with a formal "green light" given by the studio or the production team. The case study of *The Silence of the Lambs*, discussed in the prologue of this book, shows a different type of turning point—that is, a moment in time when the movie project is perceived as "real" by the central players in such a way that they decide to fully and officially commit, reinforcing in so doing its chances to be brought to completion.

In addition, there is not one single sequence of steps or set of formulas following which a movie gets green-lighted. Each studio or production entity develops its own arrangements, which are more or less institutionalized and formalized with green-light committees. With international and other coproductions, green-light moments and involved entities multiply. Most important, the process by which things are set up to come to life in Hollywood is not as simple as the image of the green-light moment suggests, in light of the diverse categories of participants who get involved in this collective endeavor.[8] Understanding how a film comes to life thus implies to recreate a complex chain of interdependent perceptions and actions.

> To better understand it, let's take a fictional example: the case of a book that ends up in the hands of a producer, whom we will call P, sent by the author's agent or manager.[9] P loves the book and is ready to try making it into a movie. At this stage, nothing is more uncertain. P and the author's agent shop the book around at studios. P's company has a preferential ("first-look") deal with a studio to which they have to present the book first; if this initial choice aborts, they will try to convince other studio executives, with whom they also have cultivated a relationship, that the book would make a great movie.

Say the initial partner studio is interested and decides to buy the rights to the book. S is the studio executive who will take the lead on this project but who also needs to report to levels above within the structure of the studio when decisions have to be made. Thus each decision that the studio takes involves in fact a multilevel negotiation process within this institutional structure. S is now on board with P in the adventure of making the movie come to life. Buying the rights to the book has involved the participation of the agent, possibly the manager, and the lawyer who represent the author of the book, of course. They and their organization are now also engaged in the filmmaking dynamics.

P needs to hire a writer to adapt the book and does so—this again bringing in whoever represents this writer. The writing process takes time; the writer eventually turns in a first draft; P and S evaluate it, reject it, and ask the writer to revise it, and eventually they accept a second draft (but the process could just as well have ended here, had the studio decided after reading the second draft that "this is not a movie after all," or had another project considered too similar been initiated in the meantime, or had a similar project just failed at the box office, or had the people in charge changed or changed priority, etc.). In the same movement, what also gets assessed is the *type of film* that this might become: the budget range, the type of director and other talent that will be attached, the kind of marketing and distribution strategies deriving from what the film's audiences are imagined to be, and so on. At this point, the participants in the process might start imagining, "This is a movie; it might be done for this much money, and with these types of people." A preliminary image of the film, fragmentary and kaleidoscopic, gets outlined.

Now that they have an accepted script, P and S—the buyers—need to hire a "critical talent element" to give some reality to the "project." This can be a star actor or a name director (at various levels of fame and recognition, depending on the type and scope of the project), or a combination of both. Let's imagine that P and S agree on a director, D, who is contacted through his representative, typically his agent. In the simplest scenario, D and his agent (possibly his manager too, and his lawyer, who formalizes the deal at this point or later on) enter the fray. D is hired; otherwise the "name-dropping game" continues until a director who adheres to the project comes out of it. At this stage, if not earlier, D's agent, A, might be in a position to package him with other clients in the movie and sell this turnkey solution altogether to the studio. Thanks to a *relationship* with P and/or S, A may have been aware of the existence of the project ahead of time, and therefore able to work within the agency and with clients on the definition of this package.

The "project" still needs to be in quotes at this point because its *content and substance*—what the project is—are still to be defined. For instance, D is on board but does not quite relate to the script as it has been written and wants to have it revised according to his own "vision" and "aesthetics." A new writer is hired (again, talent representatives join the dance). The process backtracks for a few months as D and the new writer work on another version of the film, with creative inputs from their talent representatives and the production team. What comes out of it—that is, the new script—still needs to be "a movie" in P and S's eyes, and one that they'd be willing to make. Otherwise, this point would be another dead-end.

Then, if this was not part of the film package, the protagonists already in the game still need to find one or two name actors/actresses for the movie. Five or six "good choices" might come out of this new name-dropping game. A star actress accepts, and her agent jumps into the mix, negotiating with the production team that the movie be postponed for a few years so that she can honor other engagements or priorities, adding yet another layer of complexity to this intricate game. The key elements are gathered for a movie to now become "real" in the eyes of all participants, whether it gets officially green-lighted and legally formalized at this stage, or whether the protagonists keep operating in the fuzzier context of oral agreements and implicit understandings.[10]

If all participants stay committed throughout this long process, what matters is *the alignment* of the heterogeneous "visions" of the production professionals, the different categories of talent, their agents and other representatives—all of whom belong to diverse organizations and express distinct agendas and interests, priorities and preferences, calendars, and sets of constraints. Yet they are tied into an interdependence dynamic that *never leads to unifying the various principles behind their action* but relies on their convergence at a moment in time, in the context of a given project. The *convergence of visions* built through their negotiation in interactions, and *not* their identical nature, is what is required.

In our example, now a project exists. Casting can start. An interviewed literary agent once told us, "Until the first day of shooting, nothing is real."[11] However, at this stage, the participants know that a movie will probably be physically produced, and later be offered to audiences. This unlikely adjustment of perceptions and projections is what industry insiders sometimes call "the magic."[12] But this alignment does not just "happen," firstly in the sense that it consists of collective *work*. Secondly, it does not happen *once and for all* in the room where a project gets pitched to a studio. It stems from a *complex interdependence process* that often goes on for years and seems at risk of falling apart at every step. Even if the efforts, time, and money invested in the endeavor can become an incentive for the participants to bring it to fruition in spite of the obstacles they face, many projects and the associated financial investment are abandoned, or sometimes interrupted for years before coming back to life in a different form and in different hands.

Keeping this story in mind, let's now come back to what happens and is at stake for agents every step of the way. At the beginning of this process, it's first within the organizational framework of the agency that an agent has to position him- or herself and find allies. In the case of a studio movie and Big Hollywood agents, the focus is placed on packaging clients around projects, and the structure of the agency (its formal divisions, smaller groups, teams around clients, regular meetings) partly dictates the tempo and operating procedures. This illustrates how organizational logics intersect and interact with that of the evaluation community. The agency is therefore never only a static setting in the background of agenting activities; it directly forges some of the conditions of action in evaluation communities.

[Say you have a script you like.] You'd bring it up on Monday—"I read that during the weekend, I think it's great, here's what I want to do with it"—and you can follow up Tuesday, Wednesday, the following week, about what you're doing with it, and you hope that a fish hooks. The real objective here is just to package something. You want to put as many elements attached before you sell it to the marketplace. So you want to represent the director, the producer, and the star ideally. And then sell it competitively to a studio, to a buyer. That's why you have these meetings, to *package* things, to put them together. And you also want to present what the studio has that's not our material. Say, I can also come in on Monday and say, "I've read a new script that's at Fox, so-and-so wrote it and I think it's right for these clients." (Literary agent, big agency, December 2013)

Packaging is thus about enticing others and engaging them in the process, in the service of the goal an agent pursues for a client and ultimately for him- or herself, especially when this agent does not represent "marquee names" and depends all the more on the support and resources of the agency. Indeed, most agents, even in Big Hollywood, do not handle a major star and are in a position to experience not only the highly collective nature of the endeavor, but also their situation of dependency: they may need to package their midlevel actor with other artists (a bigger co-star, a writer/director in demand, a few somewhat renowned actors in supporting parts)—*that is, to mobilize other talent and literary agents* internally, and possibly at other agencies if they endeavor to create a joint package; or, in other situations, they may need to put together the elements of an "indie movie," in which case getting the agency's specialists in international financing and packaging to cooperate also becomes crucial.

In both examples, what is at stake is "the value" of a package as the agent *anticipates it to appear* to production counterparts. The transactional nature of this mechanism is explicit in the story that the talent agent quoted below reported: the expected trade-off is that the studio buys a script that they don't want so that they also get to work with the A-list comedy actress whose name has been associated with it (or even simply so as to build a relationship with her on this occasion). The package serves the best interest of the agency as a whole, but not always as clearly that of all the clients and agents individually enrolled in it. The collaborative dimension of packaging should not overshadow the existence of potential conflicting strategies within it, as well as the hierarchization of agents (and of clients) that the package reveals and reenacts.

We have a client who I work with who's a writer and an actor—she's written a movie for Sony and Good Universe. They [Sony] have read it and their inclination is *not* to make it, and we are trying to get an actress of ours who we know Sony really wants to work with to read the script and commit to the project so we can go to Sony and say, "We know you're on the fence about this script, but [this star actress] wants to do it, and I know you want to be in business with her, so would you then make it if she says she wants to do it?" Ideally Sony says, "Oh, well, [*she*] wants to do it, then that changes it and yes, let's put it into development." And then that helps our writer client who was about to get it shelved. (Talent agent, big agency, November 2014, her emphasis)

Agenting in this context means strategizing about others' strategies, anticipating others' anticipations. It means asking such questions as: How does this other agent perceive his or her clients' needs, his or her interest with the studio, his or her best career strategy in the agency? How does this studio executive or producer see his or her own interest in making this movie or not, and in relation to what and whom does he or she form these expectations? What are this client's hopes and stakes in this project, or how should they be shaped and oriented through agenting? And consequently, what are the probable outcomes of various scenarios in which these different positions, perceptions, and inclinations to act in one way or another combine, and what are the levers by which they can be influenced? Agenting is therefore a highly reflexive (including self-reflexive) activity. It is about deciphering the visions and projections of representation, production, and talent counterparts so as to navigate this complex game in the best way—it being sometimes to protect specific relationships, sometimes to conclude a lucrative deal, sometimes to build new connections, sometimes to get involved in innovative projects, or any combination of this non-exhaustive list. This senior agent described how it played out within a team of agents employed by the same major agency who had been jointly assigned the management of a big client's relationship with a studio. Even though the internal workings of the agency are here the focus, the same dynamics of strategic interdependence and interaction also apply to the agent's relationships with all the other participants (studio employees, producers, managers, lawyers, artists) involved with the project and the specific problem at hand:

[Listen to a conference call] where you have three or four agents working as a team to solve the problem with this client or with the studio. And what you'll hear if you're careful—either by silence or the words, or tone—is each agent's specific neurosis and agenda. Even though it's all connected to this one mission of the call, and one client, and one goal, they all have a different *stake* in it. This one might be thinking of another piece of business with another client at the same studio, this one may be thinking about the fact that he needs this client to make this money for his bottom line, this one may be thinking: "I'm not really involved in this, I don't know why I'm on this phone call at all," this one may be thinking: "I *only care* about the studio relationship, and I'm kind of on *their* side," and it's interesting to see that and hear that. So you have to understand when you do see that and hear that, what must be going on inside the individual offices when the agents are in there alone, working as a team on behalf of a client list—some of which are theirs, some of which are not theirs, some of which they share—and how they position it based on their own take of the situation *for them*, their perspective. (Talent agent, big agency, December 2013, his emphasis)

In this way, in the context of the inception of a project, agents know that the participants in the filmmaking adventure do not share similar agendas, nor do they have a common vision of what the concerned project is or should be. It is the *systemic complexity* of the enterprise, made of the combined calculations and strategies of diverse types of participants positioned at different intertwined levels—in other words, it is the *interdependent and relational nature* of these professional configurations—that results in the uncertainty of a project or in the instability of the arrangements made around it, that many observers have noted but often referred to the opacity and the lack of information regarding the quality, competence, reputation, or trustworthiness of the participants that are supposed to characterize cultural/art markets. This is why agenting requires being able to "dance on a shifting carpet," in the words of an experienced literary agent.[13] The motion picture world appears to this other established literary agent as oscillating between multiple "power centers" whose importance or weight vary, depending on the project: "It could be the studio, it could be the producer, it could be an outside financier, it could be the insurance company, a big brand-name insurance. It could be the writer. It could be the star. And it could be a combination" (Big Hollywood, July 2014). These cooperation systems are even more multipolar and potentially evanescent when it comes to independent or international film projects and to the contrasted and disjointed visions, tempos, interests, stakes, routines, institutional contexts, and sets of labor rules proper to all the artists, as well as to production, distribution, representation, and financing professionals in the various countries involved.

In such a complex configuration, "dancing on a shifting carpet" refers not only to the diverse participants whose goals and interests are sometimes contradictory but also to the frequent and often unpredictable pulling out of some of these key partners, sometimes causing a project that took years to put together to fall apart. This talent agent at one of the major agencies mentally reviewed the "things that can go wrong" with a film project, to which should be added the defections that come from the agency's talent side, when a star or pivotal talent element in a project withdraws:

The director falls out of a movie, a co-star falls out of a movie, [. . .] or financing falls out, the movie gets unfinanced, the financiers pull out, or the studio decides—as Sony just did with [the film] *Steve Jobs*—that they don't want to make the movie, so when you put your client in the movie . . . and in that case [of *Steve Jobs*], I think it's going to end up at Universal, so it'll still be okay. But sometimes they just don't happen. I mean, that happened to a producer who I was talking to yesterday. He had a movie at Disney that was going and was casting, and all of a sudden, for reasons unknown, they decided not to make it. Or, studio heads will change, network heads will change, and so things that were hot to the person then in charge—that person is replaced with somebody else and they want to start their own thing. So, those are things that can go wrong: personnel changes at the studio, and a movie that was on a fast track suddenly slows down. (Talent agent, big agency, November 2014)

Part of agents' work has to do with managing these potentially unforeseen circumstances of the cinematic process that impact them, and their organization as directly as it affects their clients. "Solutions" can consist of making the other parties commit more substantially and materially to the project so that they'd have more to lose if they abandon the project: constraining deals signed by studios, "pay-or-play" agreements (following which an actor will get paid the agreed amount whether the film gets made or not), publicity given to a project so that withdrawing from it might become embarrassing, and so on. Because agenting is fundamentally not a project-based activity, if such protective techniques are put into place and the client's job and earnings are guaranteed in that sense, it might not be crucial in the eyes of the agent that the film eventually gets made. Retaining partners in the circle of a project is also achieved through relationship work and the maintenance of personal loyalty ties. In addition, developing several backup plans at the same time and playing on numbers to counter the hazardous nature of each project is a common strategy. But multiplying projects is also counterproductive *at a collective level*, as it generates potential causes for defection on the part of studios or artists who have committed to more than they can eventually really pursue. During the prosperous time of the 1990s in particular, producers and studios systematically acquired intellectual property rights (concepts, specs, scripts, or books), sometimes as a precautionary measure against competitors (to avoid the risk of leaving the next big hit to someone else), and mostly in the spirit of accumulating a stock of material to choose from, partly developing some of it, and following through to the point of completion with only a small proportion of the potential projects.[14] Even today, although the economic changes have led to a decrease in the number of projects developed and completed, this model is still partly in place.

Telling a Relatable Story

The carpet is also shifting—to extend the metaphor—because of the indetermination that continues to characterize the creative content or the *meaning* of a project over a long period of time. This is an important and consubstantial dimension of the creative process in Hollywood: even though cooperation circles have formed and investments of different sorts have been made by the protagonists, it is often difficult to imagine, until relatively late in the process, what a movie, show, or any other type of product will exactly look and sound like. This is especially true when a project develops from a pitch, as this television literary agent observed:

[Judging] from the script, it's at least somewhat easier; from the pitch, it's really hard [to imagine what a project will become]. [. . .] Clients always come and we have the debate of: "Is this something to pitch or is this something to spec?" And I still side with pitching, because I think the network wants to have their fingerprints on something and feel their involvement. Unless it's the sort of thing where you could never convey that tone or what it really is in the pitch. [. . .] But yes, it's hard to [convey a vision]. A lot of times it happens, and it's where the creative process breaks down, if development originates from that pitch where I can pitch something to you, to me it is clear as day because I've lived with it and I'm pitching it to you. But as I'm pitching it to you—and you ultimately are going to buy it—but you have a completely different vision in your head of what it is. So you then get into the actual development process and you start butting heads. Not because anyone was at fault; it's just that you believe it should be this, this person believes it should be that, and not until you're really in it do you realize: "Wait, we don't see this the same way!" (Television literary agent, big agency, November 2014)

Consequently, on top of the misalignment of stakes and agendas of the multiple participants, and on top of the possible desynchronizing of the process (a star gets another offer, the director defects, a financier falls out), comes a dynamic of fragmentation that concerns the very definition of the project: part of it simply and inevitably derives from the complexity of this interdependence game, but keeping the contours of the project somewhat fuzzy may also be a strategic way of extending the circle of potentially interested counterparts who can imagine a version of it that they can easily relate to. When agents do their job, when they sell and service, and especially when they pitch a project (or a client for a project), they create and circulate *narratives* of this project and the associated artists. They do not just deliver their vision of a movie (or pass on their client's), for instance, but they work at creating a common ground for coordination mechanisms on the basis of what they perceive of others' expectations. The use of specialized sales techniques takes the form of *storytelling*, not only as far as the story line of the movie is concerned, but also as regards the staging of the filmmaking process and its protagonists themselves. Pitching, or selling in general, is putting on a performance, which is *a show about the show*. A successful talent agent described, for instance, how he used to sell a rising comedy actor he was representing by painting to his studio counterpart on the phone, in a detailed and dramatized way, the image of the actor's messy place, his posture when he writes, the crayons he uses, his bohemian lifestyle—as many ways of representing the uniqueness, the charisma, the creative strength of the artist, all qualities by which the buyers recognize what they look for in a talent.[15] Of course, I do not mean to suggest that this actor's past credits, other practical elements of his relevance for the project, or the agent's pre-established relationship with the studio did not matter for the concerned studio person. But I insist on the fact that feeling the passion of the other side is really decisive. Assessing the enthusiasm of one's counterparts is an integral part of the process of evaluation "quality."[16] Therefore, for the agents, arousing such emotions and beliefs, in line with what production counterparts are likely to recognize as creatively and commercial promising, is a carefully crafted effort. Another illustration of how agents frame a potential hit when selling a film project or a piece of material can be found in the example of a script in which the agency physically incorporated newspaper clippings from the time period during which the story was set, in order to give it a feeling of historical accuracy and newsworthiness, and make it stand out from the mass of competing projects. This does not contradict the fact that the project also had to be immediately classifiable with reference to preexisting categories of movies and with past box-office successes, and was constructed as original and salable in both ways.

If agents are actively engaged in the collective definition of a project, if they contribute to shaping and inflecting the "visions" of key participants, the manner in which they operate is not random or a question of purely personal style or ability. There are marked paths and predefined ways of doing it. It is in fact so codified and standardized that an interviewed literary agent could refer to his pitching methods with self-derision: "It's like a joke at this point—it's like, 'where *American Beauty* meets *X*.' Because you're giving [the buyers] that relatability, or 'this is what it is.'"[17] To describe how he would go about selling a piece of material, a junior literary agent at one of the major companies explained:

Nowadays especially, you have to be able to point to something in the past, you have to point to: "It's in the vein of . . ." When you hear the greatest agents, when they present a piece of material to the room [that is, in this case, during the agency meeting] for the first time, they often compare it to another piece. So they'll say, "This is a great science fiction film, we can do it for a price, it doesn't have to be expensive, it's in the vein of *Chronicle* or *District 9*." And immediately people know, a buyer or another agent—you have to first sell to your colleagues before you can sell to an executive or a producer— they'll immediately know: "Okay, this is a great sci-fi, but it can be done for a certain price so it doesn't have to be expensive." So I think the comparison is important, but again it's very important to *also* make it feel fresh and new. So it's not tired. You can't be like: "It's like *Inception*," but if it's a rip-off of *Inception* you can't sell it. A good example is a script called *Reminiscence*, it just sold—it was actually a UTA writer, it was not even a client of ours—but it was very much in the vein of *Blade Runner*, and it was how it was being pitched: "It's in the vein of *Blade Runner*, but it's a very new idea and it feels fresh." That's a great way to sell it. [. . .] So it felt immediately like, "okay, so we know what it is, we know what the poster looks like, we know what the trailer looks like, we know what the one sheet is, we know the marketing already," so it feels safe for the studio to buy the script, which feels fresh enough but people think an audience will want to go see it. (Motion picture literary agent, big agency, December 2013)

What this agent evoked are ways of talking about projects that are not only specialized but standardized. Projects are partly patterned after well-known movies (associated with a certain type of success, not exclusively commercial) that have thus become *prototypes* and entered a *reference system* to which new endeavors get referred, and by association with which they take meaning. New projects are often composite images built in the way of a Frankenstein creature from recognizable pieces of this reference system. This manner of making a project imaginable and *cinematic*—by suggesting what it will look like, what it will sound like, how it will fall within a certain film tradition, what it will imply in terms of technical or acting prowess, and so on—is achieved through rationalizing techniques that dismiss the notion of radical singularity of an artwork. At the same time, this never overwrites the need to demonstrate the novelty and the uniqueness of a project, in what remains a *distinction game*. This is why projects and people always need to "feel fresh," as our interviewee put it. The relative originality of a categorizable project, performance, or piece of material is a matter of commercial value *and* of quality.

Let's now examine the reference system according to which projects are labeled. Through repeated exchanges in evaluation communities, *central categories* have formed, and the perception and description of what a film is like are organized around them: for example, one might evoke "a duo-based family comedy," or "this subcategory of romantic Christmas movie, in the vein of what this or that star does"; that is, a subtype within a genre organized around a series of different movies and stars thought to be paradigmatic of it. Certain movie references have become *focal points*, in Schelling's (1960) terms. In other words, they serve as tools for tacit coordination on the basis of past shared experiences and common cognitive repertoires that make these references seem obvious or naturally relevant to the members of evaluation communities. For instance, we all know what a "James Bond movie" is; or we can recognize what the "*Gravity* type of spaceship-adventure movie with an aesthetic and technical quality" refers to. There are, to keep it simple, three levels of reference with which to categorize: the general level of genres and subgenres (a horror movie, or that subtype of horror movie), that of paradigmatic titles (that is, a generic type of movie or film series—a James Bond movie), and that of legendary or outstanding one-time success. Especially in the latter category of the "great movie" that everyone knows and that has become a classic, for it not to be a recent box-office hit is not an obstacle to its relevance as a classificatory tool.[18] Referencing a project in that way defines at once its artistic profile, its budget range, and the categories of people that might be attached to it (artists and other members of evaluation communities). Mechanisms of mutual reference tie together the process of talent categorization, analyzed in chapter 5, and that governing the definition of projects. In other words, the cues and categories with which people are evaluated and labeled (manifested in the words used to describe them and in the "typecast identities" or prototypical profiles that their combination forms) and the categories used to label types of projects respond to each other and mutually consolidate: people's categorization indicates who can be a good match or a driving force in a film or a show. These categorization processes are both segmenting (constituting and reinforcing specialized crowds) and hierarchizing mechanisms. At this stage, the hierarchy mostly reflects the expectations attached to the evaluation of the quality of a future movie (its reception in the industry) and its salability to audiences: Is it an Oscar movie? Is it potentially a big box-office hit?

However, selling to audiences and seducing the critics and one's peers is not so much a direct concern for agents as it is an indirect one, because their production/distribution counterparts worry about it. Instead, what is directly at stake for the agents is to engage *their own counterparts in evaluation communities*—whom we know to be artists, production professionals, and possibly other talent representatives—and build common ground for that purpose. This means making something that is intrinsically uncertain "feel real" and safe enough to allow for major financial investments. It implies that a project or a performance is made imaginable, *representable* to others—who can now conceive what it is. In that, literally, agents *represent* not only the people but also the projects they handle, in the sense of giving the projects a relatable image. Agents are of course not alone in doing this. But their activity remains oriented in this direction, including after a studio has manifested interest in a project. For instance, during a session of observation alongside a senior talent agent in Big Hollywood, I witnessed one of his phone interactions with a studio head regarding a film starring an A-list actor represented by the agent, a film that the studio had already committed to making. The conversation started with the agent asking his counterpart how he was seeing the project and how he would describe it to him at this particular point of development. By asking his counterpart to expose his perspective, to tell *his* story of the movie, the agent was both forming his own approach and subtly remodeling, in the course of this verbal exchange, his counterpart's point of view. The construction of common "visions" emerges from such mutual and continual repositioning and reshaping. Comparably, the literary agent quoted below stressed the importance of the *translation work* at the heart of his agenting practice, being the one who converts the vision of the production side into the language of the artist, and vice versa:

You play the middleman and you play the communicator between both sides [talent and production]. Because what happens is, a lot of the networks or studios never want to be the bad guy—and especially if it's [regarding] a writer they care about, who is a hot, well-respected writer. So what can sometimes happen is the studio gives notes, or the network gives notes, but they don't hit some of the notes as hard as they should, or they dance around something, or they're not fully clear about something, because they don't want to be overly critical, and the writer will address the notes given and then the studio isn't happy because they thought [the writer] didn't address all their notes, but you didn't *give* all of the notes! [. . .] And, by the way, at the same point the writer might feel it's [already] in there. [. . .] But what it should make you do is go back and look at what you have and realize: "Okay, is this coming across the right way? Is there something I can do to what I have to tweak it or to . . . ?" So, a lot of the times, it is that bridge between [the writer and the network executive], it is brokering that. (Television literary agent, big agency, November 2014, his emphasis)

These words bring out the *brokerage of perceptions* that agents do. This is of course self-interested brokerage, since the operations of translation and assemblage of participants' "visions" that agents perform are not devoid of stakes for the agents themselves. When these "visions" and anticipations appear to converge enough for chain commitments to follow (the name director is in, therefore the studio is in, and therefore the star actor is in . . .), what participants call the "magic" happens: the combination of expectations starts to gel, the disjoined perspectives that formed it appear to come together, and the project is known to exist "as a whole." Certain narratives of the project also become prevalent. However, participants' "visions" never get fully unified, the plurality of stakes remains, and there is always space for play and possibly for tension in the definition of what is being made.

What takes place through the evaluation of people and projects in evaluation communities is a process of *collective transformation of frames of meaning*; it evokes the confrontation of various "fabrications," in

Goffman's sense.[19] In the circle that forms around a film or television project, each player frames reality in a particular way and works at inducing others into sharing this definition of the situation and acting accordingly.[20] In this context, *framing disputes* can arise, and agents also act as experts in the avoidance of such conflicts or in *relationship repair*. For participants in evaluation communities (talent representatives and their production counterparts alike), keeping their interrelation going is a priority, and so is for agents the preservation of strong and harmonious relationships with their clients—all of which tend to take precedence in agenting over the shape and fate of any particular project and to govern what the right moves are perceived to be. This stands true when the commercial dimension of relationships comes into play, as I will now explain.

Pricing the Unique

"There Are No Rules on the Money"

Making deals and pricing appear at first sight to be a rational and technically equipped type of practice, reflecting the laws of the market and based on facts, data, and numbers. Indeed, a lot of numbers circulate in Hollywood. Measuring instruments of various types exist, seemingly paving the way for the definition of economic value (of an artist, a piece of material, a project).

First of all, artists have "quotes." The quote refers to the amount that someone got paid for his or her last job in a category of project comparable to the one presently being negotiated.[21] In theory, an artist's quote tells a buyer how much it will cost to get this person to work on a project. As soon as a movie is out, "tracking numbers" are produced to closely monitor its theatrical box-office earnings; "tracking boards" provide industry insiders with all sorts of information regarding ongoing projects and finished products;[22] social media feedback on artists, products, and projects (in the form of tweets, online views and comments, followers, etc.) is also scrutinized, not only to learn about what is already out, but increasingly to anticipate future trends and probable successes. The question of knowing how the attention that a talent receives online—objectified in the number of "followers" this artist can claim, for instance—really translates into box-office revenue or in the success of a television show is not only of interest to studios and production professionals, or to film financiers: agencies are also involved in using and even in creating measuring tools with which to objectify elusive social media "sentiments" by putting a figure on them. The stakes for the agencies are first to factor how their clients are discussed online into the management of artists' public images, as well as to use "online popularity" as an argument in the negotiation of a deal.

It sometimes goes further than that: in 2014, United Talent Agency, one of the major organizations in the agency business, partnered with the established movie monitoring company Rentrak to conceive and launch PreAct, a device designed to allow studios and distribution companies to predict box-office success a long time before a film is released, based on social media conversations around this project.[23] The agency's pre-established relationships with production professionals certainly helped it to sell this tool to these counterparts, placing the agency in an even closer collaborative position with studios, and also in a position to have one foot on each side: providing tools with which production and marketing decisions are made and at the same time selling—potentially on the basis of the same numbers—the talent component of these same projects. For the production side, being able to monitor months in advance how a movie is going to perform resembles reaching the holy grail. However, what is measured is not so much an anticipated image of the movie's reception as it reflects the present reception of an early marketing campaign, the causal link between the two being here implied.[24] In any case, the idea of "reception by anticipation" reinvents the notion of reception itself. It also redefines movie audiences by forming them out of an artist's imagined demographics or reference groups (the followers, viewers, etc.) at a time when a movie is not yet out. It thus carries out social effects, let alone the question of knowing if the produced numbers are in fact accurate or not.

These elements could lead us to imagine that pricing and deal-making mechanisms are standardized, systematic, and formula based. This is, however, not the case. What is true is that studios and production entities, who support the heavy financial risk attached to making sometimes extremely onerous projects (let's remember that a big production can reach a budget of $200 million), have tried to develop rationalizing and risk-reducing techniques: producing numbers is part of it, and so is the weight that marketing departments have gained within studio divisions. Marketing specialists are often involved at an early stage in the discussions around projects. The notion of "pre-awareness" of audiences who are expected to be more inclined to go see something that they are already familiar with, and the standardized formats of movie franchises, as well as "reboots" or sequels of previous hits—also seen as more predictable in terms of economic outcome—are another response to the concentration of financial risk deriving from the studios' investment on fewer very expensive productions (as opposed to a strategy of diversifying investments to balance risks). All of this, however, is also designed to manage another risk than the financial risk taken by the studio, strictly speaking—that is, the fear that a particular executive might have to be blamed and possibly fired if a project he or she championed ends up losing too much money. Scientific-looking predictions and numbers are then justification tools used a posteriori (the movie did poorly but the numbers were good) employed in the context of corporate entities in which one has to report to superior levels and possibly to managers and shareholders who expect return on investment.

However, in interviews, both agents and production professionals commonly expressed skepticism as regards the use of marketing techniques and tools for rationalizing financial decisions. The reliability of the techniques and the accuracy of the numbers they generate were called into question, and their "noncreative" nature inspired more contempt than interest. Of course, agents recognized that reference can be made to such numbers during discussions here and there, and that such data are undoubtedly brought up by marketing professionals who are consulted during negotiations with a studio. But they also described the operations of quantification surrounding a movie project as a much more intuitive process. This former agent and agency manager in Big Hollywood turned producer spoke about his ability to figure out a film's budget—and all the associated prices/costs—as a craft that formed through experience and is practiced in an artisanal manner:

I don't believe in any of it. It's not being rational, really. You know, they try to make it rational, but running numbers: "Oh, well then, this'll do this in Germany . . ." You know, they're not . . . no! I say, whatever you're running is wrong, it's too little or too much. It's not right. [. . .] You have to always assess the risk factor. Because everything that was supposed to be a sure thing never worked. All the sure things failed.

So how can you asses the risk factor if you never know what's going to happen?

That's the beauty of it. That's what makes it fun, that's why everybody isn't doing it, because it's somewhere between taste, experience, and luck. You learn all the time. By the end of my career, I'm pretty good at reading a script and knowing what the budget of the film is. Yet, I could not make a budget of a film; I don't know what anything costs. All I'm doing is processing thousands of scripts—"That script had a budget of that. That script had a budget of that, this script has a budget of that"—even though I couldn't make the budget! You say: "Okay, well, show me how you got that number."

I go: "I don't know!" I just *know* by comparing four thousand scripts and four thousand budgets, I know what this one costs. It's like a computer, you know, it's just algorithms. (October 2013, his emphasis)

If this figuring is not a rational process, it is not because participants are not behaving in a coherent way: they assess situations, strategize, and reflect on their practice. It is because these valuation activities are embedded in the interdependence process that I described in the previous section of this chapter. Consequently, monetizing creative activities in the context of specific projects is always conducted, at least in part, in the service of keeping this interdependence system running, of maintaining the relationships that are at the foundation of this entire system of activity. This is also what keeps creative and economic values so intricate.

At this point, I need to make a distinction. In *Little Hollywood*, agents explain that there is little "negotiating" going on: the deals are relatively standard, and in fact, most of the clients make either "scale"— that is, the fixed minimum wage according to the guild scale for a type of labor on the production—or they climb a little higher in terms of pay scale but following steps that are pretty predictable and predefined (and not always negotiable—it is whatever the TV network pays for this or that role or job, for instance). Therefore, most of the time, it does not require aggressive transactions or inventiveness in the crafting of financial arrangements.[25] It's mostly in *Big Hollywood* that making deals, negotiating, and pricing becomes a subject of attention. Prices do not present themselves here as an obvious and objective reality simply given by some external market mechanisms. What agents insisted on is that, *at that level*, there is just "no rule"; "it's random." It is the reign of the unique: "Every situation that's unique completely requires a completely different code of conduct, order of events, tone and timing."[26] Much like in Lucien Karpik's analysis of the "markets for singularities," the radical singularity of artists would imply incommensurable performances and erratic pricing mechanisms (Karpik 2010).[27] A talent agent who represents several movie stars at one of the major agencies expressed it in the following terms: "In Hollywood, there are really no rules on the money. The quotes the people use are reference quotes. An actor can make twenty million dollars on a studio movie and then make a hundred thousand on an independent. Yes, he can have more back end [profit earnings] maybe on an independent, but never as much back end as he had on that studio movie. So there is really no rhyme or reason. It's a crime of passion" (April 2013).

The following pages strive to contribute to elucidating the mystery of incommensurability, and the paradox of pricing something that is deemed to be priceless: uniqueness, originality, quality, talent. How do agents price the "singularities" at the heart of their transactions—that is, artists and artworks? We can easily follow Karpik in the observation that the "rules of the market" as neoclassical economic theory imagines them—with regulation through the equilibrium market price and linear price scales—are not very helpful for understanding what happens in this context. There are indeed huge variations and a gap in the scale of prices separating the prices of performances comparable in format (spending that many days acting in a movie, that much time writing a script, etc.) accomplished by A-list artist, on one hand, and by a mid-level or unknown actor or writer, on the other hand. Completely different logics of evaluation seem to apply. Karpik suggests that the extreme price variation and the sometimes outrageously high amounts earned by the most successful artists reflect and justify, in fact, the idea of incommensurable quality in which such markets are rooted. Admittedly; but this leaves us with the question of *how* the tension between this incommensurability and the need to put a figure on it regardless is negotiated in practice, through daily interactions and activities in Hollywood. How do agents price the unique? Or, how do these pricing operations that agents and their counterparts conduct relate to the shared belief in the incomparable quality of the object of their transactions?[28]

In their accounts, agents insist on the reference to the intrinsic strength of the "good project" or the "great talent." The general belief in quality (which is not incompatible with the distance that agents can take when they recognize that the highest price does not systematically go to the best-quality project or to the most outstanding performance) is associated with the conviction that pricing mechanisms cannot be reduced to formulas, standards, or any systematic set of rules. In Big Hollywood—and especially at the top of this game—people who are already well identified among a handful of agents, artists, and production professionals who operate at that level are in a position to engage counterparts in projects and form alliances within these circles to get a movie financed. Therefore, what is primarily at stake for the agents is to satisfy their clients' artistic aspirations and experiences—what a senior agent at a big agency called "the joy":

The trick of agenting is not making deals; the trick of agenting is finding things worthy enough to make deals on. If we can find things to make deals on, we make deals. It's a small town—it goes around, it comes around. If you find an artist who is happy enough to find a project, [the deal] rarely falls apart over money. Not in my world. If I get an artist who fucking loves something and I can't get them their price, I convince them to do it for not their price. It's about the joy! It's about the joy, the love, the experience, the process, the making it. (April 2013)

The legitimacy of high prices is justified by the general belief that, in the end, talent always pays off, "the money finds you," so much so that success indistinctly means money.[29] That all the paths to success in this field—even in the so-called independent world—are associated with the accumulation of economic capital, in proportions that vary, is undeniable. This is not, however, what gives primary meaning and legitimacy to the game, even in the eyes of those who are supposed to embody its "business side." The strictly commercial repertoire of justification, which would treat Hollywood as *a marketplace like any other*, is altered or even trumped by the reference to quality, originality, the artists' "voice and their attributes," their personal mark on the work, their centrality to the existence of a collective project such as a movie—as many reasons for them to "deserv[e] bigger upsides." By saying that he felt entitled to ask for a raise of several millions of dollars in an actor's salary in comparison with what his quote then was, as well as for a significant percentage of the film's profits, *because he "knew the movie was great"* and anticipated it to be successful, the same interviewed agent was not being disingenuous or naïve as regards the real nature of the game. In fact, what he expressed is the participants' core belief and professional ideal, which give raison d'être to the practice, which we identified earlier.[30] We observe here that this mental frame incorporates an *economic dimension*, since the perception of quality or talent and that of economic value are inextricably entangled.

This professional *ideal* is of course not what comes out of the experience of each particular negotiation and deal-making process for the agents. Their approach to pricing different categories of people and projects in specific situations is more elusive and changing; it certainly doesn't follow preset hierarchies of quality and price, which would always vary concomitantly. On the contrary, agents paint a fuzzy if not messy picture of this activity in which, in the absence of a unified rationale for pricing, the assessment of value for each component of a film project is highly circumstantial and attached to the specificity of their interactions with particular buyers, financiers, talent, and other possible counterparts, and of the piece of material at the heart of the project. As far as pricing artists is concerned, quotes are fallacious precisely because no *impersonal* scale of value really applies. Several interviewees took the example of one of their star clients who could be paid $20 million or more to act in a big studio production or be in a position to direct a $100 million movie, at the same time as the exact same artist would also act (and/or direct) for almost nothing in a "small" $10 million independent film. The conclusion is well synthesized by this talent agent: "What does this quote thing mean? It means nothing. It's just chatter, to justify your file. [. . .] It's not like [the artist says]: 'Oh, I don't work for less than my quote,' or [the buyer says]: 'I don't pay that quote, because our budget doesn't . . .' There's none of that. That's just chitchat dialogue on top of the reality of it." The fluctuation of roles that an artist can occupy (acting, directing, producing), the variation in the type and budget of the projects, the specificity of the professional configuration formed for the negotiation of each project (the position of this agent at this agency facing this executive at this studio, these financiers, etc.)—all make up the radically contextual nature of the process as the agents perceive and describe it. The same talent agent continued:

That's the beauty and the curse of Hollywood—the esoteric, ephemeral gray area, [the] cloudiness of almost every value system: the value of the artist, the value of the time, the value of the location, the value of the amount of crew, the value of the amount of extras, the value of the amount of detail in the costumes, the value of the amount of writers to do rewrites, the value for a director who owns a piece of the movie, like a huge ten-million-dollar director, versus the value of some great young director—the *value* of it, and the assessment of those values is different. In other businesses, glass has a value, iron ore has a value, wood has a value, *labor* has a value. In show business, values are very much intangible, fluid. [. . .] The reality is that the values of that client, of that project, and the way they interface is dictated by the time and the moment of *that* project and that client, not by the quotes, not by any formula: by the moment in time right now. (Big agency, December 2013, his emphasis)

Despite such a perception that each case is unique and that negotiating is a purely situational and improvisational craft, conventions in the practice of deal-making are identifiable, price variations are intelligible, and a standard price may even emerge, for a time, for the compensation of the supposedly incommensurable performance of (specific categories of) star artists. In other words, activities get *coordinated*—systemically so, and not by any orchestrator who would stand above the crowd, be it a powerful mogul or an international movie star. In that sense, prices are not "random"—that is, totally unpredictable[31]—but they can be understood and explained with reference to specific logics of action. If agents do not behave in the rational style of a *homo economicus* or in the manner of the bargainer of the bazaar economy,[32] their actions *do* form certain patterns that I will now trace out.

Writing an Economic Narrative

First, the interaction systems within which the definition of worth is located and people/projects get priced, even if they are partly arranged in the context of each particular project, are never completely reshuffled. They form among a limited group of already acquainted participants, for the most part. What seems to be circumstantial and based on chance ("I just basically had the right buyer in [this studio executive], the right timing, the right studio, the right collaboration, the right spec project, and I was able to pull the deal off"[33]) exists within the limits of specific evaluation communities to which the participants belong for a long time and in which a small number of players are repeatedly dealing with one another. The evaluation community delineates the professional sphere within which "chance" happens. Preexisting familiarity with counterparts in evaluation communities and experiences of past interactions are also what makes the "right" combination of partners and the "right" moment to close a deal recognizable. This is how agents can evoke situations in which they were "feeling the market, feeling the momentum, understanding the competition"[34] and were able to act strategically in a world that is seemingly fluid and chaotic. Negotiating and pricing mechanisms are therefore structured in a way similar to that I have already described regarding the creative definition of a project. The interplay of participants' evaluations of others' positions, motives, agendas, anticipations, expectations is here again crucial to decipher action in the particular circles that form around projects within the limits of an evaluation community.

The negotiation game in this context is based on *work* to create and circulate a commonly accepted *economic narrative* that is associated with the making of a project's creative narrative that I previously analyzed. The agent's position defines a narrative framework based on the division between two groups of players in the negotiation game. One group is formed by the coalition of the representation side and the concerned talent: the agent and the corresponding agency; maybe other agents, managers, lawyers, and clients who are involved and the creative and financial partners who are attached to their person. The other group includes whoever appears to be with the "buyer(s)": the studio and/or leading production company, and associated financing, production, distribution, marketing/ publicity entities. This mental divide organizes the construction of conflicting interests ("us" versus "them") in the definition of the "best deal" as the agent sees it. But this is only true to an extent: because the agent draws his power from *both* his tie with the client *and* his relationship with the buyer, antagonizing strategies and scorched-earth policy are usually not considered an option, even by agents who are known to be "tough in negotiations." On the contrary, negotiating is about bridging the opposite positions that the agent concurrently depends on. The position of the agent in such interdependence games determines what will look like a doable negotiation and a good deal—that is, one that preserves, above all, the possibility of further playing the game.

The super-agent at a major agency quoted below gave an expressive illustration of the *collective process* by which the value of a deal is defined or sometimes revised. In this case, a studio was looking to renegotiate an agreement previously signed with a star regarding an expensive film project.[35] This situation is therefore somewhat of a dispute; but at a more general level, it reveals that relationships are potentially destabilized when any transaction crystallizes, materializing conflicting interests:

It is how to tell the story. The studio is telling us in some other language that is unfortunate and difficult to understand, that they are having a difficult time dealing with the deal they made. That's their story. Our story is: we have a deal, but we get that wink-wink. Can we find a way where we don't have to negotiate against ourselves, for you to find some comfort that we can live with?" That's our story. The story I have to tell to [the head of my agency] or I have to tell to [the star client], or that [the client] tells to [the agency's head], or that [one of the client's lawyers] tells to me, or that I tell to [the other client's lawyer], or that he tells to [the client's cowriter and creative partner] or that [he] tells to [the client]—which is all happening—our little stories, based on the belief system that each of us as individuals have and the interpretation of how to manifest those beliefs into reality. And so, we start interpreting and telling the story *as we see it*; and that narrative hopefully starts to become *accepted.by all*. Right?! And when that happens, there's a united front, and then there is a leverage within that, and you hope to win your negotiation with that narrative. Not with your contractual legal teeth, but with the power of your persuasion, the spirit that you're conveying that you are united, that: "You got a problem with [the studio head]? You got a problem with [the star]. You got a problem with [the star]? You got a problem with [his lawyers]. You got a problem with [them]? You got a problem with [the studio head]. You got a problem with [him]? You got a problem with [me]. You got a problem with [me]? You got a problem with [the agency's head]." Then you're building a case! But one not that you're willing to argue in court, ironically; one that hopefully you're using just in the Hollywood phone game. (December 2013, his emphasis)

The negotiation process is one of mutual influence, successive shifts, and eventual convergence of perceptions and anticipations, following the same lines that I described regarding the definition of the substance of the project itself. It first takes place within the circle that ties the agent to the client, and to other representatives and partners of the client who take part in the transactions with their own goals and perspectives. Working toward the alignment of positions, by way of rhetorical persuasion (agents and their counterparts operating mostly on the phone) rather than through a more technical approach or through direct confrontation, is characterized by our interviewee as finding "how to tell the story." But the construction of this (collective) economic narrative is not completed (and stabilized, at least for a moment) until the studio head and his associates are enrolled in the story, and a somewhat shared frame can be defined that protects the horizon of a common tomorrow. What is at stake here is not simply the economic outcome of the exchanges—the amount of money the client will eventually get out of the deal, the commission the agency will receive, the bonus the agent will be granted, and the various financial dimensions of this economic process; rather, it is to put back into balance the relational game between participants in the same evaluation community that was shaken by the dispute, this game being precisely what underpins these economic activities.

Negotiating is also about engaging institutions in the process and using organizational force to induce motion in a certain direction: getting production counterparts to believe that whoever has a problem with the agent has one with the manager of a large and powerful agency, and/or with a top entertainment law firm, creates strong incentives for cooperation in the case at hand on the basis of the common knowledge of all other present and potential occasions for transactions between the same big agency and the same major studio—maybe with other artists, agents, executives, and lawyers, and regarding other projects, but *within the framework of the same evaluation community*. The interplay between the weight of organizational resources and the dynamics of evaluation communities is here again visible. Because negotiating and pricing are so deeply embedded in segmented professional relations, the art of "not making enemies"—especially among potential buyers—is central to it: "One of my rules, if you will, about being an agent selling material [is]: it's easy to sell material for a lot of money; it's very hard to sell material for a lot of money and not make enemies. And not making enemies is the key to being able to represent more high-end material."[36] Face work (Goffman 1955) in evaluation communities includes allowing others to save appearances and making sure that counterparts do not leave the negotiation table feeling embarrassed or defeated. An agent needs to "make sure everyone leaves the room happy," as a former agency manager explained.[37] Similarly, a former agent who specialized in packaging and financing movies insisted during our interview on the counterproductive nature of getting a studio deal that would be "too good," not for economic reasons attached to the film itself (if the studio expects to keep a higher percentage of the profits the film generates overall, they might be incentivized to work harder on it, invest more on marketing, give it a better release date, etc.), but mostly in the spirit of not "souring" the relationships with these production counterparts.

On a more general level, a top talent agent revealingly expressed the systemic reason why the logic of evaluation communities outweighs the stakes of any particular deal: "We're all in this fishbowl together, we've all done a million deals together, we're going to do a million more, we have a lot of artists. There's this artist. But don't we all want to remain friends? Don't we want to make this [situation with this particular] movie *not* affect the future of all of our future businesses together?"[38] Aware of the fragility of each particular "house of cards" that a project represents, agents tend to invest in the relationships that make it possible rather than in the project per se (although the two are of course closely interconnected). If the subtle balance between taking advantage of a position of dominance in the short term of a project, on one hand, and sparing one's durable counterparts in evaluation communities so as to not create acrimonies for the future, on the other hand, becomes untenable, the scales are generally tipped in favor of the second option, which in fact conditions the possibility of transacting on any particular project thereafter.

The same logic sheds explanatory light on the relative rarity of lawsuits despite the high number of potentially very conflictual situations, with heavy financial repercussions, that one can identify in Hollywood. Entertainment lawyers themselves, as they are an integral part of evaluation communities and are therefore also interested in preserving their functioning, often prefer "not to get legal"—in an agent's words—or at least, not to threaten to take adversaries in a difficult negotiation to court. Agents actively work at keeping legal scenes at a distance from the relationship work that they perform. Their particular form of power resides precisely in the *strength of the informal*; it's a type of legitimacy built against legal technicality in that sense. It is thus not surprising that going to trial (or even threatening to) is in their eyes a solution of very last re-sort as well as the supreme (undesirable) weapon in the scale of threats, which is also likely to publicize a confrontation. Suing often implies a "scandalization strategy," all the more if it becomes the focus of the press (especially the trades): the crisis gets externalized outside the se-lect circles of the evaluation community where it failed to be solved. By contrast, the dynamics of evaluation communities are those of infor-mal ties and common history, suggested risks and implied consequences rather than open threats, push-pull and give-and-take, oral exchanges and coordination based on the given word rather than systematic for-malization in written instruments. The "rules" that agents follow do not derive from the formal structure of a legal system, and the degree of legal enforceability of an agreement (a memo, a letter, a contract) does not always translate into the effective strength that this agreement has for the implied participants, in context. In other words, while contracts are practically renegotiable—irrespective of their supposedly binding and compulsory nature, legally speaking—participants often prefer to remain in the more flexible area of oral transactions and soft instru-ments.[39] What members of Big Hollywood's evaluation communities collectively build and maintain in their day-to-day transactions is an "order without law" (Ellickson 1991) in that sense.[40] By contrast, more formalized and standardized deals involving little price negotiation are the daily reality of Little Hollywood agents.

If the structuring of pricing mechanisms in evaluation communities is not governed by formal rules, patterns are nevertheless observable. Forms of shared professional wisdom that new participants learn as they get so-cialized to agenting define the "maxims of action" that most of them are able to recognize and articulate. Repeated experiences with long-term counterparts in evaluation communities strengthen the participants' abil-ity to read the cues sent within these circles that signal that something or someone is "real," "good," and "fresh," and, inseparably, *to associate them with a certain category of transaction*, to identify potentially interested buyers, and to "guess" how much it could be worth. The memory of transactions within an evaluation community provides reference points. The *practical meaning* of quotes and their "good use" in different types of negotiation are construed by the protagonists throughout repeated ex-changes in this context. The process examined in the previous section of this chapter by which a project gets defined, assembled, and put on its way to be brought to completion—a process in which agents take ac-tively part—is also the first step of *a value definition process* regarding a project and the salient elements that characterize it (the lead actor, the most important supporting actors, the director, the writer, etc.—as well as the studio and the executive[s] in charge here, the main producer[s], the packaging agent and agency, and possibly the involved lawyers, managers, etc.). This value definition process affects the entire system of participants in the concerned segment of an evaluation community; it also includes the perceived value of the relationships that tie these participants together. This intertwined value attribution mechanism goes therefore beyond the strict question of pricing the performance of artists that agents sell on a labor market.

Price Variations and the Emergence of a Standard

Cases in which the value attributed to a star or a project—and consequently, the amount of the associated deal—suddenly rises or decreases are especially revealing situations. In Big Hollywood, competition among buyers to create preferential ties with a rising or an established star, or for ownership of a "promising" piece of material, can lead to what participants label as a "bidding war": buyers (mostly studios) outbid one another until one of them "takes the pot," which usually means that a significant investment has been made in a project and an artist. The studio is buying "futures in talent" and "futures in creative content," hoping not to have overpaid for the promise that this investment represents. The projective and relational dynamics through which price is collectively imagined is not devoid of similarities with what ethnographers of financial markets have described regarding traders and other financial operators (Boussard and Dujarier 2014; Godechot 2001): there also, elaborate professional cultures prescribe attitudes and define "scripts" that dictate who the players are and what are the right manners of playing the game (Abolafia 1996). Beyond the appearance that there is nothing more at stake in the activity of financial market professionals than economic profit and the exercise of individual self-interest, these works show that the rules players follow are deeply embedded in social relations and broader cultural mechanisms, also shedding light on the highly local dynamics of the so-called "global financial markets" (Knorr Cetina and Bruegger 2002).

In Hollywood too, selling and buying is not evaluating the current price of a star and a movie that exists and is about to be released; it is guessing what these values might be months away—and often years—from the point of transaction. Let's imagine that a studio has granted a contract for the development of a film project to a rising star who has had one very big box-office success in the recent past and who has another movie about to come out. The star seems able to mobilize other A-list talent in the project, whose genre and main story lines sound familiar enough to the studio to seem like a salable idea. The studio has invested a high amount in their own eyes (maybe $50 million or $80 million) in this project, but importantly, *in the relationship* with the artist as well, based on the studio's perception of the potential of the star and in the context of their experience of working with the agent, the agency, the lawyers, and the managers who were involved in this particular deal. All these elements together *make the value* of the deal *when it happens*. And they make the *value of the artist* at this particular point in time, as far as a certain type of project is concerned.

However, participants in the concerned evaluation community all know that the variables defining the "situation" will change in combined ways that they can't control, despite their calculations and expectations. At the early stage of the definition of a project where these transactions take place, the protagonists operate at *temporal distance* from the question of knowing what will happen when the finished product gets released. I suggested earlier that, for agents, the buyers are never the audiences, just as talent agencies are not consumer-facing organizations. Consequently, evaluating and pricing are not thought of by agents as a matter of what audiences will want to consume. This is why agents' "business is not the outcome"[41]—that is, the reception and commercial success or failure of a project *in the end*. Agents "can't control it," but they *can* treat it as an independent variable because this is not *directly* at stake in what they do at the specific time of their intervention in the filmmaking process. By the time a given film is out, many other conversations, transactions, and deals will have happened within the concerned evaluation community, and the stakes between the protagonists will have shifted accordingly.

Let's get back to the story of the expensive deal I imagined above, and let's extrapolate about what might happen next. Now, two years have gone by since the deal was made. The film starring the artist at the center of the deal, which was then about to come out, was a commercial flop. The project has not attracted the expected co-stars and does not develop as smoothly as expected. Anticipations have shifted in correlated ways. In the eyes of all the protagonists, the "value" of the star, the "value" of the project at hand, the "value" of the previous movie that didn't succeed as anticipated, the "value" of all associated relationships have changed. The studio executive who closed the deal is worried that the studio head and higher-ups might become unhappy with it, jeopardizing the executive's "value" for the studio and career. The artist might now be a less important client in the eyes of the agency (as well as the management company, and the law firm also involved in the initial deal). This depreciation of all the values evoked above might materialize in economic form, inseparably from the symbolic devaluation that already occurred, whether it means renegotiating the deal or just affecting later transactions involving the artist. By going along with it, the agent manifests being in line with the general perception that the client's value had become overinflated, and thus participates in restoring the collective alignment of interpretations in the new context. This also accomplishes what is absolutely central for all agents: preserving *their own relationships*, especially those built over time with production counterparts, from devaluating.

But the relative commercial failure of a project does not mechanically mean depreciation, especially for the agents. In other words, the "success" or "failure" of a film can retroact on the agent as it does on the client, *or not*, depending of a combination of elements: if a big blockbuster film loses millions to a studio, it will probably affect the bankability of the star of the movie and the ability of the agent to make things happen in this star's name (at least for a time); it might have repercussions on the agent's career and on the agency if this was *the* major A-list talent they represented; otherwise, or if this remains an isolated incident, it might not have a major effect on the agent's credibility, career path, or ability to do things. The nonperformance of certain movies or shows, and the collapse of an artist's career, do not disturb the functioning of giant organizations who represent many more stars and up-and-coming artists, such as WME or CAA, not to mention their involvement in sectors other than the talent representation business per se. In addition, if the concerned film was a smaller independent movie, which generates different expectations, not making money out of it might be a price that the concerned studio is willing to pay in order to maintain its relationship with a name talent, as it often happens. The effect on the agent of what happens in the "consumers' market" is always filtered through the relational dynamics of evaluation communities, rather than deriving from the success or failure of any particular project.

In the example I just made, the two *imagined values* of the artist and the project, and all related elements—the value at the time of the initial deal, and that collectively defined two years later—were eventually discordant, leading the participants to adjust their creative and economic arrangements according to their new anticipations. This is revealing of how value is created in Hollywood in a more general sense; that is, by *successive and interdependent adjustments of the imagined worth* (both creative and monetary) *of something or someone, within evaluation communities*. When this imagined value extends to a whole category of artist associated with a particular type a project (a film format, a sub-genre, a budget scope) and remains stable over a certain period of time, a *standard*—which never becomes formalized or permanent—nevertheless forms.

What happened in the mid-1990s in a segment of the comedy film world illustrates this. Jim Carrey was then the first comedic actor to reach the sum of $20 million paid as an advance (against 15 percent of every dollar at the box-office worldwide) for the movie *The Cable Guy* (then budgeted at $38 million to $40 million), Sony being the studio that negotiated this deal with Carrey's agent at UTA. This was immediately perceived as a "coup" and an event in Hollywood, and it was indeed a significant salary jump for the actor compared with the $7 million he had received for his previous movie, *Dumb and Dumber*, and even more with the $450,000 his labor was worth only a year earlier, when he worked on the movie *Ace Ventura: Pet Detective*. A succession of major box-office hits,[42] in a prosperous economic context in which betting huge amounts of money on stars was not unthinkable in the eyes of studio heads, had started to change the perceived realm of possibilities: production professionals, just as talent representatives and artists, could anticipate such huge box-office returns to continue coming in, or even growing, in line with the trend that they were reading in this succession of past successes (regarding a type of comedy, associated with Carrey's name and a comedic milieu). This interpretation of the situation made the combination of an unprecedented salary and gross participation seem like a "good decision" and was even perceived as a windfall for Sony Pictures' chairman, Mark Canton. It was, however, anything but obvious to other Hollywood professionals, outside of the specific segment of the evaluation community that was making this shift happen—for instance, former Orion production head Mike Medavoy expressed his fear that this deal would set a "perilous and dangerous precedent," and James G. Robinson, owner of Morgan Creek Productions (which produced *Ace Ventura*) stated his perplexity in face of both the amount and the structure of the deal (the high percentage of gross participation), which didn't "make business sense to [him]" (Natale 1995).

While the general economic context in Hollywood provided exogenous conditions that made this creation of value possible, the *endogenous process* that led to its materialization played the most important role. It involved the already acquainted members of *a specific evaluation community* who shared a prospective definition of the situation: this interrelation circle tied rising star artists in a distinctive genre; a talent department and an agent building a strong specialized position in this area (within a fast-growing agency, UTA); and a studio executive competing with a small number of top buyers at the same level and working at being "ahead of the curve" at Sony with the promotion of a new format of lucrative, star-centered comedy. The stability of this interaction and interdependence circle within which participants were repeatedly dealing with one another is also why and how Carrey's valuation in the context of a particular movie did not remain an isolated "accident." Because the members of this evaluation community kept transacting with one another regarding categories of projects that they construed as comparable, these interactions were also conducive to reiterating the use of the same pricing logic ($15 million to $20 million plus 15–20 percent on the back end) among the same players first, and soon to the propagation of this model to contiguous circles of agents and studio executives elsewhere, who felt like they couldn't afford not to keep up with what was going on. A *self-reinforcing process* formed, in which asking for this type of deal for top comedy clients became a goal and then a norm for the agents (and other talent representatives); granting it in a whole series of projects became unavoidable in the perception of studios executives; getting it became a measure of one's self-importance and worth for the concerned artists. A precedent had been established, despite the fears that were initially expressed. The press also took notice, framing what happened as a potentially lasting change, and participated in the alignment of perceptions. In the end, *The Cable Guy* did not reach the box-office summits that some previous hits had[43] and its critical reception was disappointing, but the success of *Liar Liar*, which came soon after, confirmed the participants' general perception of a larger trend that they felt to be part of. The imagined value of top comedic talent persisted and extended in the manner of a contagion process: more "$20 million stars" were made within the narrow circles of evaluation communities. A *standard* had emerged. It did not only concern pricing mechanisms and conventions of economic value; it also outlined the contours of a subgenre at the same time as it consecrated a category of stars.

When such $20 million deals are revealed outside the circles of this Very Big Hollywood—through trade magazines in particular—they can take the appearance of magical numbers, or seem to be the result of pure market mechanisms, since the real interdependence dynamics that produces them remains for the most invisible to those who are not insiders of these evaluation communities. Agents within these circles have to master the dance associating the management of the unique (that is, the artists they represent) and the definition of tendencies in pricing that challenge the very notion of singularity. On one hand, agents and their counterparts in evaluation communities believe in the incommensurability of quality that derives from the notion of talent, genius, or gift, which legitimizes that two actors be paid radically different amounts for a comparable type and volume of labor;[44] and they are in fact *makers and keepers of artists' incommensurability*. While this "uniqueness" of the artists is celebrated, it is in a more discreet manner that agents are also engaged, on the other hand, in valuation practices that intrinsically induce to measure, compare, and order, as I just explained. In practice there is no contradiction there, but more of a continuum and a combination of commensuration mechanisms and the proclamation of the unique.

The emergence and stabilization of a standard is, however, always precarious, as it does not get objectified in formal instruments or institutional mechanisms. The same dynamics can work in economically reversed ways, and did a few years later. In the mid to late 2000s—in what is now perceived as a difficult time for global financial markets, impacting conglomerated studios, especially after the writers' strike of 2007/08—new mental frames defining the situation formed and came to prevail. The new shared visions fell in line with the conviction that "$20 million deals are over" and associated coordination mechanisms inflected the scale of prices downward, this time.[45] This is not simply the effect of an exogenous factor, the "market change"; what the market allows for is always mediated and, in the deepest sense, constructed through the convergence of perceptions in evaluation communities. Changes that matter are those that *directly* impact counterparts in the same evaluation community—their respective positions, organizations, resources, interests, and ties. The historical, relational, and segmented dynamics of price-making in Hollywood is structured through activity in evaluation communities.

Specialized Economic Conventions and the Making of Value

More generally speaking, evaluation communities are also the framework within which economic conventions take specific form, get circulated and reinforced through reiteration, and are learned by newcomers, but also inflected and continually (though usually imperceptibly) reshaped. Olav Velthuis (2003) has pointed to the existence of two "pricing norms" governing the activity of art dealers on the market for contemporary art, norms that are anomalies to price mechanisms as they are understood by mainstream economic theory. The first one is the avoidance of price decreases at all times; the second one is to avoid pricing differently two artworks of the same size by the same artist (even though dealers know that some works sell more easily than others). If pricing conventions in Hollywood have some family likeness with such norms—agents hope to consistently increase their clients' quotes; the budget size of a production partly determines the price range of the various performances of the involved artists—they are primarily *specialized conventions*.

The (e)valuation process in Big Hollywood associates *types of project characterized by a specific price range* with different *dimensions of value*; and agents define professional strategies for creating overall *worth* by playing on their combination. Let us now explore what this exactly refers to. The system of conventions with which agents construct value is a dual one. On one hand, in Hollywood and in agenting (for the client and the agent alike), *success is measured by the rise in price* as much as by box-office numbers, popularity scores, and other elements that derive from a consecration system attached to the evaluation of a finished product and to its reception by critics and audiences. Price is, in addition, an *early* measure of an artist's success in terms of stage in the filmmaking process: it comes before other "tournaments of value" (Appadurai 1986) and with expectations; it contains the promise of other successes. It's a *sign of greatness* granted in evaluation communities. For this reason, doing a big-budget studio film, which is always the type of production that generates the highest-paying jobs for "name talent" (both in terms of advance and in terms of gross participation), means more than just the economic endeavor and opportunity that it represents. *Price signals status* and professional importance here: it makes the "big" player (star, agent, or producer alike). It's because the meaning of high price is not only an economic one that a decrease in the amount a successful artist can get for doing a studio movie (compared to his previous "quote" for a similar type of blockbuster production) comes to signify more than monetary loss: it is "about him, his life, and his art," as an interviewed super-agent stated. He feels that his symbolic value is depreciated as it is intrinsically attached to the price that he can get in this context, for a type of production that signifies, and in fact *constitutes*, his worth in the industry beyond the strict question of financial value.

On the other hand, in Hollywood, there is also a *specific value of small price*. Doing "arty" independent-style films that are made for a modest budget is the aspiration of most artists who can and do get the big production deals just mentioned and are "big stars" in that sense.

Small price, in this case, *signals quality*. Indeed, talent's participation in such "independent films" is always compensated at a much lower level than it would be on a big-budget project, the type of movie dictating the pricing of the artist's performance. Movie stars notoriously do such "arty" movies for amounts that are out of proportion by comparison with their earnings on studio films. The definition of what a small price is in this context remains relative to the dual structure of success in Big Hollywood that we are presently examining: it could still be millions, and these indie films are not the semi-amateur movies that are put together through thick and thin with no funds at all in Little or Very Little Hollywood. However, what matters here again is that, beyond their economic relevance, prices and rates are cues that manifest noneconomic value.

An artist's worth in Big Hollywood always emerges from some combination of these two modes of assessing value. Correlatively, an agent's worth does as well. More complex criteria for classifying and evaluating movies (and entertainment products) exist, of course. But balancing elements from these two repertoires of value—in proportions and ways that vary depending on the artist's profile and career stage, an agent's position in an evaluation community, and so on—is at the heart of agenting in Big Hollywood. The formula of doing "one for us, one for them" (meaning that the artist has to do one movie for his or her own satisfaction, one to please the studio) is repeatedly invoked by the agents, who also explain that they have to convince their clients to embrace this strategy and conceive the progress of their career in terms of its gradual rearrangement: from "two for them, one for us" to "one for them, two for us," ideally.[46] The "one for us" is the small price/quality value project dear to the artist's heart. The small one is for "us" in the agents' words: the worth of the client is inseparable from the greatness of the agent who speaks in his name. These parallel hierarchies are *signified* by prices. Worth comes out of this combination not simply as a result of a mechanism of economic balance, but because of embedded signs of artistic value. Economic and artistic types of capital, even if we might want to differentiate them analytically, cannot be dissociated in the process by which they are produced and accumulated. Studios play along by contributing to the production and more often to the distribution of smaller "arty" movies, so that they can be in business with the most desirable artists when it comes to making the most lucrative projects. Each type of project conditions the existence of the other, and they conjointly signal worth by offering complementary marks of value. This combined system of signs informs the hierarchy structuring this professional space.

Agents—just like their counterparts in evaluation communities—have had to learn these conventions that associate various categories and scales of price with various approaches to value. Learning the pragmatic rules of agenting implies mechanisms of "semiotic socialization," to borrow Zerubavel's (1997) expression. Successful agents in Big Hollywood are experts in the manipulation of signs of value: it means recognizing them and mobilizing in their strategies for clients the correspondence between monetary and extra-economic dimensions. With argumentative practices (selling/pitching, advising) that rest on the cognitive frame formed by these conventions, agents "make worth with words" through activities that always remain deeply rooted in the materiality of evaluation communities. Their transactions are therefore central to the making of value—indistinctively economic and creative—that takes place in evaluation communities, and not exclusively (like Bourdieu's analysis of what makes the symbolic value of an artwork could lead to imagine) at the later stage of the consecration process by critics, journalists, professional authorities, and audiences.[47]

As a result, through relationships between professionals in evaluation communities, the mechanisms that produce economic and artistic value in Hollywood are inseparable. Relationships and transactions that have to do with naming, gauging, classifying, and pricing talent make economic and creative value in the same movement, even if negotiating deals and defining the key points of a contract imply a particular expertise on the part of the agents. Prices and forms of quality are not simply interconnected; they *signify each other* following a correspondence system that the participants have assimilated, that they embody and bring into play in their daily practice, and that their interactions collectively and imperceptibly affect over time. Besides its obvious material consequences, pricing is a *symbolic operation* made possible by interrelations in evaluation communities: it makes worth (of artists and other evaluation community members) by signaling *both* quality and economic value. Therefore, in the everyday activities of the occupational system that evaluation communities form, economic dimensions and creative ones are *co-constitutive*.

If I need to state it so forcefully, it's because these two aspects are defined in other works not only as two principles that are analytically distinguished, but as opposed or contradictory mechanisms for the explanation of action in this world. For instance, Bourdieusian approaches are built around the idea, visualized in the statistical construction of cultural fields, that the tension between a pole of "art for art's sake" and a commercial pole structures the field of cinema (and any field of cultural production) and therefore accounts for what makes action meaningful, possible, and successful in the field. In such a perspective, the world of Hollywood seems paradigmatic of what stands at the strictly commercial pole of cultural production. This representation is, however, deceptive.

On the contrary, what the case study of Hollywood agents shows is a professional world in which the creative and the commercial are intimately embedded *without constituting conflicting dynamics* in the process by which careers and products are made. What we therefore observe goes way beyond the simple mention of cultural consequences attached to economic activities. It contrasts with analyses that deal separately with economic and artistic dimensions, or divide these activities as belonging to distinct social spheres. It also questions the approach pointing to (and often denouncing) the influence of economic constraints over "pure" artistic activities, commercial forces being then seen as operating from the outside of the artistic sphere itself and "polluting" it.

The "good taste" and the "sense of talent" that agents have acquired through professional socialization, accumulated and executed in evaluation communities, also operate at the intersection of the commercial and artistic dimensions of evaluation. Taste-forming and taste-making are two interconnected faces of a collective process. All decisions regarding what should get made and with whom are judgments that assess at once the creative and the commercial potential of a project and of the people attached to it. When professionals involved in pitch meetings evaluate a person or a piece of material in terms of "creativity"—which they do—what they name "creativity" is not only the anticipated capacity to be or do art (to write a script, run a show, play a part, direct a movie in the way the buyer wants it), it is *inseparably* the name of economic viability and desirability. It is the signal that there is business there, and the legitimate label for it. Conversely, the judgment that something is not "creatively promising," "fresh," "relatable," or "exciting" means "no deal." For the same reason, a perceived lack of quality is understood as an economic handicap in this professional world. This is why agents who represent actors with little artistic legitimacy or celebrities of the reality world, for instance, fight to label them as artists and real talent, and work at getting them recognition as such. This is also why the generalization of the idea that cable television offers "quality programming" and can compete with motion pictures in that regard enhances the social value of the media as a whole. Labeling activities in which agents and their counterparts in evaluation communities are involved almost always convey double-edged meanings of this sort. They express salability in the language of creativity and signify artistic worth with economic categories.

The social judgments and activities that construct the artistic as separate from the commercial come into play for the most part a posteriori in respect to the time of the conception and early assemblage of a project, which is the period during which agenting activities take place. They mostly correspond to the moment when critics, journalists, commentators of all sorts, and other professional authorities enter the fray and express competing opinions about a finished product: a film or a show that has come out. The processes and principles of artistic legitimization, the categories with which something is labeled and consecrated as "good art" (in a given society at a given time) *at this later stage*, are partly specific to this moment of social reception of a product and to its particular system of participants. Before this phase of public (dis)qualification of an artwork and of associated (de)legitimization of its official creators, the categories used to grasp what a project is and evaluate its contributors are significantly different. They refer to cognitive and practical arrangements that are *specific to Hollywood's occupational configurations*, which only marginally interfere with the frames of perception and action organizing other social spheres.

I don't mean to suggest that there aren't any circulations and exchanges between evaluation and valuation repertoires proper to Hollywood and those that operate in other social spheres. But outside judgments and activities become relevant for Hollywood professionals and affect their action only once converted into the order of priority, categories of understanding (ways of measuring quality and worth, especially), and divisions and hierarchies that are specific to Hollywood configurations. Even within the realm of entertainment activities, the practices and interventions of film critics or commentators that take place at a later stage of the entertainment-making process are meaningful to the agents and their counterparts only insofar as they relate to the workings and stakes of their particular evaluation community. This is why agents can state that agenting is "not about the outcome"; that is, about the completion and later fate of the artistic product.

SEVEN

Agents of Change: The Formation of New Evaluation Communities

This final chapter takes our exploration of evaluation communities one step further by questioning how such circles form and transform. The formation of new evaluation communities is indissociably linked to mechanisms of professional specialization and the emergence of new agenting roles, which, at a more general level, contributes to the diversification of activities in the very large organizations that populate Big Hollywood nowadays, described in the second chapter of this book. The rise in the late 1980s and the 1990s of the "indie film agent"—an expert in coordinating, from the very start of the filmmaking process, the necessary financial and creative elements that make up an independent film production—illustrates the dynamics by which new evaluation communities take shape and their participants imagine new markets (Roussel 2016). This chapter focuses on this paradigmatic case study in order to draw more general lessons from it. Another revealing case study—which is the focus of an ongoing research—would be the constitution of a "digital world" in terms that are relevant to Hollywood (and its business side especially): this happens, from the mid-2000s on, in the same process by which a specialized evaluation community progressively emerges, bringing together newly created "digital agents" and their counterparts (gradually identified as a limited circle of "digital buyers"), who relationally define "digital talent," "digital products and formats," "digital strategies," and so on.

In the late 1980s and early 1990s, the premises for the constitution of a new expertise in the agency world arose, which gradually consolidated during the 2000s: a few agents who represented the rare few foreign star directors or actors started focusing on foreign coproduction and distribution opportunities, developing alliances with European or Australian counterparts who had access to sources of film funding. Those who built such a new field of specialty regarding independent film packaging and financing talked during our interviews about their ability to foresee the emergence of a new market. Indeed, the practice that they invented went beyond the traditional work of foreign sales agents who usually only came into the mix at the distribution phase. This birth of the indie film agent that I will now retrace sheds light on how evaluation communities come into existence and how markets are constructed.

Until the late 1980s, the major Hollywood studios were the only companies that had the power and structure to produce and distribute content *directly* to audiences globally. Smaller production companies could find distribution domestically but had to go through foreign sales agents in order to find independent, local distributors around the world. This process was seen as uncertain, as well as somewhat precarious for the artists (who didn't know to what extent their working conditions and benefits would be preserved since they weren't going to be in the perimeter of the guilds that protect their rights domestically). In the agencies, traditional talent agents (and even those representing the few foreign star directors and actors) weren't any more familiar with foreign financial players, rules, and institutions, and were reluctant to dive into something seen as too adventurous, if not perilous. The "independent route" was thus considered a solution of last resort for projects that the studios wouldn't support or which were too small for them, at a time when most "talent representatives were seriously lacking in being able to navigate, or even explain, the independent environment to the client."[1]

At the turn of the 1990s, the development of cable and home video (centrally DVD at that time, but also VHS, and VOD [video on demand] later on) created new potential revenues, beyond box-office profits, domestically as well as internationally. Such socio-technical change was construed as a window of opportunity by the professionals of the ancillary exploitation of motion pictures, especially for the distribution of independent films produced in English language. However, the development of such distribution outlets does not mechanically explain the expansion of independent film packaging. What mattered was the *perception* of a new potential demand for such films; in other words, the progressive constitution of an *imagined market* for transactions that did not yet exist at this initial point, other than in a marginal and restricted way. This perception led a few pioneers—including a handful of agents—to "venture into the independent world"[2] and, through experimentation with a succession of film projects that turned out to be successful, to change their own anticipations into a self-fulfilling prophecy.

This process started with individual "entrepreneurs" acquiring distinctive skills, both in film finance and in film production, and penetrating into neglected geographic territories—mostly Europe (France, Germany, Ireland) and Australia, at first—at the same time as into new areas of practice in the agency business. What they did was more than just being present alongside clients at international film festivals and markets. They inflected their usual relationship work toward creating familiarity with the local players at such festivals. This included, for instance, identifying relevant foreign buyers, reading the cues with which to recognize trustworthy local financiers and funding institutions, enlisting local talent representatives, and making allies of sales agents or lawyers interested in this sort of deal. This particular relationship work also implied distinguishing oneself from the crowd of American agents who were just revolving around the artists they were servicing without mingling with local film professionals, in order to be recognized as a serious and knowledgeable counterpart. These agents had to adjust their style to the different professional cultures of their local partners (whose conventional ways of speaking, communicating, transacting differed from those usual in Hollywood). It also required developing a unique knowledge of the formal and informal rules organizing local film industries and ties with the foreign authorities in charge of supporting and regulating the production of movies (including governmental and professional bodies, local unions, etc.) These few pioneer "international agents" had the specific background allowing them to quickly grasp the ins and outs of these international transactions, and to find interest in them. The case of WMA agent John Ptak is especially revealing.[3] In August 2015, he shared with me a written account of his efforts to make the movie *Green Card* happen, at the turn of the 1990s. What he called his "tale of *Green Card*" both illustrates the process by which the strategies of a few maverick agents (who were operating inside the core agency system) gradually contributed to shaping a new field of specialty in agenting, and gives us clues for understanding the process by which a new evaluation community formed when these strategies met with the activities of other categories of film professional, on a transnational scale:

I represented Peter Weir, beginning with *Gallipoli* [1981], with *The Year of Living Danger-ously* [1982] and *Witness* [1985] soon to follow. His value was rising and he had many studio opportunities. One day he sent me a story that he had written. It took place in Southern California and was a love story between a young American woman and an English fellow who was trying to get his papers in order so that he could stay in the US and get a job. In Peter's words, it was meant to be a "charming soufflé." It was too small for the studio system. Being an Australian, Peter carried a certain financial value for that part of the production that could be defined as Australian. That value was his profile in the Australian market, coupled with the government incentives that existed to encourage domestic labor. However, I realized that the UK just didn't provide enough, creatively or financially. Peter then met Gérard Depardieu while Gérard was in Australia promoting one of his films. Peter thought that Gérard was perfect for the film. Gérard was certainly a star in France. I then explored the possibility of an Australia/France coproduction. I had always been a Francophile and Eastern Australia reminded me of my own Southern California, so I was comfortably at home! Gérard, however, wasn't immediately available and Disney had been discussing a project with Peter that he quite liked. *Green Card* was pushed and Peter made *Dead Poets Society* [1989] first. The tremendous success of that film, particularly in France, served to insure my coproduc-tion strategy for *Green Card*. We decided on New York as the proper location.

I encouraged Peter to write the screenplay and become the film's Australian producer. He then "owned" the film, particularly the Australian rights. We secured a French pro-ducer and hired an actual line producer, Ed Feldman, to manage the physical produc-tion itself. Peter had worked with Feldman on *Witness* and they had become friends. On behalf of the production I made all of the personal service deals with the various parties, utilizing the participation of their attorneys so as to avoid the appearance of any conflict. I personally approached the government bodies in France (the CNC) and Australia (the AFFC) to begin the process of a formal France/Australia coproduction. I secured approxi-mately $3.5 million for a buyout of all French rights, as well as approximately $3.0 million for the various Australian rights. The benefits from those two countries alone resulted in my bringing 50 percent of the financing to the $13 million production. Once these were locked down, I went to Disney's head of production, Jeff Katzenberg, to make a distribu-tion arrangement for Disney to handle the release of the film in all media for the rest of the world. By this time, because of the success of *Witness* and *Dead Poets*, Peter and Jeff liked and trusted each other, so it was the only call that I made. [. . .]

Weir and Feldman then set about choosing the production personnel. The film was physically financed by taking the Australian, French, and Disney distribution contracts to a Dutch bank, Pierson, Heldring & Pierson, and borrowing the production cost by using the financial guarantees payable upon delivery of the completed film as the collateral to pay off the loan. Peter had total control over the choice of his crew. The film was delivered in completed form to Disney on what is called a "negative pickup" basis, meaning that the administrative control over the film remained in Peter's hands until such delivery. He continued to have strong rights with regards to the subsequent marketing campaigns. Part of the deal with Disney allowed us to use their marketing materials in France and Australia, so as to maintain continuity in the marketplace.

The result was a $13 million production that garnered over $100 million at the box office around the world and has generated profits every year to this very day. It enabled Gérard to subsequently create a career in English-language films, which, in turn, enhanced the export value of his French-language films. It was the first Australian full-nationality coproduction that returned profits to the AFFC [Australian Film Finance Corporation], after more than eighty previous film investments. [. . .] In addition to commissioning Peter Weir for his multiple services as producer, director, and writer, plus commissioning Gérard and Feldman, I also received a small consultancy fee and profit participation for the William Morris Agency for my additional services in representing the film itself as well and received a very nice sole-card "Special Appreciation" credit on the film. I was offered an executive producer credit, but felt that that would be inappropriate. This was the first time that an agent had taken on the responsibility of guiding such an independent film. Such chores are generally considered to be for the producer or executive producer to handle, but I took it upon myself to provide the services as a result of my talent representation, as well as my curiosity to learn and further enhance my value as a talent agent. [. . .]

I was also able to create an agency fee structure for the service, beginning with a guarantee equal to 1 percent of the bonded budget of the picture, plus 2.5 percent of the profits. That structure was soon adopted by the other agencies and is still in place today. I was quickly able to sign a number of other foreign national filmmakers and represent other independent productions, particularly from Australia and France. As a talent agent, I was alone in being able to say that independent production could be an initial option and not a court of last resort for major talent.

Agenting activities of this type converged with the strategies of other types of participants in the filmmaking process: because agents discerned this alignment of perceptions, they were inclined to increasingly invest in the orchestration of international independent coproductions, reinforcing, in return, this circle of mutual adjustments. As these activities developed, relationships between mutually constituted groups of "sellers" and "buyers" of indie projects got routinized; reliable foreign territories and local counterparts became well known; Hollywood agents in these circles built more homogeneous client lists by refocusing their attention on top foreign talent. The subsequent formation of groups of cognitively and tactically interdependent players delineated the contours of *new, transnational evaluation communities*:

Local distributors around the world were willing to provide pre-negotiated financial guarantees, payable upon the film's delivery, for the right to secure territorial, regional, and media distribution rights to independent content for their territory. Independent foreign sales companies were created in order to represent the films in this global market, service the delivery elements, and track the subsequent exploitation of the film through theatrical, television, cable, and home video use. Major banks created film departments ready to provide loans to the production companies, using such guarantees as collateral. [. . .] The independent film option blossomed, driven largely by financially secure production companies that had the connections and experience to put the creative and financial elements together and manage the film through to delivery and use. (Former independent film agent, big agency, February 2015)

This new manner of agenting initially seemed like a risky "coup": its initiators engaged in a marginal dimension of the agenting practice. They mostly faced skepticism and defiance on the part of their colleagues who occupied more traditional positions, who considered only the projects that studios backed up as "real," and who tended to discourage their clients from getting involved in what they saw as uncertain independent/international endeavors. However, the success of a handful of movies (*Green Card* [1990], *Dances with Wolves* [1990], *Shattered* [1991], *Until the End of the World* [1991], etc.) quickly shifted perceptions in the agency world. As a result, in a business in which being one step forward from competitors is key, "international agents" were rapidly taken seriously, increasingly so as their new role got progressively institutionalized at the biggest agencies.

[I] signed a lot of people, put a lot of movies together. And then, after a point in time, I ended up representing some movies where we didn't represent the client at all. [. . .] Then, because of that becoming important, what was really funny was that, you know, agents aren't stupid, their basic antenna is always looking around to whatever they should know and do, or that guy is going to be ahead of them, you know, it's like this. So I would say, within six months to a year, all the agencies hired somebody who was their international person. (Former talent and independent film agent, big agency, September 2013)

This transformation of anticipations in the industry derived from the observation of repeated success with international coproductions, which functioned like successive *experimentations*: while most industry professionals were initially not on home ground with such packaging activities (not expecting great success with them, but also not knowing in practical terms how to accomplish them), they progressively came to make out the contours of a new domain of practice in agenting. The managers and leaders of the big agencies played a key role in the constitution in this new area of specialty by stabilizing specific positions, and soon after by organizing entire departments around international packaging and financing activities. In 1991, CAA hired WMA's pioneer John Ptak to build such a practice and create a team of specialists at the top agency, and the competitors followed. Interdependence between the major agencies was such that none of them could afford not to offer the services of "an agent or consultant that could speak to their clients about the values of independent production," in what had become dominantly seen as "a quickly growing business."[4]

Over the course of a few years, entire divisions dedicated to assembling independent movies grew within the large and midsize agencies.[5] Today's "Global Finance and Distribution Group" at WME or UTA's "Independent Film Group" illustrate it. In addition, independent "indie film" consultants and financial advisors multiplied, contributing to the formation of a whole professional sector. Among the first generation of international packaging specialists, many converted themselves to agenting from the world of film finance. With time, a new generation of agents, which is now at work, rose from the ranks of agency assistants and mailroom trainees, embracing this field of specialty from the start of a career. Unlike their predecessors who had to forge in practice, in collective transactions, by trial and error, the very definition of their specific competences and distinctive identities, younger generations find them ready to use and adopt. Even if an agent may want to engage in the exploration of new national territories (such as China, typically today), the essential know-how relative to international financing and packaging has already stabilized. Correlatively, a relabeling process has taken place: this agenting role, which was initially defined mostly as *international* arrangements and deal-making (with foreign financiers and distributors) has been progressively reframed in reference to the manufacture of *independent* films, as this new subfield of agenting was getting organized. The "indie film agent" has supplanted the "international agent" in that sense.

As previously noted, the "independent film" dynamics that I just retraced began at the end of the 1980s, and it developed during the 1990s, in a time of prosperity when the studios were spending a lot of money on hiring stars (granting them both generous salaries and percentages on the back end). It was thus not initially a mechanism counterbalancing the lack of studio options for agency clients. However, the conditions for this new area of specialty to stabilize were given and reinforced by the studios' strategy to almost completely withdraw from the production segment of "big independent" films during the 2000s. From the mid-2000s on especially, studios increasingly focused on making film franchises and sequels of previous box-office successes, and in general developed fewer projects. New "solutions" had therefore to be found to respond to the decrease in job offers, and to the desire of commercially successful artists to do more "arty" movies. This agent in charge of financing and packaging independent movies at a midsize agency described his changing relationships with studio divisions:

We can be with the independent divisions of the studio, we can be with Focus of Universal, we can be with Searchlight of Fox, or [the] Weinstein [Company], or Lionsgate, or whatever. But Disney is not generally buying a lot of independent films. Warner Brothers is not buying a lot of independent films. Right? The companies that have such massive overheads, you know, if they buy a four-million-dollar movie that goes off and makes ten million dollars in profit, it so doesn't even matter. The bottom line is they don't even want to waste their time. [. . .] They produce less. But it has changed, right? The studios in the '70s and '80s and '90s, it has all changed. It's like now all the studios are owned by conglomerates. It is all about the stock price. So, they have to do things that move the stock. Financing a new movie doesn't necessarily move the stock. (April 2013)

With the interdependent transformation of agency structure and studio policy, the *symbolic turnaround* changing what was initially seen as an option of last resort into the new normal avenue for one-off movies that do not fit the new studio formats is complete. This evolution fortifies an approach to independent films as international assemblages in terms of financing, production, and distribution; and agents as packagers become increasingly central for the orchestration of this type of project. That a group of specialized agents from big agencies holds such a decisive coordination role directly affects, in fact, not just how (big) independent films are made, but what they are and how they circulate. The same process that has shaped a new evaluation community has also redefined the corresponding film genre and artistic categories. What an "independent film" is and how one can get made have been partly reinvented, way beyond—and even at a distance from—the reference to aesthetically "vanguard" projects and/or those made for no money. These changes have consequently opened wider the paths for the international circulation of talent, especially actors and directors; and in general they have crystalized new options for artistic choices and careers.

Correlatively, the relative importance inside a big agency of the agents who specialize in putting together such arrangements—and especially the relationships that indie film agents have with talent agents who handle artists who have somewhat of a name and aspire to be the leading force (or a part) of an independent production—also changes. This talent agent at a big agency explained during our interview that agents in her position can no longer afford not to team up with colleagues in the independent financing departments who have now gained a central role in orchestrating "Hollywood indies." The professional standing and importance of the talent agent become increasingly dependent on cooperations with "indie film agents":

The independent financing group at any agency is super important when you're talking about putting movies together. That's what they do, because they're in the business of putting those packages together and selling them as a package. So yes, the collaboration is really significant between the independent group and talent agents for sure. [. . .] The more interesting version of [agenting], from a talent agent perspective, is if a client has an idea and they come to you and say, "I want to get this off the ground." And then *you* go to the independent financing department *here* at [big agency's name] and say: "Client X wants to star in this movie, can we get it financed?" And then *those* people will go out to different financiers, and all of them will check the value of a given actor, and hopefully somebody says, "Yes, I'd like to finance that film." And then a casting process starts there. The client is a producer, and then you sort of supervise it. (November 2014, her emphasis)

In contrast with talent agents who represent individual clients, these specialists of independent financing/packaging are therefore in a position to claim a distinctive legitimacy, based on the specialized competence that enables them to represent *a whole movie*, and not just the artists involved with it.[6] Like John Ptak in the *Green Card* story recounted above, these agents often point to the specific structure of their remuneration—unlike their colleagues in other areas of agenting, they receive a consultancy fee—to underline the exceptional nature of their service. Their specific role relies on the valorization of a "unique skill" when it comes to "blending art and commerce,"[7] and on the exhibition of familiarity with and recognition from the world of film finance (and its bankers and investors). Several of these specialized agents have indeed worked in finance before joining an agency. The agency that hires someone with such a background is looking for both a level of technical expertise and a set of preexisting relationships with potential film funding sources, all the while expecting the new agent to approach movies as an "investment" like any other.[8] However, for the most part, the financial dimension of the practice is not what takes prevalence in these agents' self-definition. As their job consists of assembling various eclectic pieces that make up an independent production, "indie film agents" can pride themselves with both expert knowledge and creative autonomy. As a matter of fact, they coordinate the participation of diverse players—from financiers, producers, and distributors in various countries to creative personnel and their representatives (agents, unions, managers, etc.)—in a complex project. They draw symbolic power from this position that places them "above the crowd."[9] Because they have the responsibility of putting together entire movies, these agents promote their area of specialty by stating that they accomplish "more than ordinary packaging." Their overarching position is what protects them from the fragmentation that usually confines agents to the preproduction phase, with little control over the filmmaking process as a whole; by contrast, it places these specialists closer to the position of a director or a producer: "It's not packaging, because packaging in my mind is just bringing on the director and an actor into it. If you're also organizing all of the financing, you're structuring, you're setting up the distribution; it's much more than packaging. It's executive producing without the executive producing title" (independent film agent, big agency, December 2013).

The value of working on international independent coproductions and the very meaning of "independence" for these agents have precisely to do with this self-attributed "producerial" power that associates them with creative personnel, and therefore detaches them from the image of the pure salesman or the technician in finance. This observation goes beyond the case of indie film specialists. It manifests what makes up worth in Hollywood: unearthing and bringing to the table one or several of the key elements that determine the existence of an artwork. This ties the agents to content creation through its economic as well as its artistic determinations, and in many ways beyond this distinction: "The producing that we do as agents, whether it is finding the money, or finding the other artists, or finding the script, or developing the script, or whatever it is: the not-just-making-the-deal-and-putting-them-in stuff, the other stuff, is rewarding and creates dimension to your service, and also separates the smarts from the clinicians" (talent agent, big agency, April 2013).

In the end, the professional role of indie film agents is now well established; the largest agencies and their specialized divisions are centrally positioned when it comes to putting together independent productions of midlevel or higher budget, relative to this type of film. Even though in the realm of motion pictures at the big agencies, studio productions remain the priority and packaging for studios the main focus, being at the top of the international indie game is important—not so much for strictly economic reasons, since other sectors generate more revenue for the agencies, but because this category of projects is what sustains the loyalty of key clients. Not only does this illustrate how artistic classifications operate in Hollywood, it also exemplifies how segmented markets are practically and symbolically constructed: it shows how a handful of Hollywood professionals who felt like they were "alone in pursuing such a market"[10] really *defined* it by forming, with foreign counterparts who were equally inclined to internationalization strategies, a new space for exchanges. These repeated relationships gradually formed *a new type of evaluation community* (including a small number of Hollywood agents, particular artists, specific international and domestic distributors, identified independent producers, trusted equity and financing partners, international sales entities, etc.). But this imagined market for indies only came to full existence—that is, to producing social effects as a framework for coordination identified by certain players, associated with certain lines of action, partnerships, instruments, and so on—when the wider perception shift that I described in this section led dominant players to share the interpretation that a promising business had emerged and to institutionalize the roles that this market required.

By building relationships with international partners in production and distribution according to their perception of a shrinking domestic market, indie film agents and their counterparts also participated in feeding a self-reinforcing process. Independent film teams gained more importance in the agency business as the international versus domestic box-office revenue numbers got more visibility. The inversion of proportions between foreign and North American film revenues (respectively 70 and 30 percent,[11] when it used to be the contrary) has become a basis for anticipation and strategy in the industry, partly rearranging internal professional hierarchies. As international numbers and projected foreign sales are considered increasingly important, the unique skill of those who have firsthand knowledge of international markets gains value. For experts in international packaging, it means moving the boundaries of relevant "territories" in line with what they foresee to be viable future markets (from Canada, Australia, Western Europe to China, India, Russia), therefore contributing to the construction of such anticipated markets and to the collective reshaping of "global Hollywood." This extension of the confines of Hollywood does not translate into a relocation of agenting activities, or only very marginally.[12] The physical core of Hollywood's evaluation communities, even in this domain, remains Los Angeles, and even Beverly Hills and Century City, where the major agencies have settled.

The case study of indie film agents illustrates more than the changes at play in this particular segment of the industry. It is paradigmatic of how show business at large changes, and is currently transforming in significant ways. It shows *how the extension of the domain of Hollywood* that I pointed to in the second chapter of this book *concretely takes place*, through successive transformations that existing professional configurations structure and frame, rather than in impenetrable and erratic ways. The emergence of "digital media agents" in the mid-2000s is another salient manifestation of such processes, although it is only one among many others. The constitution of a new evaluation community whose activities gradually defined "what the Internet meant for entertainment,"[13] including in terms of imagined market, went hand in hand with the institutionalization of this field of specialty in the agencies, as the opening of the first agency's digital division with UTAOnline in 2006 and the creation of the new position of global distribution strategist in the same agency in 2014 illustrate.

The dynamics that rearrange Hollywood professional configurations is always two-faced: one is the constitution of new evaluation communities, shaped by those who practice the day-to-day activity of agenting and by their counterparts, and the other consists in the institutionalization of these new systems of professional relations through organizational transformation (of the agencies, in particular). Both dimensions are closely interdependent. The strategies of organizational and financial growth that the top managers of the major agencies have recently been pursuing, because they induce rearrangements in existing evaluation communities, contribute decisively to such transformations. In particular, the recent development of WME's activity in the world of sports in the wake of its spectacular merger with the giant of athletes' representation IMG in 2013, followed by financial operations and the acquisition of companies specializing in the organization of live sport events (including the $4 billion acquisition of mixed martial arts organization Ultimate Fighting Championship, UFC, in July of 2016), does not only mean business diversification. The new model of company attached to this acquisition strategy changes the face of the agency not just by de-centering it from the core film and television business,[14] but also by adding a content creation and distribution component to its talent representation activity (and its other preexisting activities).[15] It comes, for WME agents, with the injunction of inventing ways to connect their existing business in the traditional sectors of Hollywood with the new domains that the growth of the agency as an organization adds to their realm of activity. This redefined perimeter of agenting and show business not only results from a top-down process guided by financial strategies, but depends for its very existence and its stabilization on the formation of new evaluation communities, experienced by those who perform agenting on a daily basis.

It is also why such transformation processes stem both from participants' strategic behaviors and from unintentional mechanisms. As powerful as a Hollywood mogul or the CEO of a giant agency might be, no one is ever powerful enough to control the general transformation mechanism here at work. It is carried out collectively and interdependently by Hollywood players at all levels, from those who prescribe models to those who craft the daily manifestations of these transformations.[16] A senior agent at one of the biggest companies made a revealing comment regarding the strategies of growth by mergers and acquisitions that he was seeing take place up close at his company, addressing the question of knowing whether or not the agency leaders had a precise vision of the future that their initiatives contributed to bringing into existence:

I don't think so. I think that they have a precise vision as far as the company they're targeting. [. . .] So you start to focus on that thing, and you start to craft a reality around that notion, and then you start to build a business plan around that transaction, and then you kind of feel your way through it. The precision is more about taking our Hollywood business and plugging it into the world, taking the world of sports and broadcast and life entertainment business and plastering it back into Hollywood, and scrambling the eggs! (Talent agent, big agency, January 2014)

In the end, if all participants, from top players to ordinary Little Hollywood agents, face a time of drastic change in Hollywood, this transformation of what entertainment means and of the relative value of people and projects derives from specialization processes forming and reshaping evaluation communities—that is, from the simultaneous evolution of relational (and cross-organizational) systems, as well as, at the same time, from processes of organizational growth and concentration that have given rise to an oligopoly of giant players, of which the evolution of WME as an organization is typical. These transformations change what agents are and do; they blur the boundary between production and talent brokerage, increasingly placing agencies into the content creation and distribution business, therefore affecting the balance of power between studios and big agencies. They also, inseparably, redefine what talent is, who the artists who are seen as worthy of representation are, what their career paths are expected to be, what the "good formats" and "promising genres" that agents are likely to look for are. It affects how to price people and projects, or target the right Hollywood buyers—in sum, how audiences and markets are envisioned; that is, constructed by the participants.

Although they don't control these changes at a global level, agents hold a pivotal role in their development because they are both central to the organizational restructuring in play and to the functioning of evaluation communities. They are in a position to be catalysts of transformations that also redefine their own activity.[17] In that, today's agenting goes way beyond just selling talent in the traditional sense of the term. In the age of multimedia conglomerates, Big Hollywood agents are at the heart of the transformation of entertainment.

Conclusive Word

The ambition of this book has been to understand how the inconspicuous activity of Hollywood agents impacts the making of cultural products and artistic careers. It sheds light on the complex dynamics of professional configurations that fundamentally shape the cultural production process at the distinct but combined levels of Little and Big Hollywood. While the empirical investigation unveils the importance of the relationship work learned and performed by the agents, the concept of the evaluation community is what allows us to grasp how agents and their counterparts affect the shaping of reputations and career paths in Hollywood, the making of professional powers and power balance behind the scenes, and the collective definition of entertainment projects and products. Through their inclusion into a particular evaluation community, not only do agents affect what and who is made in Hollywood insofar as movies, television shows, and the associated artists and stars are concerned, but they also play a significant role in the emergence of new categories of "talent" and new formats of projects which discreetly reinvent what "creative content" means, as we currently see it happening for instance in the area of digital media.

In cultural industries, the relationship work that participants, including agents, perform, when successful, operates as "magic work." The stable workings of evaluation communities *create* worth; they generate belief in value and quality on the part of Hollywood participants. These combined activities also contribute to the production of belief in art and artists in our society at large. In other words, they participate in shaping what we—who are external to this occupational sphere—perceive as the "Hollywood magic." By showing that the creative process does not happen "as if by magic" or just by virtue of the inexplicable gift of a few individuals, but derives from structurally determined forms of labor, this book pays tribute to the activity of the invisible makers of popular culture who decisively affect the fate of artists and entertainment products, not simply *while* remaining hidden but *because* they remain so. The puppeteers' invisibility makes up the magic of the show.

However, what is at stake with the study of agenting is more than just bringing out of the shadows formerly invisible participants in the manufacture of popular culture. There are lessons to learn from this case study for understanding other types of activity and social worlds, and first of all other art and entertainment industries. It is the case because certain modes of action and organization proper to Hollywood have circulated and been appropriated in other parts of the world, partly as a result of Hollywood's expansionist strategies. Agencies' globalization strategies (when they open offices in new territories, for instance) contribute to transferring professional models and roles. At the same time, the inner dynamics of the European cultural industries has also led to the emergence and development of middlemen within increasingly professionalized and institutionalized systems. The case of Hollywood agents can therefore be illuminating by comparison and sometimes by contrast.

Beyond the sole creative worlds, studying "talent agenting" also has an important analytic impact because it sheds light on the crucial role of *intermediation and brokerage* in highly specialized, differentiated societies. With the increased division of labor characterizing our society, "intermediaries," "auxiliaries," "middlemen," "brokers"—all are invisible actors whose activity oils the system in a decisive way. They are the cement of their professional world, as go-betweens or connectors (in networks) and long-lasting players, who do the job of *translating* the vocabularies and stakes of certain occupational groups into the language of others, making the participants seemingly speak with one voice. On the other hand, occupations that derive from a mandate to speak and act in someone else's name and interest, to *represent* others, are also comparable to the profession of talent agent in this respect, and similarly raise the question of the interplay of positional power and relational power. For instance, the specialized skills and legitimacy of the lawyer or those of the political representative have to do—much like in the agent-artist relationship—with the management of a "relation of representation" that oscillates between the dependence of the representative toward the source of his or her delegated authority and the representative's objective power over the represented by virtue of his or her inclusion into a specialized game.

Finally, at a more structural level, what this book unveils of Hollywood may be useful for exploring power and action in other social worlds that are also experienced by the participants as relationship driven all the while being highly institutionalized and organizationally structured spaces. In that regard, lines of comparison could be drawn, despite obvious differences, with the worlds of finance or politics, for instance. In such worlds, in which the state of informal relations within stable professional circles plays a decisive role and affects what becomes of institutions, it would be worth exploring what specific forms of relationship work are performed by the participants, what types of occupational community they delineate, and how this relates to the perception of trust (or lack thereof) and the building of reputations and professional powers.

Acknowledgments

I am immensely grateful to all the agents and industry professionals who have agreed to participate in this study, taking time out of busy schedules to share irreplaceable insights with me, sometimes over the course of long and repeated conversations. This book wouldn't exist without them. Beyond this, I wish to pay special tribute, for their particularly critical support at one or more points in this adventure, to Jeff Berg, Bob Bookman, Chris Day, John Ptak, Glenn Rigberg, Tom Rothman, Nick Stevens, Maureen Toth, and Harry Ufland.

My most sincere thanks also go to the colleagues who have helped me at various stages of this work, especially to Ann Crigler, Michael Curtin, and Michael Renov. I am indebted to the scholars and staff of my research center (LabToP-CRESPPA) and department at the University of Paris 8, as well as to Emmanuelle Zagoria for her invaluable assistance throughout this project.

This study received financial support from the European Commission in the form of a Marie Curie International Outgoing Fellowship for Career Development (7th Framework Programme, Project FP7-PEOPLE-2012-IOF).

Notes

1. All quotes in this section are from Bob Bookman, who was an agent at Paradigm when I interviewed him in Los Angeles in 2014. He left this agency to become a manager/producer in March 2017.
2. See below, chapter 6.
3. *The Silence of the Lambs* was an author-written sequel—that is, a sequel to a book—"as opposed to studio sequels, which give a studio the right to make their own sequel and make a passive payment to the author," Bookman explains. The "author-written sequel" right reserved by the author (Thomas Harris) in this case allowed him to make a movie based on the second novel of the Hannibal Lecter series. But Harris's right was limited in drastic ways when combined with the "first negotiation/last refusal" right included in the *Manhunter* initial production deal, as I will later show.
4. Tensions between the client's interest and the agency's are possible, as I will later explain.
5. Foster and Hopkins were respectively represented by Joe Funicello at ICM and Rick Nicita, Bob Bookman's colleague at CAA.
6. This provision was indeed included in the initial Warner Bros. contract that De Laurentiis inherited. It compromised the interest that another studio might have of turning the second novel into a film, and was in fact intended to produce such an effect.
7. *Hannibal* (2001) was adapted from the novel of the same name, directed by Ridley Scott (who also coproduced it with Dino and Martha De Laurentiis), and distributed by Universal/MGM. It stars Anthony Hopkins and Julianne Moore. Made for a budget of $87 million, it commanded

$351,692,268 at the box office (domestic and foreign combined). One year later, another sequel was adapted from the first book of the series, *Red Dragon*. Also produced by Dino and Martha De Laurentiis and distributed by Universal and MGM, it was directed by Brett Ratner, with a screenplay by Ted Tally, again starring Anthony Hopkins. Its budget was $78 million, and the total gross was $209,196,298 (source: Box Office Mojo). In 2013, the *Hannibal* TV series was released on NBC.

8. On network repair, see Jones and Foster 2015.

CHAPTER ONE

1. According to the Hollywood Representation Directory (2012, last published edition), there are about six hundred licensed agencies. The Association of Talent Agents (ATA) organizes the majority of agencies in activity (at least one hundred in LA, not including ATA's sister organization in NYC). But all agencies do not belong to ATA. Some agencies are directly franchised by artists' unions, which also deliver partial lists of companies.

2. ATA used to have an agreement with SAG, including rules governing payment for agency services to their clients. Although this union agreement hasn't been renewed since it expired in 2002, these rules have remained stable, the interdependence system between the various players in Hollywood guaranteeing their permanence better than any legal agreement could have.

3. *Fortune*, "Put Their Names in Lights," September 1938, 67–73. Cited in Kemper 2015, 100.

4. It refers to partly different financial arrangements in film and television: unlike in television, agencies do not receive a separate fee for the activity of film packaging itself (they are remunerated from their individual clients' contracts). However, film packaging has developed from the 1980s on and is now a central dimension of agenting in Big Hollywood.

5. Regarding scholarly studies on celebrity and stardom, see, for instance, Gamson 1994, Ravid and Currid-Halkett 2013; on the economic dimensions of celebrity, Rosen 1981, De Vany 2004.

6. John Thompson (2010) has examined the role of agents in the radical changes altering the publishing world in a digital age (esp. pp. 59–100). Showing how publishing practices are (re)shaped by a field that has a specific structure and dynamics, his approach is not devoid of similarities with ours. This is also true of Hortense Powdermaker's pioneer approach to moviemakers ([1950] 2013), even though agents appear only marginally in her study.

7. A few books by journalists provide useful data about agents either at a very specific and early stage of their career (Rensin 2003) or at particular agencies (Rose 1995; Singular 1996, Miller 2016). Some professional handbooks and practitioner-oriented publications also feature former or senior agents delivering advice and "tricks of the trade" to beginners or simply to people

looking for a way to become part of the "Hollywood dream" (Hurtes 2000, Martinez 2012).

8. Some of these centers also have ascendance in terms of potential consumer market, like China; or have symbolic value, like France (Schwartz 2007).

9. Publicists and unions are also part of this grouping, but this is less important to this discussion because they interact more marginally with agents.

10. Agents in other national industries have received more attention; for the French industry, for instance, see Lizé, Naudier, and Roueff 2011.

11. For critical discussions of the notion of cultural intermediaries, see Hesmondhalgh 2006; Roussel 2014.

12. So do popular books—for instance, Longstreet's novel about a talent agency, *The Flesh Peddlers* (1962), or more recently, Matthew Specktor's *American Dream Machine* (2013).

13. In *Swimming with Sharks* (1994), the studio world is the place where the moral norms that are supposed to prevail elsewhere in society are suspended, leading a naïve writer-assistant to learn that he has to lose his own scruples—all the way to murder—in order to earn success in Hollywood. In *The Player* (1992), a studio executive also murders an aspiring screenwriter he believes was sending him death threats.

14. From Lew Wasserman at MCA (McDougal 1998, Bruck 2004) to Michael Ovitz at CAA (Singular 1996, Slater 1997), Jeff Berg at ICM, and today Ari Emanuel at WME. On the studio or the management side, the names Jeffrey Katzenberg at Disney or David Geffen also come to mind.

15. Even if the whole point of a movie might be to tell the extraordinary story of an agent's epiphany (like Tom Cruise in *Jerry Maguire* [1996]).

16. "It's rough and it's empty in a lot of ways. So people, I think, have an indication about that—there are jokes about lawyers and agents and things like that. [. . .] That's the nature of flashiness, the nature of *Broadway Danny Rose*'s kind of things, or agents like Martin Short, or the way agents are being depicted in cinema" (talent agent, big agency, October 2010). NB: In *The Big Picture* (1989), Martin Short plays Neil Sussman, an eccentric Hollywood agent who appears as shallow, falsely caring, and in fact manipulative, and overall a rather ridiculous character.

17. Owner, below-the-line boutique agency, October 2010.

18. For hypotheses regarding comparable professional configurations and fields of practice, see the conclusion of this book.

19. I adapt it from Faulkner 1983. See below, in chapter 2, under "Agenting in Big versus Little Hollywood."

CHAPTER TWO

1. Although Hollywood can be conceptualized as a social field, in Pierre Bourdieu's terms, what I mean to insist on here are the occupational dynamics that structure interactions and interdependences in this world.

2. Statistics published by the Motion Picture Association of America (2013, 22), show that in 2004, 489 movies were released in theaters in the US and Canada, including 179 films produced by the major studios and their subsidiaries (36.6 percent), whereas in 2013, 114 of the 659 releases were studio movies (17.2 percent). The increase in global production combines with a decrease in the proportion of big studio movies. The same source provides data by production cost, for full-length feature films which began production in 2011, produced by a US production company in English language: out of a total of 818 produced films, 100 are studio movies, 399 are nonstudio films with a budget over $1 million (but only 14 percent of which have a budget over $15 million), and 319 have a budget below $1 million. This does not include student films, documentaries, and films created for video release.

3. "Roughly half of the global box-office revenues for 2013 stem from the year's top 50 films. Of the 622 movies released in 2013, fewer than 160 had production budgets exceeding $1 million and fewer than 100 had budgets exceeding $15 million. In short, relatively few 2013 films accounted for the majority of 2013 box-office revenues. [. . .] Of the 108 [studied] movies released by the Majors and Mini-Majors, reported production budgets ranged from $1.25 million to $225 million. The average production budget in the sample was $71 million" (FilmL.A. Research, 2014, 6).

4. A former Little Hollywood agent interviewed in 2012 shared with us the following data he used in the course he was teaching, which was aimed at helping actors find a job: "There are approximately five hundred new and unique roles released every day in Los Angeles for television, film, theater, commercials, industrials, and print work, including public submission sources like Actors Access (Breakdown Services), Casting Billboard (LA Casting), Now Casting, and Backstage. Across all fields, there is an average of forty auditions per role per day (more per commercial role, less for theatricals). That's twenty thousand auditions per day. There are approximately four hundred agencies in Los Angeles, representing nearly 120,000 actors. There are approximately 80,000 unrepresented actors in LA as well. That makes 200,000 actors in the Los Angeles area. Statistically, if all things were equal and everyone was on a level playing field, an actor should have a 10 percent chance of getting an audition every day, and .025 percent of booking a job every day. Using these statistics, the average actor should expect thirty-six auditions and one booking per year. But we know it's not like that, since there are more roles for certain categories, and skill and looks, and the quality of an agent are instrumental in obtaining auditions and getting booked for a job."

5. Breakdown Services is an online company that publishes precise casting information to talent agencies, allowing agents to submit the résumé, photos, and videos of the actors they represent to registered casting directors. See below, chapter 5.

6. In between these two contrasted levels—full packaging or purely casting—an intermediate position characterizes midlevel agents at top agencies (and sometimes top agents at the main midsize agencies), whose clients have enough success in the eyes of the producers/studios to be approached before the casting process formally starts without being "bankable" enough to justify an investment based on their sole name.

7. Respectively current or former CEO/director/president of WME, CAA, UTA, and ICM.

8. This is so even though Paradigm Talent Agency expanded into the music business, totaling over 150 agents in early 2015. At the same time, the Gersh Agency counted about sixty agents and twice as many employees.

9. Big Hollywood, April 2013.

10. During interviews, studio heads and executives mentioned several cases of box-office failure in which the "green-lighting person" was fired for being perceived as responsible for losing a lot of the company's money. The risk of losing a relationship with key talent on the basis of one single misfortune is considered even more real by a studio chairman interviewed in January 2014: "Failure is horrible. It's horrible. I hate it. [. . .] If you're running a studio, you just have to have many more successes than failures. [. . .] But in individual relationships, basically no failure is acceptable. If you fail with a big piece of talent, they're going to blame you and you're going to be out of luck with them, mostly."

11. First-look deals are offered by studios that pay the overhead of certain companies (in order to keep a preferential relationship with star actors, directors, and/or producers) in return for a first option on financing and distributing a pitched property. Indeed, successful actors often set up production companies with the goal of carving for themselves a stronger position of partnership with studios for the making of films that they are creatively interested in. Sometimes, a studio signs a "vanity deal," providing the star's company with offices and money in exchange for a closer relationship with the actor and a "first look" at the scripts that the star wants to make into films. These companies are not so much production entities in the traditional sense of the term as they are the provider of star-controlled material, for projects that the star is willing to act in and sometimes direct, as well as coproduce. In this way, star artists create an organizational vehicle for their aspiration of making more arty, indie-style movies.

12. For instance, among the movies released in 2013, *Iron Man 3* was made for $200 million (Disney), *The Hobbit: The Desolation of Smaug* for $217 million (Warner Bros.), and *World War Z* for $190 million (Paramount).

13. All 12,000 screenwriters and television writers in the Writers Guild of America, East (WGAE), and the Writers Guild of America, West (WGAW), were part of the strike, which started in November 2007 and concluded in February 2008, lasting for one hundred days. The writers sought increased funding in comparison to the profits of the larger studios; at the resolution

of the strike, they were granted a new percentage payment on the distributor's gross for digital distribution.

14. The strike was quickly presented in the trade press as a consequential confrontation destined to last and threatening the whole television season 2008/09. Leaks from various types of industry players and plethoric online comments from insiders put top reporters in a position to arbiter the conflict as well as to play a key role in defining the prevailing frame for players on both sides. This led to the shared perception that the events marked a turning point for studio production, associated with the idea that film production should preferably be based on internally owned material and that, in television, reality programming was a viable and cheaper option compared to the more uncertain production of scripted shows.

15. Studios narrow their interest to stars who are popular with foreign audiences and to film genres that are known to sell abroad, such as comedy.

16. This is of course not to suggest that the targeted producers and studios, members of the Alliance of Motion Picture and Television Producers (AMPTP), did not privately confer (among themselves and with other powerful industry players, such as the big agency managers) on how to handle the situation.

17. Distance from this type of profile is probably one of the reasons why Amy Pascal stepped down in February 2015 from her longtime position as the head of Sony Pictures, even though several movies produced during her recent tenure at Sony were just nominated for an award, leading some industry insiders to prognosticate that she wouldn't be forced out despite the crisis that had surrounded a hacking attack against the film *The Interview* in November–December 2014.

18. Even if corporate interest in the studios isn't a new phenomenon, recent changes have given them their current form of components of larger media conglomerates: after the purchase of 20th Century Fox by Rupert Murdoch in 1985, Paramount, Warner, Columbia, and Universal all changed ownership between 1989 and 1994 in a series of purchases and mergers. Only Universal changed corporate hands thereafter (acquired by Vivendi in 2000, and Comcast in 2011).

19. "It does not mean you cannot be an advocate and make a living as an agent but your clients won't be a Tom Cruise or a Jack Black. These guys were the last of the pinnacle. Who are they now? Name a female movie star. [Silence] That's exactly the problem, isn't it?! Name one comedy actor with a franchise going. [. . .] The movie star is no longer the golden ticket. The TV show that goes into reruns is no longer the golden ticket" (talent agent, big agency, March 2010).

20. As of this writing, film buyers are down to six major studios (Sony/Columbia, Disney, 20th Century Fox, Paramount, Universal, and Warner Bros.) and a handful of mini majors. Meanwhile, television buyers are simultaneously multiplying: in addition to the four major US television networks

(ABC, CBS, and NBC, and Fox) and their affiliates, cable networks are plethoric, and digital platforms (such as Hulu, Netflix, Amazon) have recently been added to the existing buyers in television, extending the forms that "television" takes.

21. Scripted television agent, big agency, November 2014.

22. Ron Meyer, William Haber, Michael Rosenfeld, and Rowland Perkins are the other four.

23. Along with visible individual agent figures such as Sue Mengers; see Kemper 2013.

24. On this process and the rise of independent film agents, see Roussel 2016, and below, chapter 7.

25. The technology-focused private equity firm based in Silicon Valley, Silver Lake, invested $200 million in WME in 2012 acquiring a 31 percent stake in the agency, while the agency, in turn, also invested in digital startups. The two faces of the mechanism are in fact inseparable: Silver Lake backed WME's acquisition of IMG (International Management Group) in late 2013 and invested an extra $500 million in the combined group increasing its stake in it to a 51 percent majority. Later on, WME/IMG and their equity partners acquired properties such as the Professional Bull Riders and the Miss Universe Organization (2015), as well as the Ultimate Fighting Championship (2016), drastically diversifying the scope of the agency's activity. CAA sold a 35 percent minority stake to investment firm TPG Capital for $165 million in 2010, and an additional $225 million gave TPG a 53 percent majority stake in 2014. TPG has also backed CAA in a series of acquisitions. Similarly, after selling a minority stake to hedge fund manager Jeffrey Ubben in the summer of 2015, UTA bought the Agency Group, whose ninety-five agents represent music artists. Between 2010 and 2015, Wall Street investors have injected more than $1 billion into the two largest agencies, WME and CAA, enabling their expansion in other arenas than the traditional business of artists' representation. See, for instance, Rottenberg 2015.

26. "Sport is television—we are in the television business. Athletes and models are artists—we are in the artist's representation business. [. . .] Either way, it's advocacy; either way, it's connecting the dots; either way, it's sales; either way, it's talent; either way, it's content" (Big Hollywood agent, January 2014).

27. "It's my relationship with talent that's going to help drive [the other businesses that the agencies pursue] because that's still sexy and romantic. But how do I use outside money to create other businesses? By leveraging my relations with talent. And so, if you look at CAA and WME, that's what they're doing with that capital, and that's why there's money coming in, because they understand that the economics are changing" (former independent film agent at a big agency, producer, November 2012).

28. This talent agent at a big agency described "the most important change" she felt she had witnessed so far in these words: "Agents are really now trying to figure out other streams of revenue, getting more involved in campaigns, like branding and licensing and clothing lines and promotional campaigns and product endorsement, and that's an area that we were sort of never involved in before. You're looking for a lot of different ways to monetize your clients [. . .] because the idea of making money on a pure actor who just goes to work as an actor is more and more difficult, so you're looking for ways to make them more financially solvent for you" (November 2014).

CHAPTER THREE

1. The data used below are drawn from the 122 interviews that I conducted for this study, and complemented with various secondary sources (including data from the Hollywood Representation Directory; online data on agency partners/top managers; archive work at the Margaret Herrick Library of the Academy of Motion Picture Arts and Sciences). No systematic data of larger numeric importance is currently accessible to develop a quantitative study of the agents' backgrounds and careers, which would make any attempt to analyze their profiles and identify their "dispositions" with statistical methods unrealistic.

2. Nonwhite agents are a small minority; they form only 13 percent of my sample of interviewees. They are found mostly in Little Hollywood, and among those who occupy symbolically dominated positions; that is, who represent artists who are undervalued in the symbolic and economic hierarchy of talent (below-the-line talent, reality television celebrities, "digital native" talent) or who operate outside of the core activity of representing artists directly.

3. She recounts her experience in David Rensin's book, *The Mailroom* (2003, 209). Cases of successful female agents were not completely unknown then, but they remained a rarity. Sue Menger's visible career in the 1970s and 1980s, representing stars such as Barbra Streisand, Candice Bergen, Faye Dunaway, Gene Hackman, and Burt Reynolds, stands out as an exception.

4. According to the Hollywood Representation Directory of 2012 (which is the most recent edition published to this day), among CAA's 353 agents, executives, and agency managers, 25.5 percent were women (that is, 90), while WME had 31.5 percent (94 out of 298), ICM 35.4 percent (56 out of 158), and UTA 33 percent (38 out of 115) female agents. Eleven of the thirty-eight partners at ICM Partners were women in October 2013. In my sample, a quarter of the interviewees are women.

5. Professional conversions to agenting from the world of finance or on the part of lawyers were also seen in the 1990s through 2000s. Specialists in

(film) finance have, for instance, been hired by the big agencies to head some of the international financing and packaging departments, mostly since the 2000s. However, those who reinvented themselves as agents in this way, taking the risk of interrupting a career that has already started, often come to Hollywood with a strong desire to express a "creative self" that they had to suppress in a previous job. Consequently, such trajectories do not necessarily mean a "business-oriented" approach to agenting.

6. One of the well-known historical narratives of how Hollywood was invented includes the journey of Jewish entrepreneurs, with homogeneous backgrounds, who came to Los Angeles and built "an empire of their own," in Neal Gabler's terms (1989). Past and present prominent figures of the business side of the industry have become incarnations of this narrative. For instance, Ron Meyer—former CAA cofounder, successfully turned studio head, and now one of the top executives of NBCUniversal—told his story as that of a California native, born to Jewish immigrant parents who escaped Nazi Germany, and who overcame his troubled youth to become one of the most powerful men in Hollywood (Rensin 2003, 101–7). However, nothing would be more fallacious than suggesting the image of a homogeneous group bound by religious ties concertedly ruling the top level of the entertainment world, which is nothing more than conspiracy theory applied to power in Hollywood.

7. That is, how religious schemes and norms, models of success, and occasions for interconnections and sociability shape (or don't shape) mental frames that are professionally relevant and translate into agenting practices.

8. Without reifying what such "identities" mean and how identification processes occur. See Brubaker and Cooper 2000.

9. Talent agent, Big Hollywood, April 2011.

10. A former actor who trained at one of the large agencies before becoming agent and partner at a boutique company, September 2010.

11. One agent at a major agency explained how he embraced this career in spite of the fact that he wasn't initially drawn to the work, and how he discovered on the job that this professional role was a perfect fit for him: "I didn't really think I wanted to be an agent, never aspired to, because I didn't really love a lot of the other agents and sometimes what they represented. And one person gave me very sage advice and said, 'That's why you need to be an agent.' And so, that's kind of what happened. And I decided to go for it. And I've been incredibly fortunate. [. . .] And I've really loved it for a long time now. So I've been really, really fortunate to do what I'm doing" (October 2010).

12. University programs in film and television production (within film schools and departments) sometimes include a class on "the business of Hollywood" and less often on "talent representation" per se; these dimensions remain very marginal. Only very recently have we started to see the

development of programs that focus on "art business/art management" (often under the umbrella of business/management schools), integrating the study of talent management/agenting among the courses offered.

13. Primarily, this is so for the four giants of agenting (CAA, WME, UTA, ICM) and, to a lesser degree, the most important midsize agencies that imitate them in this matter (Gersh, Paradigm, etc.).

14. Which is why a book could be dedicated to this experience; see Rensin 2003. On these dimensions, see also Roussel 2015a.

15. Coordinators are often unofficially doing part of what a junior agent does, including more direct service to agency clients and unofficial scouting for future personal clients (that the future agent "hip-pockets"). They can also be in charge of creating the "grids" that list the projects that studios and major production entities are developing at the moment, a key tool used by agents.

16. The order in which such phases present themselves and the ways in which positions are labeled may vary slightly, depending on the agency, but the general process remains comparable.

17. Potentially, any agent can become a mentor. Agents' professional socialization often predisposes them to think of it as an integral part of their mission. But those who are both high up enough in the organizational hierarchy of the agency and in a position to still practice agenting on a daily basis (in contrast with top agency managers in large companies) are more likely to be targeted by aspiring agents; thus mentoring also becomes a more important dimension of their practice.

18. "When I look at [agents], myself as well as people who have succeeded in the company, the majority of them had at least one strong mentor. One, because I think it's that person who's going to take you under their wing and advise you and steer you in the right direction, and also that person that eventually is going to be able to champion you in terms of being able to get you promoted, and onward" (television agent, big agency, November 2014).

19. Talent agent, Big agency, November 2012.

20. Agents are the "tenpercenters" who "package" and "pitch," negotiations happen in "the room" with "the buyers," participants distinguish "above the line" from "below the line" clients, "talent agents" differ from "lit [literary] agents," and so on. This shared language defines a community of professional meaning and practice. It also comes with norms regarding the proper style and tone of communication: for instance, constantly and intensely expressing passion and enthusiasm is expected. Subtypes of specialized languages corresponding to different specializations in agenting coexist as well.

21. In that sense, assistants are in a position comparable to that once occupied by the domestic staff of the aristocracy, indispensable and exploited at will, invisible and silent witnesses whose "inferior" status allows them to

go unnoticed—with, of course, the major difference being that assistants expect and are expected to be promoted out of this status: they are considered to be on track to become those whom they silently observe.

22. Interviewed agents explicitly make this difference, most of the time. "Personal taste" is a judgment system that existed prior to one's first job at an agency and often led the concerned to engage on this professional path (the passion for "great movies" or "great shows" is often mentioned by interviewees), and that persists in parallel to the acquired "professional taste." The formation of a professional taste that remains distinct from one's personal taste manifests the differentiation of social spheres and its effects on the coexistence of distinct interiorized evaluation systems.

23. And: "You have to read ten thousand scripts before you really know how to read scripts. I don't think I'm there yet, but I do [know] that as opposed to five years ago, I'm one hundred percent better at spotting something special. I used to read a script from page 1 to 120, then I had to read to page 60, I think that now already by page 30 or 10 you could tell if the writing is anything special. Sometimes you still have to finish the script, but in terms of writing, if something isn't good by page 10, you can guarantee it's not a good writer. Or not yet. Five years ago I couldn't have done that. I just wouldn't have known."

24. Reference to WMA, Endeavor, CAA, UTA, and ICM, before the merger between WMA and Endeavor that formed WME in 2009.

25. Similar to a junior literary agent who mentioned during our interview that he still hadn't signed a contract formalizing his appointment at one of the major agencies two years after he was made an agent there, this below-the-line agent recounted how he started at a boutique agency, learning in the course of a conversation what his title was: "[The agency owner] introduced me to a new assistant she had hired, and she said, 'This is [name]. He's our new junior agent.' And that was the first time anybody had said what my job title was" (Little Hollywood, November 2012).

26. During our interview, this agent explained the unusual circumstances in which she was hired at one of the major agencies from a small boutique and the efforts she then had to make to get accepted in this new environment: "People don't tend to go from one to the other. [. . .] The challenge is that a lot of these [big] companies like to grow people from within, and they don't actually take you as seriously. People take you seriously if you go from one big agency to the next, but if you're hired from a smaller agency into a bigger agency, the underlying feeling is: you're lucky to be here, you have to prove yourself a lot more, because the assumption is you don't totally know what you're doing, the assumption is you weren't well trained, the assumption is you probably don't quite get it and so you need to prove that none of those things are true. [. . .] But the truth is, you can sign bigger clients [by virtue of being] at these bigger agencies, so I was able to, in a very short period of time, sign a list that suddenly was worthy of

the agency that I was working at. And then I became worthy of the agency that I'm working at" (talent agent, Big Hollywood, November 2014).

27. "It's important when you start to know who everybody is, obviously, and you sort of all mature together, so the [other] assistants mature into studio executives as you become an agent. So everyone kind of grows up together, and it's almost like, you know, the generation. And so you have all the freshmen, and at another time you're all seniors—you're a big agent, your friends run the studio. Then it's just about maintaining those relationships and welcoming the new people" (former talent agent, big agency, February 2013).

28. This mostly concerns a very specific profile and a limited number of agents, in charge of financing for independent cinema, often former professionals from the world of film finance: "I had a faster trajectory. The difference is I just didn't have those personal relationships that were formed . . . where these people are hanging out together. I don't have that. Even to this day, well, I am fairly well known, [but] I am still kind of an outsider" (agent, film financing, big agency, March 2013).

29. Studies have underlined the existence of specific career models characterizing the creative industries (Peiperl et al. 2002) as a result of their project-based organizational structure, sometimes pointing to new "boundary-less" careers (Arthur and Rousseau 1996). However, exploring talent agenting leads us to unveil a more complex reality. The centrality of projects in one's career trajectory and self-perception varies depending on the position occupied in Hollywood as a professional system. Artists, producers (especially independent ones), and managers who also produce may share such a perception. On the contrary, lawyers and managers who do not usually produce, as well as certain categories of studio employees (by virtue of their inclusion in large corporate structures), relate more to the agents' experience described in this book. On Hollywood as a project-based labor market, see esp. Faulkner and Anderson 1987; Jones 1996; and W. Bielby and D. Bielby 1999.

30. Talent agent, big agency, March 2013.

CHAPTER FOUR

1. Among such approaches, see Faulkner 1983 and W. Bielby and D. Bielby 1999 for pioneer works, and more recently, Rossman, Esparza, and Bonacich 2010. For a more detailed critical discussion, see Roussel 2015a.

2. "Ultimately, you want to get the client the job, but what you also want to do is get the client in the room with the director, because part of your business, your job is to make the client feel like you're giving them opportunities. So if they don't book the job, well, it's partially their fault; but if they didn't get in the room, it's your fault—even though [the director] may not want to see the client, it's still your fault, because what they've hired you to do is to figure out how to get them in the room" (talent agent, big agency, November 2014).

3. "Like the artist, be your true self. [. . .] You have to find the creative . . . you're really into Hollywood because you wanted to make movies, to be a producer and do stuff, and you ended up as an agent that's distant from that stuff. So how do you bring your artistic ability, your creativity, your whimsy, your humor, your sensitivity, your salesmanship, your charm, your charisma to the job, as you would if you were a director or a writer or an artist like you thought you wanted to be? It starts with: are you true to yourself in the way you look, in the way you sound, and who you are trying to hang out with" (Big Hollywood agent, April 2013).

4. This has some similarity with the process of signaling expertise involved in the making of reputations, analyzed by Candace Jones (2002).

5. Former indie film agent, big agency, February 2015.

6. In the big agencies, it is also and especially a question of being able to offer successful clients a variety of agent "personalities" so that they can find the one(s) with whom they will have the most affinity.

7. "It's about a business model. I think it's about: if you're a brand, what does your brand represent? And our brand represents a high quality of representation, helping clients work through problems, and to be well compensated, and to be publicized, and to do what we can to promote them in any way that will benefit their career. [. . .] This isn't about me. This is not a show about me. This is an agency about clients. [Name of another agent], likewise, is an agent whose reputation is built on the fact that she puts her clients first. And that what you see is what you get. She's not a showman, you know. She doesn't wear a shiny suit and go to the set and hand out business cards and try to convince everybody that she's cool" (below-the-line agent, April 2011).

8. For another, converging example: "I think that William Morris, for example, is corporate—it's a corporate culture. [. . .] There's a Wall Street vibe to what that agency is; and it's an interesting culture, because it's a Wall Street vibe, but it still is creative content. [. . .] So there's a combination of those two, but at its core, there's a corporate culture at work. [. . .] I think CAA is a version of that, but there's a military sense to it, and by that I just mean there's a uniformity. That's what makes them so powerful—there's a very clear structure to how they all behave, how they all communicate, what they all do, and that's a very powerful thing. And I think that [UTA has] a culture of individuals with a common goal, which is to put forward the vision of the artist and make money doing that, monetize that in the best and smartest way possible. [. . .] Those are three different, very different worlds. You're talking to different agents at different agencies, so it must feel really different going into different companies" (talent agent, big agency, November 2014).

This last comment reveals the importance and obviousness of such distinctive "cultures" for (Big Hollywood) agents, but the significance of such small differences fades away in the eyes of other industry professionals, including former agents turned manager or producer: "It is very easy for people to put different agencies into a compartmentalized box and say: 'oh, they are like this and they are like that.' But I found out, now that I am on the management side, that they are all similar in many ways, and this idea that they are all so vastly different, you know . . . it has been very eye opening to me. I find them very much more alike than not" (manager, former talent agent, big agency, March 2013).

9. Talent agent, big agency, September 2012.
10. Producer, former Big Hollywood agent, Februrary 2014.
11. Literary agent, big agency, June 2014. This also translated in terms of position in an organization, as it allowed him to be promoted from the television department to the motion picture department—a more prestigious although globally less lucrative area of the business.
12. Such observations converge with other sociological studies that have shed light on the relational formation of personal identities. See esp. White 2008.
13. We observe here a manifestation of the pragmatic dimension of ethical principles, already noted by Hughes ([1971] 1984).
14. Agent, owner of a below-the-line boutique agency, October 2010, my emphasis.
15. "Brad Grey, who was actually the chairman of Paramount, got into trouble for that with Garry Shandling on *The Larry Sanders Show*, because he was taking a commission from Garry Shandling and also taking an executive producer fee, and I think even a production company fee. So he's getting paid three ways from this, and Garry Shandling said, 'Wait a second, it's my show!' [. . .] If you're found out, you're going to get in trouble. Is it legal? Yeah, it's legal. You know, I mean, there's no law that says you can't do that. *But, does it build your relationship? No*" (former agent, big agency, March 2010, my emphasis).
16. Digital media agent, big agency, April 2012.
17. "A lot of it is relationships. There are business affairs execs that I've been dealing with for years, that I can get on the phone with for a negotiation and we can cut through it really quickly, because we both trust each other and when I say, 'I really need this or I can't close the deal,' they know I'm not lying, not trying to scrape every penny off the table. Or when they say, 'This is all I have, I can't move at all,' I know they're . . . you know what I mean? It cuts through it so much more. [. . .] When I'm negotiating, we're on different sides of the argument, I'm going to argue this, they're going to argue this. I totally get that. I always just want someone to acknowledge that they understand my argument. There's nothing that's more frustrating than when they've already made up their decision of 'This is what I'm doing,' and it doesn't matter what you say, it's like talking to a wall. If you acknowledge me and say to me, 'I clearly understand where you're coming from, that makes complete sense, you deserve that, unfortunately, this is where we are,' then at least I feel like I'm being heard" (television agent, big agency, November 2014).

18. For Luhmann (1979), trust works as a means of reducing social complexity in differentiated societies, in which the need for anticipation and projection into the future has highly intensified. Here we observe in practice this link between trust and relationship with time. In a different perspective, Tilly (2007) has explored the emergence of interpersonal trust networks from long-term strong ties.

19. For a critical approach to this use of the notion of trust, see, for instance, Berezin 2005 and Bandelj 2009. The idea that the film world constitutes an opaque and uncertain market is the premise of many studies of cultural production; among others, see Faulkner 1983; Caves 2000; Zafirau 2008.

20. Talent agent, big agency, February 2013.

21. Indeed, "not to lie" about a client's last salary, for instance, in the context of a negotiation, is thought of both as a moral behavior and as a self-interested and rather rational one, given the anticipated risk of being exposed and suffering negative consequences. Moral philosophers such as Annette Baier (1986) have already noted that trust—even though it presupposes goodwill and can therefore be betrayed, in Baier's view—is compatible with self-interestedness and that "rational trust" exists when the truster has no reason to suspect that the trusted has motives that conflict with his or her own aims.

22. "[Studio executives] learn to trust what your taste is, and how you conduct your business. So, in other words, whether or not you have a good relationship with someone, you may constantly call them and recommend the wrong people, who are never going to get the job, who don't quite fit. Or they may know you for always having great taste. It's a big deal whether you waste someone's time or not, based on what you pitch and what you tell people to take a look at. You know, if you constantly tell people, 'This is a great script,' and everyone else thinks it's horrible . . . There's no real right and wrong, it's a very subjective business, but, you know, overall, people can formulate: 'Ah, this person tends to know what they're talking about. This person, whenever they call me, doesn't waste my time. I sit down with interesting people that I like'" (former talent agent, Big Hollywood, April 2011).

23. Former talent agent, big agency, March 2013.

24. The buildings also materialize the "culture" that the agency leaders intend to convey, whether it is to be in the temple of corporate modernity and success (as in the spacious and clean offices of WME in the heart of Beverly Hills), in a place whose heavy metal and marble structure is meant to express unrivaled power (such as the massive CAA offices in Century City), or in a more intimate and traditional materialization of "good taste" (like with the bourgeois home–looking offices of Paradigm).

25. For instance, Oasis and inEntertainment are such software and database programs commonly used by talent agencies and management companies.

26. This is why agenting involves, as a former agent put it, "getting into people's heads": "You try to get to know a client, you try to get to know a

buyer. What turns them on, what are they looking for, you know? [. . .] You can only be able to get inside somebody's head if you have a conversation with them. 'What are your tastes? Do you like hockey, do you like playing cards?' I mean, whatever it is, you get to know them and so, once you get to know them, then the object is: now you're going to see the world through their eyes. So, if I get to know you, I don't need to have a conversation with you to say, 'You know what? I think this is going to be something that you'll like.' That's fantastic when you get that kind of relationship hook" (Big Hollywood, April 2014).

27. In-person meetings appear to be a "test of the self" as well as a "test of the other," which seems to go beyond technical mastery and requires one to be a "virtuoso of people"—a "virtuosity" that is in reality inseparable from the socio-technical network that produced it. See Dodier 1995.

28. On this geography of Hollywood, see Scott 2004.

29. Bruno Cousin and Sébastien Chauvin (2014) point out, on other empirical grounds, the importance of the acquisition of forms of collective social capital that are not inherited. Other approaches to social capital, such as that of Coleman (1988) or Putnam (1995), have not emphasized the specialization of social capital and the mechanisms proper to its accumulation in professional context.

30. Interview with a studio head, March 2014.

31. "Whether they're at a small agency that's in the business or [at a big agency], with the Internet and e-mail, everybody has, pretty much, access to the same information; so it's not really about access to information. At smaller agencies, the end game is actually activity, like getting a lot of meetings and auditions for a client. But that's really not what makes the difference in somebody's career. What makes the difference in somebody's career is getting the *right* auditions and getting opportunities to make an action convert into those jobs. It's actually about *conversion*, it's not about the opportunities, it's not about volume" (talent agent, big agency, September 2012, my emphasis).

CHAPTER FIVE

1. "When I'm inspired creatively, I grab that artist and try to have them realize their hopes and dreams under my watch. If they got cold or I was wrong, I stayed with them, I never left them, I never stopped" (talent agent, Big Hollywood, September 2010).

2. Former talent agent, Big Hollywood, April 2014.

3. "Call it friendship—and a lot of people are. I have always kept a barrier there. Before cell phones, it was like: 'You've got me from seven in the morning until eleven at night, but at night when I go home and I'm with my family, you want me recharged for the next day.' Now with cell phones, you've got me 24/7, which is fine, but I'm never afraid to say, 'Let's deal

with this Monday,' because I want to make sure that I am rested when comes Monday morning. But I promise you, if there's an emergency, I deal with it.' And I'm social, I have dinners and lunches and breakfasts with my clients, I go to parties and all that. But a lot of people go on vacations with their clients, and I'm not saying there's anything wrong with it, but I always wanted to have a separate life, just so that I could have perspective. I wanted to be able to bring as much life experience to my work as possible" (former talent agent, Big Hollywood, April 2014).

4. "[Clients] don't really understand what it really takes to be a good agent. To really be a good agent, it's [a] seven-days-a-week-full-time job, you have to be on top of the business all the time, you're dealing with people's lives, their careers and their futures, and it's not something that you can, you know, come and go, you have to be available to do it all the time. To be a good agent . . . to the day I left—I had a good life—but I felt like a doctor on call, I was available to my clients seven days a week, twenty-four hours a day. The people who love you the most have to understand the most. The client in many ways has to come first, if there's an important client situation" (former big agency manager, May 2015).

5. This dimension of emotion work is also institutionally implemented—for instance, when the agencies buy personalized presents for the clients, the economic value of which varies depending on the client's worth.

6. It also shows that the strictly technical skills involved in deal-making are not central to the agents' type of competence. The type of power that agents hold is thus not drawn from "technical expertness," as has been observed in other professional groups (Freidson 1962). On the contrary, it is somewhat similar to the notion of "relational competence" developed by Milburn (2002). Nina Bandelj (2009) has also noted the importance of taking seriously the emotional dimension of relational work. For a more detailed discussion, see, Roussel 2015b.

7. Talent agent, Big Hollywood, September 2012.

8. Former talent agent, Big Hollywood, April 2014.

9. Ibid.

10. This is true for all agents who directly represent individual talent, whereas those who represent projects or companies do not have to perform emotion work to the same extent.

11. Here, we freely use the notion of the false self defined by Donald W. Winnicott (1980).

12. The flight attendants studied by Hochschild play a reassuring role with the passengers that is purely situational, detached from their experience and modes of expression of self in other contexts, including professional ones. Emotion work therefore reflects a capacity to engage in "double dealing" and to perform a dual role. Applying such a perspective without modification to the agenting world would be, however, misleading: as soon as it must be maintained over a long period of time, the emotional

engagement is not likely to remain a pure facade. Without doubt, we see the "roles" played out in work situations being inscribed in the facets that constitute the "self."

13. "I have a very professional relationship with my clients, when you have a relationship that stands, for some relationships, fifteen, twenty years, it's hard not to feel close to people, because you've lived . . . children have been born, family members passed away, you create a relationship with people, you're connected to them, and there is a bond that's unique and exciting. But I think that my clients want to think of me in terms of being their representative and not being their best friend. So first of all, I'm a representative and I want them to think of me that way, and then we have unique relationships. But, you know, we're not best friends and I don't think that they think of me as their best friend, but they certainly think of me as a very close adviser. And that definition of an adviser can oftentimes go into personal aspects of people's life, no question about it. Because, when you have long-term relationships, that happens" (talent agent, Big Hollywood, March 2010).

14. In network analysis, artists are often portrayed as isolated entities facing uncertain and inscrutable markets. The assumption that cultural markets are characterized by opacity and instability is a common feature, to the point that it is more often implied than explicitly discussed. One of the most sophisticated approaches of markets as networks can be found in Ronald Burt's (2005) study of network brokerage: for Burt, social capital stems from brokerage of otherwise disconnected units, creating ties where there were structural holes in networks (versus the idea that social capital would develop in situations of network closure). Brokerage across holes, bridging them, becomes "the solution" to structural disconnection. However, in the case study of Hollywood, our investigation suggests that the image outlined by this network analysis is likely to be an artifact. Indeed, it's the way in which networks are usually constructed—the type of data collected and the coding, especially the fact that most network approaches of the entertainment industry are artist centered and project oriented, that ties within one particular professional group are rarely incorporated to the analysis (as rightly noted by Foster, Borgatti, and Jones 2011)—that *produces* a visual representation of disconnection, which is then *interpreted* as a structural hole. This, in turn, fuels a functional interpretation of brokerage roles. In this story that network analysts tell, brokers become the solution to an artifactual disconnection problem. What ethnography shows, on the contrary, is that, in the experience of Hollywood professionals, the "small world" of Little or Big Hollywood and the given area of specialty in which they operate are relatively transparent to the participants: counterparts who matter are well known, and so are their "competence" and "worth"; and information regarding projects is not difficult to access (if not readily available). Beyond the limits of such worlds that one is already acquainted and familiar with, there is not much bridging going on.

15. To paraphrase Marx, who stated in *The Eighteenth Brumaire of Louis Bonaparte* that those who dominate are dominated by their own domination.

16. Nowadays the harsh competition between agents and managers around artist representation, which was at its height in the early 1980s, has pacified. Their jurisdictional struggle has turned into the management of a shared territory of talent representation with a routinized division of labor. But their coexistence alongside artists in Big Hollywood (where most clients have both a team of agents and a manager or a management team, in addition to a lawyer and a publicist) affects the definition of the agent-talent relationship, because the manager sides sometimes with the client, sometimes with the agent, in contexts in which projects are shaped or difficult choices must be made.

17. Talent agent, big agency, October 2010.

18. Talent agent, Big Hollywood, May 2015.

19. At an earlier stage, before any discussion with a client on a given project or job, the routinized division of labor attributes to the agents the role of operating on behalf of a client the preliminary selection among projects/potential jobs—whether this means choosing what jobs to submit an actor for in Little Hollywood, or which of the numerous solicitations for parts and projects to dismiss or present to a name artist in Big Hollywood. This delegation of initial choices to the representative goes unquestioned, as it is part of the very definition of the agenting relationship.

20. Talent agent, Big Hollywood, March 2013.

21. By analogy, on the construction of charisma, see Collovald 1999.

22. For convergent conclusions regarding charisma stabilization in a different context, that of "miracle workers," see Lainer Vos and Parigi 2014.

23. Weber opposes simple "power"—defined as the chance that an individual in a social relationship can achieve his or her own will even against the resistance of others—to "domination," which exists when a specific command is obeyed by a given group of people, therefore implying a minimum of voluntary compliance (that is, an interest in obedience). "Authority" refers to legitimate (that is, accepted, obeyed, unchallenged) forms of domination, which Weber famously divided into three major types: traditional, charismatic, and legal-rational.

24. It similarly challenges Bourdieu's analysis of traditional modes of domination by opposition with those that govern contemporary differentiated societies (Bourdieu 1976). Agents' forms of power over clients are indeed comparable to the "soft forms of domination" that Bourdieu described regarding traditional societies. For Bourdieu, in societies in which power relations are established and sustained through interpersonal relations rather than stabilized and guaranteed by institutionalized and depersonalized mechanisms, dominance stems from the moral and material debt by which one can subordinate others, as well as from the ability to inspire others to believe in one's importance or greatness. However, in order to keep their position of power, those who dominate have to consistently

work at re-establishing their ascendance through interpersonal, face-to-face relationships. Despite all the obvious differences between the traditional societies observed by Bourdieu and today's American entertainment industry, elements of such "traditional modes of domination" are observable in Hollywood. What our case study in fact reveals is the need to go beyond Bourdieu's opposition of traditional versus state societies, to better approach the complexity and hybrid nature of domination mechanisms in contemporary, highly institutionalized societies.

25. They share it with already established artists and with production professionals in the circles they form at an early stage of the creative process, and later on with publicity specialists, critics, journalists, and other authorities of artistic judgment. See below, chapter 6.

26. "*Libido* would also be entirely pertinent for saying what I have called *illusio*, or investment. [. . .] Each field imposes a tacit entrance fee: "Let no one enter here who is not a geometrician," that is, no one should enter who is not ready to die for a theorem. [. . .] One of the tasks of sociology is to determine how the social world constitutes the biological libido, an undifferentiated impulse, as a specific social libido. There are in effect as many kinds of libido as there are fields" (Bourdieu [1994] 1998, 77–78).

27. The invention of "ordinary talent" and what it implies for the definition of talent itself has been analyzed by Laura Grindstaff and Vicki Mayer (2015).

28. Talent agent, big agency, September 2012.

29. Talent agent, big agency, April 2013.

30. This is especially prominent in comedy, a genre and a field of specialty characterized by recurrent professional cooperations within a small milieu of established artists, as this agent who built his reputation on representing several of them described: "This is a family, this is the wheel of comedy! And there is connectivity, and so you draw from that connectivity. Over and over and over and over again! Movie after movie after movie, it's everything. It's everything we do" (Big Hollywood, April 2013).

31. I take here some distance with the conclusions drawn by Zuckerman et al.

32. This has been noted in other works. See esp. Faulkner 1983 and De Verdalle 2014.

33. Former talent agent, Big Hollywood, April 2014.

34. To whom the image of the great movie star primarily refers and who reach the highest salaries, even though star actors are these days few and far between.

35. In addition, in the hierarchy organizing agencies internally, "upstream" positions in the production process, allowing agents to participate to the early orchestration of projects (for instance, literary agents who control the material, talent agents who handle a star actor, "indie film" agents who work at financing and packaging movies), are more valued than "downstream" ones (for instance, sales agents who are not involved in packaging, talent agents who only put midlevel actors in jobs when casting has begun).

36. "Getting someone who is used to working in features to work in television, it is always a tough conversation. More and more people are starting to understand how fantastic and wonderful TV is. But for a very long time that was always a tough conversation, and one that you may not even be open to having because you know they will just yell at you, they will be upset, they will cry to you" (manager, former talent agent at a big agency, March 2013).
37. "Since I've been here, in our department, as far as representing line producers, cinematographers, production designers, costume designers, and editors, and some visual effects people, we've had over a hundred Oscar nominations. We've roughly had between five and ten every year. And last year we had three winners" (Big Hollywood, October 2010).
38. Agent, Little Hollywood, October 2010.
39. Reference to big names of the agency business, at CAA (regarding the first two) and WMA (as for the last one, who died in 2010).

CHAPTER SIX

1. I borrow freely this notion from Lamont 2012. From here on, I drop the parentheses from *(e)valuation* with the understanding that the double meaning is implicit.
2. Former agent and manager of a big agency, April 2014.
3. That artists also develop direct relationships with production professionals is therefore part of the normal and ordinary functioning of evaluation communities; it should not be misunderstood as a sign of what Rupert Russell (2013) called "brokerage failure," given that such direct ties do not make the relationships between these production professionals and the stars' representatives of lesser importance.
4. An established casting company in Venice.
5. Talent agent, Big Hollywood, November 2014.
6. Former agent and agency manager, Big Hollywood, April 2014.
7. On the role of middlemen in the making of value and taste in other areas, see Bessy and Chauvin 2013; Mears 2011.
8. This experienced literary agent both noted the increased role of green-light committees in vast corporate studios, as far as big-budget films are concerned, and suggested that final approval still comes from the studio head, eventually: "The bigger the budget is, the more the studios have a lot of control. And even now, as you probably know, there are green-light committees; it used to be that one person had the right to say no. Now, these committees, almost by definition, regress to the mean in terms of the most boring, easy, least edgy choices. It's always been [this way], because if somebody is there to really fight for something, it might get done, but you need an advocate. [. . .] The higher the budget, the more formal it is; it depends who the person is saying 'I want to do it.' If it's the chairman

of the studio, it's probably going to get done; if it's the head of marketing, it's probably not, right?" (Big Hollywood July 2014). In the same vein, this studio head explained: "It's different in different places. But I don't put too much emphasis on it, because I think ultimately, at every studio, the real truth is, there's one person who decides—whoever that person is—and then other people get in line or not, they take advice, and it's easy to know who that [decision-making] person is" (March 2014).

9. Of course, we know the situation with which this story starts could vary: that other types of material can initially be in the hands of the agent or the manager (a spec, or an idea to be pitched), placing different categories of artists at the root of the process; that the lawyer can be involved; that a studio executive can rediscover a piece of material that his company owned, and so on.

10. "In some cases [. . .] they'll green-light this movie and say: 'Okay, we're going to make this movie for this price,' and then the casting process happens. [. . .] In other cases it's all about the casting, so they'll say, 'If you can *cast* it, we will green-light it, so bring us a cast.' By 'if you can cast it,' it just means that you can cast it with people who have a value so that 'we see—you know, there's incentive to us—that we really can sell that movie based on who you brought us as attached; then we'll green-light it'" (talent agent, big agency, November 2014).

11. Big Hollywood, July 2014.

12. "I think that magic is perhaps the most important part of the pitch. [. . .] It's a seduction, a promise of what lies ahead. At a certain point, the writer needs to pull back and let the producer project himself as the creator of the story. And let him project what he needs onto your idea that makes the story whole for him" (Oscar-winning writer, director, and producer, quoted in Elsbach and Kramer 2003, 296).

13. Former motion picture literary agent, midsize agency, March 2013.

14. Television shows work in the same way, to an extent, with many more being developed than eventually made, pilots shot but not picked by the network, shows canceled after a few episodes even though more had already been made, and so on.

15. As noted by Kimberly D. Elsbach and Roderick M. Kramer (2003).

16. "Quality" here refers to the judgment made by members of evaluation communities—with an eye toward the authorities and institutions in charge of critical and professional consecration at a later stage—with reference to various criteria of evaluation (aesthetics, conceptual originality, potential for technical virtuosity or prowess in terms of performance, etc.).

17. TV agent, big agency, November 2014.

18. "I've heard so often people compare comedies with *Midnight Run*. I don't know why, but that movie is constantly being referenced. Oftentimes it helps to reference an older classic, because everybody knows it; it's a proven

success, a movie people grew up with, enjoyed, so you immediately know: it's kind of an action comedy with that kind of travel element to it, you know?" (literary agent, big agency, December 2013).

19. But in our case, fictional framing (the "false belief" of movies or TV shows) and the strategic framing of real-life situations (which is situated, but does not mean to be particularly deceptive—unlike what Goffman's notion of fabrication connotes) are closely intertwined. See Goffman 1974.

20. This analysis of agents' narrative competences and practices *in the specific context* of evaluation communities converges with several dimensions of the approach in terms of the "sociology of storytelling" (Polletta et al. 2011).

21. This includes the salary and possibly a percentage of the profits a film makes after it breaks even (this is called "points on the back end," which could be a percentage of the total gross or of the net amount, varying from a few points to 15 or 20 percent). Salary and back-end points are combined in various ways, depending on the type of movie and the associated budget, the status of the artist, and the context in general. Besides the artist's payment, negotiating a deal also means defining all working conditions for a client on a given project, as well as other material and symbolic arrangements (for instance, how one's name will be placed on the movie poster).

22. Online entertainment tracking boards are select networking groups that offer information to their members, such as job postings, pay rates, contracts, crew needs, contact and budget information to scripts, and screening invites.

23. PreAct is a dashboard that offers the studios the potential to adjust their marketing campaigns according to data collected on a daily basis from social media conversations months before a movie is released (based on how the trailer is commented on, how much attention the star of the film receives, etc.). Sold to many distribution companies, this instrument is far from being the only available source of data for production and distribution professionals—for instance, Fizziology is another social media research firm that provides studios with reports sourced from online discussions; Moviepilot analyzes social data and runs digital marketing campaigns; ListenFirst Media studies digital engagement, particularly for TV.

24. The assumption is that the "buzz" built up online before the movie opens makes its success in theaters, which might be true of the opening weekend, but disregards the "longer tail" of the reception process and the word of mouth that can develop after a film's release, as well as the international career of a film, which is more complex and also unfolds over longer periods of time.

25. This also tends to be the experience of agents at midsize companies and, in general, of agents who represent clients who are not "names," even at the big agencies.

26. Talent agent, big agency, December 2013.
27. In Karpik's terms, singularities are goods or services that are unique and incommensurable, whose quality is uncertain—such as movies, fine wines, paintings, books, but also the services of a lawyer or a doctor. In such markets, Karpik states, the appeal of a product for consumers is based on *quality* more than *price*. In other words, competition over quality in context of uncertain value is more structuring of such markets than competition over price. This places markets for singularities out of the scope of what mainstream economic theory explains convincingly. Quality is evaluated according to one's *taste*, which itself forms through the use of what Karpik calls *judgment devices* (*dispositifs*). Judgment devices can take personal or impersonal forms and are divided into five categories: networks, brands/names, critics, rankings, and confluences.

   This combines with the definition of seven *regimes of coordination* that structure different markets for singularities. Such regimes are also either based on personal connections, or they are impersonal (when finding the right product does not involve the activation of interpersonal ties). As far as movies are concerned, two impersonal regimes of coordination organize evaluation and choice: the "authenticity regime," rooted in criticism and the value of aesthetics, concerns judgment over independent small productions; whereas big blockbuster movies involve what Karpik calls the "mega regime," which combines references to aesthetics and profitability, and in which consumers are active but more subject to marketing and sales apparatus.

   Our analysis complements Karpik's work but also challenges some of his conclusions. We shed light on the making of value in transactions between buyers and sellers at a stage that *precedes* the availability of a product to consumers; that is, here, to audiences. This exchange system could be characterized as an extremely personalized, small-scale "market" (for labor, but not exclusively) embedded into the larger market for consumers that Karpik studies. The construction of value in such embedded multilevel markets cannot be subsumed under the traditional neoclassical notion of supply and demand mechanisms. However, it is reasonable to hypothesize that there is a link between the way in which evaluation processes happen at the stage that we explore (through the relationships tying agents and their counterparts) and the assignation of value that happens later on, through more visible means and interventions (reviews, publicized rankings, etc.). In other words, the game we investigate *sets the conditions* for the future definition of value (and the future struggles over the quality of a product), starting with the fact that it conditions the existence of the evaluated good itself. In a way, our approach looks at the specific "judgment devices" that agents use in personalized systems of relationships, but also at how they form and come to prevail: Hollywood professionals do not simply pick and choose from a choice of available judgment devices; their devices are imposed by the structure of professional configurations that they belong to.

The logic of action is a given in the protagonists' eyes (even though they can behave strategically).

28. On commensuration as a social process, see esp. Espeland and Stevens 1998.

29. "I always believed that if you make the right decisions in this business, the money will find you. Yes, it'll find you. If you *do the right thing*, you get lucky. Nobody is a success in show business that didn't make any money. If they're a success, they made money" (producer, former big agency manager, November 2013, his emphasis).

30. On *illusio*, see also "Controlling Talent?" in chapter 5.

31. The question of the unpredictability *of the success of a product* is a different one. The idea of the radical uncertainty characterizing the movie business in which even star power cannot always guarantee box-office success (De Vany 2003), as robust as the data that provide the basis for it may be, does not elucidate the question of the perceptions and logics of action of participants who are able to get their bearings, strategize, and anticipate in small worlds filled with well-known partners and adversaries.

32. Whereas the bazaar economy is characterized by a high level of "known ignorance" about quality and price, which leads the "bazaaris" to devote time and energy to searching information, Hollywood is a game where participants feel that everybody knows everything and everyone, as we already explained. A common feature, however, is the importance of repeated exchanges with acquainted partners—what Geertz calls "clientelization"—for the structuration of bargaining practices (Geertz 1978).

33. Talent agent, big agency, April 2013.

34. Talent agent, big agency, September 2012.

35. Renegotiating contracts usually happens "upwards" in terms of what the client and the agency will receive; it is typically the case when a TV show suddenly becomes a hit and the agent asks for a raise in a lead actor's salary. But, on occasion, renegotiating may also happen "downwards"; for instance, when a deal has been made in favor of a high-profile talent for the development of a project and the production side feels, after some time, that they have committed to paying too much given how the status of the artist or the project has evolved.

36. Literary agent, midsize agency, July 2014.

37. Big agency, May 2015.

38. Talent agent, big agency, December 2013.

39. Jonathan M. Barnett (2015) has observed the prevalence of "soft contracts" (unsigned deal memos, draft agreements, e-mails) with uncertain legal enforceability in Hollywood. What we see here is that this preference for flexible tools does not just derive from rational behaviors in context of uncertainty, as suggested by Barnett; it more profoundly manifests how the structure of professional configurations guides the participants' perceptions and practices.

40. Robert Ellickson, studying disputes among residents of Shasta County, California (1991), has noted that informal interactions can spontaneously generate complex institutions and, moreover, that the cost of learning and using the law for dispute resolution can very well lead social actors to avoiding legal tools and formal procedures, and to solving problems by bargaining according to informal norms, thus better preserving in their own eyes chances for future cooperation.

41. "Our business is not the outcome. Our business is to realize the hopes and the dreams creatively of the clients. Whether the clients know it or not, our job is to dig in and to understand what they are good at, and how they can have that carried in a project to the audience. Hopefully the audience pays their money, hopefully the weather is good, hopefully people don't want to be on their phones, hopefully there is not a World Series game, hopefully there is not some other competition from some movie with a guy with a cape on him, hopefully there is not some fucking bomb that goes off somewhere, hopefully, hopefully, hopefully! I can't worry about it! [. . .] We can't control it. So what can we control? We can control the movies that we choose. So I'm never focused on the outcome. And that's why I take risks with the careers. That's why I put them in different [types of small and big projects]" (talent agent, big agency, April 2013).

42. *The Mask* brought in $351 million in the summer of 1994, *Ace Ventura* (1994) $107 million, *Dumb and Dumber* (1994) $247 million (all worldwide gross; source: Box Office Mojo).

43. *The Cable Guy* (1996) had a worldwide gross of $102 million. (source: Box Office Mojo).

44. Which is rarely a subject of debate in the industry or beyond. For an exception, see, Acuna 2014.

45. Even though A-list talent can still command salaries of $15 million to $20 million, as the list (including Leonardo DiCaprio, Sandra Bullock, Matt Damon, Robert Downey Jr., Denzel Washington, and Angelina Jolie) published by the *Hollywood Reporter* in March 2015 illustrates (Galloway 2015), they don't receive a substantial percentage of first-dollar gross, as their predecessors used to. Today, back-end deals start generating money for the star only after the studio has recouped its costs.

46. "I told all my clients that they're always going to be overpaid or underpaid. Never be paid correctly—they're always going to get too little or too much. [. . .] It's my point: 'Do this little film where they're paying you very little, and then do that big film where they're paying you a lot. That's how we'll figure out this one.' It's usually kind of: one for us and one for them. It was the way it would happen" (former big agency manager and agent, October 2013).

47. Olav Velthuis pointed in the same direction in his study of contemporary art markets in which "not just the consecration process, but also the very

exchange process, contributes to the production of belief in the value of art" (2003, 184).

CHAPTER SEVEN

1. Former independent film agent, big agency, February 2015.
2. Ibid.
3. Ptak's college education at UCLA's film school and former professional experiences provided him both with the capacity to have creative conversations with directors about movies and with an understanding of the motion picture business, retail included.
4. Former independent film agent, big agency, February 2015.
5. Midsize agencies practice "co-packaging" with larger companies that have more star clients.
6. "The basic job of an agent is to put the client to work. That's what you'd call a single-point transaction. [. . .] But the thing about representing a *movie* is a whole other thing" (former independent film agent, big agency, September 2013).
7. Independent film agent, big agency, December 2013.
8. "There is a bunch of things we do, not just financing movies. . . . We'll make investments in different movies that only come after the fact in North America. So, it has nothing to do with me packaging a movie; it has to do with me saying, 'Okay, I like that *as an investment,* let me see if one of my guys wants to put money in.' We do all of the financial analysis and put them as producers on those movies" (indie film agent, midsize agency, April 2013, his emphasis).
9. They simultaneously describe this role as a challenge: they first have to overcome the reluctance of other agents who hold different positions and often have contradictory interests (primarily choosing the most secure job option for their clients). It's internally, in the agency world and often within their own company, that they fight their first battles. The precarious aspect of playing with such a composite system appears in this agent's words: "Every agent, whether they want to admit it or not, has an agenda for their client. So, to get a movie made means you have to have a hundred different agents somehow come to the same agenda at the same time. I need this male actor, this female actor, this director, this writer, this producer, this line producer, this DP, this editor, and then the financier's agent and manager and blah-blah-blah. The most difficult thing by far is trying to get everyone on the same page at the same time. [. . .] So, it is going to all the agencies, convincing talent to do a movie, convincing the team that they should do the movie for the right price, convincing the financiers that they should do this. It is getting a lot of different people to agree on one thing. To align all the different pieces and all the different agendas

and find the right financier who says, 'You know what? I'm doing that'" (independent film agent, midsize agency, April 2013).

10. Former independent film agent, big agency, February 2015.

11. In 2013. Source: MPAA Theatrical Market Statistics 2013, 4.

12. Even though CAA has opened offices not only in Europe, but also in Beijing and Mumbai, and while WME has locations in London and Sydney (in 2016), their main activity remains operated in or from the United States. Similarly, runaway production phenomena (a runaway production is a movie or a television show that is intended for initial release in the United States but whose shooting takes place outside Hollywood or in another country) have not transformed agents' work significantly.

13. Former digital agent, big agency, March 2013.

14. WME/IMG also acquired the Professional Bull Riders and the Miss Universe Organization in 2015.

15. It is worth noting that UFC was one of WME's clients before the acquisition, which means that this operation was also a way of turning this representation activity into a content/distribution business.

16. Growth by mergers and acquisitions in a highly specialized service business that is primarily based on long-lasting interpersonal relations implies dependency of the company owners who operate such financial transaction on the expert employees of the organizations that they assemble: as a senior agent noted, because of their intimate relationship with the clients, which often determines the artists' loyalty toward the agency, "the agents are the asset owners. If you buy an agency to have the clients, if you get rid of the agents, you lose the clients!" (talent agent, big agency, January 2014). This is why the professional relationships and culture that ordinary agents embody remain of central importance, and their gradual inflection *has to be* the path that transformation takes.

17. In chemistry, an autocatalytic reaction is a reaction in which one of the products involved is also reactant, and therefore triggers the mechanism of the reaction while transforming itself. It causes the reaction to have certain effects rather than others. The autocatalyst activates the transformation by which it is also altered. Padgett and Powell (2012) have adapted the notion of autocatalysis to social processes (and to the coevolution of multiple social networks) in their book on the emergence of organizational and market novelty across a wide range of cases, from the time of early capitalism and state formation to the transformations of contemporary technology-based capitalism. Agents' activity can be described as part of an autocatalytic process transforming Hollywood and entertainment at large, in that sense. Brokers and middlemen—intermediaries in relationships between the other key groups involved—appear to be in a structurally favorable position to be catalysts of transformations.

References

Abbott, Andrew. 1988. *The System of Professions: An Essay on the Division of Expert Labor.* Chicago: University of Chicago Press.

Abolafia, Mitchel. 1996. *Making Markets: Opportunism and Restraint on Wall Street.* Cambridge, MA: Harvard University Press.

Acuna, Kirsten. 2014. "Jim Carrey Was Paid 140 Times More Than Jeff Daniels for Original 'Dumb and Dumber.'" *Business Insider*, November 12. http://www.businessinsider.com/dumb-and-dumber-jim-carrey-jeff-daniels-paycheck-2014-11.

Alexander, Jeffrey C., and Paul B. Colomy. 1990. *Differentiation Theory and Social Change: Comparative and Historical Perspectives.* New York: Columbia University Press.

Appadurai, Arjun. 1986. *The Social Life of Things: Commodities in Cultural Perspective.* Cambridge: Cambridge University Press.

Arthur, Michael B., and Denise. M. Rousseau, eds. 1996. *The Boundaryless Career: A New Employment Principle for a New Organizational Era.* New York: Oxford University Press.

Austin, John L. 1962. *How to Do Things with Words.* Oxford: Urmson, 1962.

Baier, Annette. 1986. "Trust and Antitrust." *Ethics* 96:231–60.

Bandelj, Nina. 2009. "Emotions in Economic Action and Interaction." *Theory and Society* 38:347–66.

Barnett, Jonathan M. 2015. "Hollywood Deals: Soft Contracts for Hard Markets." *Duke Law Journal* 64 (4): 605–67.

Baumann, Shyon. 2007. *Hollywood Highbrow: From Entertainment to Art.* Princeton, NJ: Princeton University Press.

Becker, Howard S. 1982. *Art Worlds.* Berkeley: University of California Press.

Berezin, Mabel. 2005. "Emotions and the Economy." In *The Handbook of Economic Sociology*, edited by Neil J. Smelser and Richard Swedberg, 109–29. 2nd ed. Princeton, NJ: Princeton University Press; New York: Russell Sage Foundation.

Bessy, Christian, and Pierre-Marie Chauvin. 2013. "The Power of Market Intermediaries: From Information to Valuation Processes." *Valuation Studies* 1 (1): 83–117.

Bielby, Denise, and C. Lee Harrington. 2008. *Global TV: Exporting Television and Culture in the World Market*. New York: New York University Press.

Bielby, William T., and Denise D. Bielby. 1994. "'All Hits Are Flukes': Institutionalized Decision-Making and the Rhetoric of Network Prime-Time Television Program Development." *American Journal of Sociology* 99 (5): 1287–1313.

———. 1999. "Organizational Mediation of Project-Based Labor Markets: Talent Agencies and the Careers of Screenwriters." *American Sociological Review* 64 (1): 64–85.

Boltanski, Luc, and Laurent Thévenot. 2006. *On Justification: Economies of Worth*. Princeton, NJ: Princeton University Press.

Bourdieu, Pierre. 1976. "Les modes de domination." *Actes de la recherche en sciences sociales* 2:122–32.

———. 1984. "La jeunesse n'est qu'un mot." In *Questions de sociologie*, by Bourdieu, 143–54. Paris: Minuit.

———. 1986. "The Forms of Capital." In *Handbook of Theory and Research for the Sociology of Education*, edited by John G. Richardson, 241–58. New York: Greenwood.

———. [1994] 1998. *Practical Reason: On the Theory of Action*. Stanford, CA: Stanford University Press.

———. 1996. *The Rules of Art: Genesis and Structure of the Literary Field*. Stanford, CA: Stanford University Press.

Bourdieu, Pierre, and Richard Nice. 1980. "The Production of Belief: Contribution to an Economy of Symbolic Goods" *Media Culture Society* 2:261–93.

Boussard, Valérie, and Marie-Anne Dujarier. 2014. "Les représentations professionnelles en question: Le cas des intermédiaires dans les fusions-acquisitions." *Sociologie du Travail* 56 (2): 182–203.

Brubaker, Rogers, and Frederick Cooper. 2000. "Beyond 'Identity.'" *Theory and Society* 29:1–47.

Bruck, Connie. 2004. *When Hollywood Had a King: The Reign of Lew Wasserman, Who Leveraged Talent into Power and Influence*. New York: Random House.

Burt, Ronald S. 2005. *Brokerage and Closure: An Introduction to Social Capital*. New York: Oxford University Press.

Caldwell, John T. 2008. *Production Culture: Industrial Reflexivity and Critical Practice in Film and Television*. Durham, NC: Duke University Press.

Caves, Richard E. 2000. *Creative Industries: Contracts between Art and Commerce*. Cambridge: Harvard University Press.

Coleman, James. 1988. "Social Capital in the Creation of Human Capital." *American Journal of Sociology* 94, supplement S95–S120.

Collovald, Annie. 1999. *Jacques Chirac et le gaullisme: Biographie d'un héritier à histoires*. Paris: Belin.

Cousin, Bruno, and Sébastien Chauvin. 2014. "Globalizing Forms of Elite Sociability: Varieties of Cosmopolitanism in Paris Social Clubs." *Ethnic and Racial Studies* 37 (12): 2209–25.

Crane, Diana. 1992. *The Production of Culture and the Urban Arts*. Newbury Park: Sage.

Curtin, Michael. 2010. "Comparing Media Capitals." *Global Media and Communication* 6 (3): 263–70.

Curtin, Michael, and Kevin Sanson, eds. 2016. *Precarious Creativity: Global Media, Local Labor*. Oakland: University of California Press.

De Vany, Arthur. 2004. *Hollywood Economics: How Extreme Uncertainty Shapes the Film Industry*. New York: Routledge.

De Verdalle, Laure. 2014. "Le double travail du producteur cinématographique." In *De nouveaux créateurs? Intermédiaires des arts, des industries culturelles et des contenus numériques*, edited by Laurent Jeanpierre and Olivier Roueff, 63–70. Paris: Editions des Archives Contemporaines.

De Verdalle, Laure, and Gwenaële Rot, eds. 2013. *Le cinéma: Travail et organisation*. Paris: La Dispute.

Dodier, Nicolas. 1995. *Les hommes et les machines: La conscience collective dans les sociétés technicisées*. Paris: Métailié.

Du Gay, Paul, ed. 1997. *Production of Culture, Cultures of Production*. London: Sage.

Eliasoph, Nina, and Paul Lichterman. 2003. "Culture in Interaction." *American Journal of Sociology* 108:735–94.

Ellickson, Robert C. 1991. *Order without Law: How Neighbors Settle Disputes*. Cambridge, MA: Harvard University Press.

Elsbach, Kimberly D., and Roderick M. Kramer. 2003. "Assessing Creativity in Hollywood Pitch Meetings: Evidence for a Dual-Process Model of Creativity Judgments." *Academy of Management Journal* 46 (3): 283–301.

Espeland, Wendy Nelson, and Mitchell L. Stevens. 1998. "Commensuration as a Social Process." *Annual Review of Sociology* 24:313–43.

Faulkner, Robert R. 1983. *Music on Demand: Composers and Careers in the Hollywood Film Industry*. New Brunswick, NJ: Transaction Books.

Faulkner, Robert R., and Andy B. Anderson. 1987. "Short-Term Projects and Emergent Careers: Evidence from Hollywood." *American Journal of Sociology* 92 (4): 879–909.

FilmL.A. Research. 2014. *2013 Feature Film Production Report*. Los Angeles. https://www.hollywoodreporter.com/sites/default/files/custom/Embeds/2013%20Feature%20Study%20Corrected%20no%20Watermark%5B2%5D.pdf.

Fine, Gary Alan. 2012. *Sticky Reputations: The Politics of Collective Memory in Midcentury America*. New York: Routledge.

Foster, Pacey, Stephen P. Borgatti, and Candace Jones. 2011. "Gatekeeper Search and Selection Strategies: Relational and Network Governance in a Cultural Market." *Poetics* 39 (4): 247–65.

Freidson, Eliot. 1962. "Dilemmas in the Doctor-Patient Relationship." In *Human Behavior and Social Processes*, edited by Arnold M. Rose, 207–24. London: Routledge and Kegan Paul.

Gabler, Neal. 1989. *An Empire of Their Own: How the Jews Invented Hollywood*. New York: Anchor.

Galloway, Stephen. 2015. "Leonardo DiCaprio Makes How Much Per Movie? Hollywood's A-List Salaries Revealed." *Hollywood Reporter*, April 10.

Gamson, Joshua. 1994. *Claims to Fame: Celebrity in Contemporary America*. Berkeley: University of California Press.

Geertz, Clifford. 1978. "The Bazaar Economy: Information and Search in Peasant Marketing." *American Economic Review* 68:28–32.

Godechot, Olivier. 2001. *Les traders: Essai de sociologie des marchés financiers*. Paris: La Découverte.

Goffman, Erving. 1955. "On Face-Work: An Analysis of Ritual Elements in Social Interaction." *Psychiatry: Interpersonal and Biological Processes* 18 (3): 213–31.

———. 1959. *The Presentation of Self in Everyday Life*. Garden City, NY: Doubleday.

———. 1963. *Stigma: Notes on the Management of Spoiled Identity*. Englewood Cliffs, NJ: Prentice-Hall.

———. 1974. *Frame Analysis: An Essay on the Organization of Experience*. Cambridge, MA: Harvard University Press.

Granovetter, Mark S. 1983. "The Strength of Weak Ties: A Network Theory Revisited." *Sociological Theory* 1:201–33.

Grindstaff, Laura. 2002. *The Money Shot: Trash, Class, and the Making of TV Talk Shows*. Chicago: University of Chicago Press.

Grindstaff, Laura, and Vicki Mayer. 2015. "The Importance of Being Ordinary: Brokering Talent in the New TV Era." In *Brokerage and Production in the American and French Entertainment Industries: Invisible Hands in Cultural Markets*, edited by Violaine Roussel and Denise Bielby, 131–52. Lanham, MD: Lexington Books.

Hesmondhalgh, David. 2006. "Bourdieu, the Media and Cultural Production." *Media, Culture & Society* 28 (2): 211–31.

Hochschild, Arlie R. 1983. *The Managed Heart: Commercialization of Human Feeling*. Berkeley: University of California Press.

———. 2009. "Marchés, significations et émotions: 'Louez une maman' et autres services à la personne." In *Politiques de l'intime*, edited by Isabelle Berrebi-Hoffmann, 203–22. Paris: La Découverte.

Hughes, Everett C. [1971] 1984. *The Sociological Eye: Selected Papers*. New Brunswick, NJ: Transaction Books.

Hunt, Darnell, and Ana-Christina Ramón. 2015. "2015 Hollywood Diversity Report: Flipping the Script." Ralph J. Bunche Center for African-American Studies, UCLA. http://www.bunchecenter.ucla.edu/wp-content/uploads/2015/02/2015-Hollywood-Diversity-Report-2-25-15.pdf.

Hurtes, Hettie Lynne. 2000. *Agents on Actors: Over 60 Professionals Share Their Secrets on Finding Work on the Stage and Screen*. New York: Backstage & Garsington/Windsor.

Jones, Candace. 1996. "Careers in Project Networks: The Case of the Film Industry." In *The Boundaryless Career: A New Employment Principle for a New Organizational Era*, edited by Michael B. Arthur and Denise M. Rousseau, 58–75. Oxford: Oxford University Press.

———. 2002. "Signaling Expertise: How Signals Shape Careers in Creative Industries." In *Career Creativity: Explorations in the Remaking of Work*, edited by Maury Peiperl, Michael Arthur, Rob Goffee, and N. Anand, 209–28. Oxford: Oxford University Press.

Jones, Candace, and Pacey Foster. 2015. "Film Offices as Brokers: Cultivating and Connecting Local Talent to Hollywood." In *Brokerage and Production in the American and French Entertainment Industries: Invisible Hands in Cultural Markets*, edited by Violaine Roussel and Denise Bielby, 171–88. Lanham, MD: Lexington Books.

Karpik, Lucien. 2010. *Valuing the Unique: The Economics of Singularities*. Princeton, NJ: Princeton University Press.

Kemper, Tom. 2010. *Hidden Talent: The Emergence of Hollywood Agents*. Berkeley: University of California Press.

———. 2013. "Sue Mengers." In *Immigrant Entrepreneurship: German-American Business Biographies, 1720 to the Present*, vol. 5, edited by R. Daniel Wadhwani. German Historical Institute. Last modified October 10. http://immigranten trepreneurship.org/entry.php?rec=151.

———. 2015. "The Emergence of Hollywood Agents." In *Brokerage and Production in the American and French Entertainment Industries: Invisible Hands in Cultural Markets,* edited by Violaine Roussel and Denise Bielby, 91–102. Lanham, MD: Lexington Books.

Knorr Cetina, Karin, and Urs Bruegger. 2002. "Global Microstructures: The Virtual Societies of Financial Markets." *American Journal of Sociology* 107 (4): 905–50.

Lainer Vos, Dan, and Paolo Parigi. 2014. "Miracle Making and the Preservation of Charisma." *Social Science History* 38 (3–4): 455–81.

Lamont, Michèle. 2000. *The Dignity of Working Men: Morality and the Boundaries of Race, Class, and Immigration*. Cambridge, MA: Russell Sage Foundation Books at Harvard University Press.

———. 2012. "Toward a Comparative Sociology of Valuation and Evaluation." *Annual Review of Sociology* 38 (1): 201–21.

Lamont, Michèle, and Laurent Thévenot. 2000. *Rethinking Comparative Cultural Sociology: Repertoires of Evaluation in France and the United States*. Cambridge: Cambridge University Press.

Lizé, Wenceslas, Delphine Naudier, and Olivier Roueff, eds. 2011. *Intermédiaires du travail artistique: À la frontière de l'art et du commerce*. Paris: La Documentation Française.

Longstreet, Stephen. 1962. *The Flesh Peddlers*. New York: Simon & Schuster.

Luhmann, Niklas. 1979. *Trust and Power*. Chichester: Wiley.

———. 1982. *The Differentiation of Society*. New York: Columbia University Press.

Mann, Denise. 2008. *Hollywood Independents: The Postwar Talent Takeover*. Minneapolis: Minnesota University Press.

Martinez, Tony. 2012. *An Agent Tells All*. Beverly Hills, CA: Hit Team Publishing.

Mayer, Vicki. 2011. *Below the Line: Producers and Production Studies in the New Television Economy*. Durham, NC: Duke University Press.

McDougal, Dennis. 1998. *The Last Mogul: Lew Wasserman, MCA and the Hidden History of Hollywood*. New York: Crown.

Mears, Ashley. 2011. "Pricing Looks: Circuits of Value in Fashion Modeling Markets." In *The Worth of Goods: Valuation and Pricing in the Economy*, edited by Jens Beckert and Patrick Aspers, 155–77. Oxford: Oxford University Press.

Milburn, Philip. 2002. "La compétence relationnelle: Maîtrise de l'interaction et légitimité professionnelle. Avocats et médiateurs." *Revue française de sociologie* 43 (1): 47–72.

Miller, James Andrew. 2016. *Powerhouse: The Untold Story of Hollywood's Creative Artists Agency*. New York: HarperCollins.

Motion Picture Association of America. 2013. "Theatrical Market Statistics."

Natale, Richard. 1995. "Is Rich and Richer Dumb and Dumber? Movies: Jim Carrey's $20-Million Fee for 'The Cable Guy' Alarms Some in the Industry, while His Managers Call It a 'Genius' Move by Sony." *Los Angeles Times*, June 22.

Negus, Keith R. 2002. "The Work of Cultural Intermediaries and the Enduring Distance between Production and Consumption." *Cultural Studies* 16 (4): 501–15.

Nixon, Sean, and Paul du Gay. 2002. "Who Needs Cultural Intermediaries?" *Cultural Studies* 16 (4): 495–500.

Obst, Lynda. 2013. *Sleepless in Hollywood: Tales from the New Abnormal in the Movie Business*. New York: Simon & Schuster.

Ohmann, Richard, ed. 1996. *Making and Selling Culture*. Hanover, NH: Wesleyan University Press.

Ortner, Sherry B. 2010. "Access: Reflections on Studying Up in Hollywood." *Ethnography* 11:211.

———. 2013. *Not Hollywood: Independent Film at the Twilight of the American Dream*. Durham, NC: Duke University Press.

Padgett, John F., and Walter W. Powell. 2012. *The Emergence of Organizations and Markets*. Princeton, NJ: Princeton University Press.

Peiperl, Maury, Michael Arthur, Rob Goffee, and N. Anand, eds. 2002. *Career Creativity: Explorations in the Remaking of Work*. Oxford: Oxford University Press.

Perlow, Leslie A. 1999. "The Time Famine: Toward a Sociology of Work Time." *Administrative Science Quarterly* 44 (1): 57–81.

Peterson, Richard A. 2004. "The Production of Culture Perspective." *Annual Review of Sociology* 30:311–34.

Polletta, Francesca, Pang Ching Bobby Chen, Beth Gharrity Gardner, and Alice Motes. 2011. "The Sociology of Storytelling." *Annual Review of Sociology* 37:109–30.

Powdermaker, Hortense. [1950] 2013. *Hollywood, the Dream Factory: An Anthropologist Looks at the Movie-Makers*. Eastford, CT: Martino Fine Books.

Putnam, Robert D. 1995. "Bowling Alone: America's Declining Social Capital." *Journal of Democracy* 6 (1): 65–78.

Ravid, Gilad, and Elizabeth Currid-Halkett. 2013. "The Social Structure of Celebrity: An Empirical Network Analysis of an Elite Population." *Celebrity Studies* 4 (1): 182–201.

Rensin, David. 2003. *The Mailroom: Hollywood History from the Bottom Up*. New York: Ballantine Books.

Rose, Franck. 1995. *The Agency: WMA and the Hidden History of Show Business*. New York: HarperCollins.

Rosen, Sherwin. 1981. "The Economics of Superstars." *American Economic Review* 71:167–83.

Rossman, Gabriel, Nicole Esparza, and Phillip Bonacich. 2010. "I'd Like to Thank the Academy, Team Spillovers, and Network Centrality." *American Sociological Review* 75 (1): 31–51.

Rothman, Tom. 2004. "A Chairman's View." In *The Movie Business Book*, edited by Jason Squire, 148–59. New York: Fireside.

Rottenberg, Josh. 2015. "Wall Street Investors to Hollywood Talent Agencies: 'Show Us the Money.'" *Los Angeles Times*, July 10.

Roussel, Violaine. 2013. "Celebrities and Politics: Representation Struggles in Arenas of Public Intervention." In *Voices of Globalization*, edited by Barbara Wejnert, 107–28. Research in Political Sociology, vol. 21. Bingley, UK: Emerald Publishing Group.

———. 2014. "Les agents artistiques américains: Des intermédiaires de marché?" In *De nouveaux créateurs? Intermédiaires des arts, des industries culturelles et des contenus numériques*, edited by Laurent Jeanpierre and Olivier Roueff, 97–112. Paris: Editions des Archives Contemporaines.

———. 2015a. "'It's Not the Network, It's the Relationship': The Relational Work of Hollywood Talent Agents." In *Brokerage and Production in the American and French Entertainment Industries: Invisible Hands in Cultural Markets*, edited by Violaine Roussel and Denise Bielby, 103–22. Lanham, MD: Lexington Books.

———. 2015b. "Une économie des émotions: Le travail de relation des agents artistiques à Hollywood." *La nouvelle revue du travail* no. 6. https://nrt.revues.org/2117.

———. 2016. "Talent Agenting in the Age of Conglomerates." In *Precarious Creativity*, edited by M. Curtin and K. Sanson, 86–100. Oakland: University of California Press.

Roussel, Violaine, and Denise Bielby, eds. 2015. *Brokerage and Production in the American and French Entertainment Industries: Invisible Hands in Cultural Markets*. Lanham, MD: Lexington Books.

Russell, Rupert. 2013. "Dying of Encouragement: From Pitch to Production in Hollywood." PhD diss., Department of Sociology, Harvard University.

Schatz, Thomas. 2010. *The Genius of the System: Hollywood Filmmaking in the Studio Era*. Minneapolis: University of Minnesota Press.

Schelling, Thomas C. 1960. *The Strategy of Conflict*. Cambridge, MA: Harvard University Press.

Schwartz, Vanessa. 2007. *It's So French! Hollywood, Paris, and the Making of Cosmopolitan Film Culture*. Chicago: University of Chicago Press.

Scott, Allen J. 2004. *On Hollywood: The Place, the Industry*. Princeton, NJ: Princeton University Press.

Silver, Allan. 1990. "Friendship in Commercial Society: Eighteenth-Century Social Theory and Modern Sociology." *American Journal of Sociology* 95 (6): 1474–504.

Singular, Stephen. 1996. *Power to Burn: Michael Ovitz and the New Business of Show Business*. New York: Carol Publishing Group.

Slater, Robert. 1997. *Ovitz: The Inside Story of Hollywood's Most Controversial Power Broker*. New York: McGraw-Hill.

Smith, Stacy, Marc Choueiti, and Katherine Pieper, with Traci Gillig, Carmen Lee, and Dylan DeLuca. 2014. "Inequality in 700 Popular Films: Examining Portrayals of Gender, Race, & LGBT Status from 2007 to 2014." Report of the Media, Diversity, and Social Change Initiative. University of Southern California and the Harnisch Foundation. http://annenberg.usc.edu/pages/~/media/MDSCI/Inequality%20in%20700%20Popular%20Films%2081415.ashx.

Specktor, Matthew. 2013. *American Dream Machine*. Portland, OR: Tin House Books.

Thompson, John. 2010. *Merchants of Culture: The Publishing Business in the Twenty-First Century*. Cambridge: Polity.

Tilly, Charles. 2007. "Trust Networks in Transnational Migration." *Sociological Forum* 22 (1): 3–24.

Velthuis, Olav. 2003. "Symbolic Meanings of Prices: Constructing the Value of Contemporary Art in Amsterdam and New York Galleries." *Theory and Society* 32:181–215.

Waxman, Sharon, and Lucas Shaw. 2014. "Leaked! Inside Details of $2.45 Billion WME-IMG Financing and Why an IPO May Loom." *TheWrap*, April 13. http://www.thewrap.com/leaked-inside-details-2-45-billion-wme-img-financing-ipo-may-loom/.

Weber, Max. [1905] 2002. *The Protestant Ethic and the Spirit of Capitalism: And Other Writings*. London: Penguin.

———. 1978. *Economy and Society: An Outline of Interpretive Sociology*. Berkeley: University of California Press.

———. 1958. "Politics as a Vocation." In *Essays in Sociology*, translated and edited by H. H. Gerth and C. Wright Mills, 77–157. New York: Oxford University Press.

Wei, Junhow. 2012. "Dealing with Reality: Market Demands, Artistic Integrity, and Identity Work in Reality Television Production." *Poetics: Journal of Empirical Research on Culture, the Media and the Arts* 40 (5): 444–66.

White, Harrison C. 2008. *Identity and Control: How Social Formations Emerge*. Princeton, NJ: Princeton University Press.

Winnicott, Donald W. 1980. "The Fear of Breakdown: A Clinical Example." *International Journal of Psychoanalysis* 61 (3): 351–57.

Zafirau, Stephen. 2008. "Reputation Work in Selling Film and Television: Life in the Hollywood Talent Industry." *Qualitative Sociology* 31 (2): 99–127.

Zelizer, Viviana. 2005. *The Purchase of Intimacy*. Princeton, NJ: Princeton University Press.

————. 2012 "How I Became a Relational Economic Sociologist and What Does That Mean?" *Politics & Society* 40 (2): 145–74.

Zerubavel, Eviatar. 1997. *Social Mindscapes: An Invitation to Cognitive Sociology*. Cambridge, MA: Harvard University Press.

Zuckerman, Ezra W., Tai Young Kim, Kalinda Ukanwa, and James von Rittmann. 2003. "Robust Identities or Nonentities? Typecasting in the Feature Film Labor Market." *American Journal of Sociology* 108 (5): 1018–73.

Index

Academy of Motion Picture Arts and Sciences, 134–36

Ace Ventura: Pet Detective (film), 172, 224n42

Actors Access, 110, 202n4

Agency Group, 205n25

agency system: compartmentalization in, 45, 47, 191; crossover agents, 48; distinctive cultures in, 84–86, 211n8, 213n24; divisions of labor, 32, 45, 116, 217n16, 217n19; energy in, as palpable, 96; evaluation community, 147; globalization of, 181, 195; group styles, 84; incoming-call business and outgoing-call business, 42; and mailroom, 64–70; mentors, importance of, 59; as organizations, 13; relationship-based, 72; studio coverage, 32–33; studio system, 12–13; talent vs. literary, 133–34; team agenting, 32; transactions, as institutionally and technically equipped, 95; transformation of, 44, 48–49, 51–52. *See also* agenting; agents

agenting, 15, 23, 151, 179, 182–84, 192, 195; acting, as part of, 107; and American dream, 61; as autocatalytic process, 226n17; coded exchanges of, 66–67; common conventions to, 11–12; and coordinators, 208n15; and creativity, 119, 224n41; ethics in, 93; experience of, 50;

foreign talent, 185–86; founding myth of, 119; as hierarchized, 16, 72, 116, 125–26, 131, 133–36; as informal, strength of, 167; interconnections, preexistence of, 78; and interrelations, 7–8; intimacy, creating of, 81; invention of, 12–14; mailroom, as entry point, 60–62, 72; negotiating, art of, 89–90; physicality of, 51, 98; playing by the rules, 62; playing the game, and art of negotiation, 89–90; power of naming talent, 119; and pricing, 157–58; professional images of, 11; reinvention of, 52; relationships, making of, 79–80, 213–14n26; relationship work, as cornerstone of, 27, 74–75; secrecy, culture of, 21; as self-reflexive activity, 148; semiotic socialization, 177; strategic roles of, 12–13; strategizing of, 148–50; styles of, 86–88; symbolic division of labor, 20; systemic complexity of, 149–50; and typecasting, 122–31; as vicarious vocation, 59; worthy things, finding of, 161–62; as "young person's job," 60. *See also* agency system; agents

agents, 1–2, 10–11, 16, 35, 58, 193–94, 206n28, 209n26, 225–26n9, 226n16; aesthetic judgment of, 114, 119–20; art and commerce, 17–22, 188; artists, relationships

237